# Toward a Manpower Policy

Edited by **ROBERT AARON GORDON**

*One of a series of books from the
Research Program on Unemployment
Institute of Industrial Relations
University of California, Berkeley*

**JOHN WILEY & SONS, INC.**

**NEW YORK LONDON SYDNEY**

Copyright © 1967
by John Wiley & Sons, Inc.

Library of Congress Catalog Card Number: 67-19443
Printed in the United States of America

# Contents

CONTENTS

# Preface

In 1962, with the help of a generous grant from the Ford Foundation, a four-year research program on the subject of Unemployment and the American Economy was begun at the University of California. During the first three years of the program, Arthur M. Ross and I served as codirectors of the program. Since the fall of 1965, Mr. Ross has been on leave from the University serving as Commissioner of Labor Statistics in the U. S. Department of Labor.

Our program grew out of widespread and deep concern over the persisting high level of unemployment in the United States. It was our hope to stimulate research on the underlying forces at work which were affecting both the demand for and the supply of American workers—not merely in the aggregate but along all of the significant dimensions of what is probably the most heterogeneous labor force of any industrialized nation. Through such research and the convening of groups of specialists to exchange views on various facets of the unemployment problem, we hoped to make some contribution to the formulation of policies, both public and private, that would help to move us closer to the goal of full employment.

An important element in our program has been an annual conference on unemployment which has brought together key people involved in research and in the formulation and administration of policy. The first of these conferences, in 1963, resulted in the book, *Unemployment and the American Economy*. The second, a year later, led to the publication of a substantial volume of research papers under the title *Employment Policy and the Labor Market*. The third conference in June 1965, by which time the national unemployment rate had fallen to 4.7 per cent, resulted in *Prosperity and Unemployment*.

By the beginning of 1966, the national unemployment rate had fallen to 4 per cent, the figure most often associated with the goal of full employment in the United States. Increasing attention was being paid to the *pattern*, not merely the overall level of unemployment. This concern over the unequal incidence of unemployment led the federal government to undertake in the first half of the 1960's a series of manpower programs to improve employment prospects for the less privileged parts of the labor force. A good deal of this effort formed part of broader programs to reduce poverty, improve the position of Negroes and other minority groups, and, more generally, to achieve the "Great Society."

It seems appropriate, therefore, that the fourth and final annual conference conducted by the Berkeley Unemployment Project should concern itself with the goals and instruments of manpower policy. This book is the result. I hope that it will prove of some help to those, in and out of Washington, who must concern themselves with the question: What kind of manpower program does the United States need to have in the years ahead—years, hopefully, in which the rate of unemployment will be even lower than it was in June 1966, when the papers in this volume were presented.

I wish to acknowledge my indebtedness to Mrs. Barbara Palmer for her help both in organizing the 1966 conference and in preparing the papers for publication. My thanks also go to Ruth Parker and Brian Motley for their assistance. As always, I have had the advice and help of my wife, Margaret Gordon, on whom I have leaned at all stages in arranging the conference and editing the resulting volume.

R. A. GORDON

*Berkeley, California*
*January, 1967*

# Toward a Manpower Policy

CHAPTER **1**

# Introduction

## BY R. A. GORDON

When the research program on Unemployment and the American Economy began at Berkeley in the summer of 1962, the major economic concern of Congress, the Administration, and the American people was the high overall level of unemployment. The national unemployment rate averaged 5.6 per cent in 1962 (the fifth consecutive year in which this rate, on an annual basis, had not fallen below 5.5 per cent). Already the debate had begun as to whether this poor record was to be attributed primarily to a persistent deficiency of aggregate demand or to a worsening of "structural unemployment." The issues involved in this debate were the main focus of attention in the volumes that resulted from the first three annual conferences conducted by the Berkeley Unemployment Project.

It can fairly be said that the third conference, held in June 1965, helped to wind up this debate.[1] By then the unemployment rate had fallen to 4.7 per cent and a further decline was clearly in prospect; the tax reductions initiated early in 1964 had proved successful beyond any dispute; and there was coming to be increasing agreement as to the nature of the structural-unemployment problem which the United States does face, and the respects in which this problem has, in fact, worsened in recent years. This is not to minimize the problems of adjustment in the labor market created by rapid technological change and the changing composition of total output; but it was being increasingly recognized that these problems of adjustment were, on the whole, manageable if a satisfactorily high level of aggregate demand were maintained.

### Evolution of Present Manpower Programs

While total unemployment was still at a distressingly high level in the early 1960's, the federal government took its first tentative steps to aid specific groups in the labor force to find jobs, and thus a federal manpower program began slowly to evolve. Some instruments of manpower policy, such as the federal-state Employment Service, had of course already existed for a long time, but it is fair to say that only in the last few years has the United States set out to develop a significant peacetime program aimed at helping substantial parts of the labor force to become better qualified for the jobs that were or might become available.

Garth Mangum traces how a national manpower program evolved in the 1960's, beginning with the Area Redevelopment Act in 1961. As Mangum points out, the federal government began a "structural approach" to the problem of excessive unemployment before it tackled the basic difficulty—deficiency of aggregate demand—by a large-scale tax reduction in 1964. As aggregate demand expanded, at an accelerated pace after the tax cut, additional manpower legislation was put on the statute books. This legislation is described in Mangum's essay, which traces out the expanding scale of the federal government's manpower programs and the increasing emphasis on broad socio-economic goals that came to be reflected in civil rights legislation, the "War on Poverty," and federal aid to education. This leads John Dunlop, in his concluding essay, to distinguish sharply between manpower policy in the narrow sense, aimed directly at influencing the labor market within a given institutional framework, and a broader or "gross" concept of manpower policy, concerned with the impact of changes in the institutional framework on the operation of the labor market. Somewhat similar distinctions are drawn by a number of the other contributors to this book.

Thus today the United States has on the books a variety of pieces of manpower legislation. Part of this legislation stems from a growing sensitivity to broad social needs and seeks to meet these needs in part through influencing the labor market. This is manpower policy in the broader sense. Other legislation is more narrowly and immediately concerned with meeting specific manpower goals. The question of how narrowly or broadly to define manpower goals also comes up in Philip Arnow's paper, and it underlay a good deal of the discussion at the conference regarding how specific manpower programs were to be evaluated in cost-benefit terms. In this connection, it is worth citing Harbison's definition: manpower policy in the broadest sense is concerned with the *development, maintenance,* and *utilization of* actual and potential members of the labor force. One might also cite Arnold Weber's useful dichotomy—between manpower programs that are "client-oriented" and seek to alleviate the plight of particular disadvantaged groups, and those longer-run programs that seek to improve the functioning of labor-market institutions, from the educational system to private training programs.

Our federal manpower policy has emerged out of a succession of pieces of legislation, and the manpower programs themselves are administered by a number of different federal agencies. Cooperation from state governments is required, and, more important, initiation and implementation of local programs are the responsibility of thousands of community organizations and agencies of local government. In view of all this, are we getting the coordination and overall planning needed? Joseph Kershaw, addressing himself to this question, makes a distinction between planning, especially at the national level, and coordination, particularly coordination at the local level. While strongly in favor of planning and while recognizing the need for a better coordination of local efforts, he also warns against pushing coordination too far. He suggests that "a certain amount of competition in the public sector will bring good results even as it does in the private sector." Frederick Harbison agrees with this position, although he believes Kershaw has too narrow a view of the scope of manpower policy, while Thayne Robson, Dunlop, and Levitan take a stronger and more positive stand in favor of coordination than Kershaw.

So we find ourselves today with a fairly elaborate and not very well-coordinated set of manpower programs, which seek to achieve a set of not too clearly formulated objectives along several different socio-economic dimensions. The driving force has been the growing sense of the need to aid particular underprivileged sectors of society, and some of the manpower programs are merely parts of broader legislative attacks on such social ailments as poverty and racial discrimination. Indeed, as several of the conference participants noted, it has required the political pressures generated by these social needs to bring into being a large part of the manpower legislation enacted by Congress in the last half-dozen years. There has, in addition, been further federal action—notably in the form of federal aid to elementary and secondary education—which has strong manpower implications.

Much of this greatly expanded manpower activity relies to some extent, directly or indirectly, on a long-established and much criticized piece of labor-market machinery, the federal-state Employment Service. Clearly the Employment Service has an increasingly important role to play in an expanding manpower program, but opinions differ as to precisely what that role should be. The issues are set forth in the Report of the Employment Service Task Force, presented to the Secretary of Labor in December 1965, and reprinted here in Chapter 6. The problems involved are further developed by George Schultz, who was Chairman of the Task Force, Leonard Adams, and Daniel Kruger in their comments on the Report of the Task Force. As this is being written, legislation is before the Congress that would significantly strengthen the Employment Service and permit it to play a more effective role in implementing federal manpower policy and, more generally, in improving the functioning of the labor market.

## The Present Situation

How effective a manpower program have we developed and what are the criteria to be used in judging its effectiveness? As we have noted, the approach thus far has been piecemeal, so it can hardly be said that an integrated and comprehensive labor-market policy has yet emerged. To a considerable degree, the emphasis has been on helping underprivileged sectors of the (actual and potential) labor force—primarily through counseling, training and retraining, and job creation.

Informed observers generally take the view that the spate of federal manpower programs in the 1960's have thus far made only a small contribution to reducing unemployment among those most in need of help in finding jobs. This view is expressed by Mangum, although Stieber offers a more optimistic evaluation. It is probably fair to say that the chief value of our manpower efforts thus far lies (1) in their long-run effects (this is particularly true if we include the expanded investment in education), and (2) in the background and experience they provide for formulating and implementing future manpower policy. In this connection, we would do well to heed the pleas by Dunlop, Somers, Rothbaum, and others at the conference for more and better evaluation of the results of the programs that have been begun. Vigorous support for this view comes also from Curtis Aller, Director of the Office of Manpower Policy, Evaluation, and Research.

There was agreement at the conference that an effective manpower program must place heavy reliance on private action—considerably more so than is the case today. This raises the question of the precise role employers and labor unions now play in the functioning of the labor market and also of what can be done to induce organized labor and business to make a more effective contribution to present and future manpower programs. Charles Myers takes a judicious look at the present and potential role of employers, and his paper draws little dissent from two leaders in the field of personnel management, William Caples and Edward Robie. Richard Lester offers a constructively critical evaluation of labor's activities and attitudes and draws a long and vigorous reply from Nat Weinberg of the UAW, one of the most progressive of the national labor unions. In his comment on Lester's paper, Adolph Holmes of the Urban League discusses the restrictive and discriminatory practices to be found among some unions, particularly at the local level and feels that the answer lies not in voluntary action by the unions but in strong federal legislation.

In connection with the role employers might play, there seems to be widespread agreement that greater emphasis needs to be put on on-the-job training (OJT) than has been the case in the past. This point is made by Somers, Myers, and others. Among the issues here are employer willingness to participate in OJT programs and the related question of the most appropriate form of government financial help. Another question raised by Somers, Thurow, and Rothbaum, and a difficult one, is how to bring more of the disadvantaged—those relatively far back in the hiring queue—into OJT programs. It might be noted in passing that OJT is now coming to play a more important role in the total Manpower Development and Training (MDTA) program than it did in the first few years.

Despite the effort and thought already expended, we are still uncertain as to how to blend most effectively general education and vocational training—and what forms both should take. As David Bushnell points out, there is still a distressing gap between the actual functioning of our educational system and "its potential capability of fully developing the nation's human resources." His paper provides a useful review of the manpower aspects of recent developments in this area, and additional comments are offered by Burton Weisbrod and Louis Kishkunas. The latter speaks from personal experience in a metropolitan school system. As an economist, Weisbrod's emphasis on the need to evaluate the results of our efforts in education and training repeats a theme that runs through many of the papers in this book.

Despite Kershaw's defense of some degree of competition among different government agencies and programs in the manpower field, it can hardly be denied that lack of coordination and overlapping efforts seriously impair the effectiveness of present manpower programs, however we choose to judge effectiveness. As was repeatedly emphasized at the conference, this lack of coordination is particularly serious at the local level, but it is aggravated by the variety of federal agencies and programs through which local authorities must operate.

Now that we have moved into a period of high employment and growing labor shortages in some occupations and regions, another deficiency in the present manpower policy begins to take on increased importance. We need more and better information on present and prospective skill shortages and more systematic and intensive efforts—through education, training and retraining, and other means—to eliminate such shortages and prevent future ones from occurring. Our manpower policy must deal with excess demands for particular kinds of labor as well as with cases of excess supply. Supply needs to be related to demand regionally as well as by occupation and other characteristics. It is clear that American manpower efforts thus far have not put sufficient emphasis on the geographical relocation of workers. This fact is brought out by Kershaw, Somers, and Stieber, among others. American deficiencies in this respect stand out in contrast to the emphasis placed on the relocation of workers in Sweden. This and other features of Swedish manpower policy are described by Bertil Olsson, the distinguished Director of the Swedish National Labor Market Board.

## The Present and Future Setting for Manpower Policy

By peacetime standards, the United States is experiencing a moderately low overall rate of unemployment. We are close to the goal of full employment, as that goal has been defined in recent years, although pressure is mounting to lower unemployment still further. The Clark Subcommittee is not the only group to insist that full employment in the United States should be defined in terms of an unemployment rate of 3 rather than 4 per cent. Mr. Goldfinger, in his discussion of Lester Thurow's paper in this volume, suggests a goal of 2 per cent unemployment "to be achieved within the next several years." What is the role of manpower policy in a full-employment economy, and what can manpower policy do to raise our standards as to what constitutes a full employment goal?

A number of issues are involved. Some are raised in Philip Arnow's paper and in the comments by William Bowen and Arnold Weber. Part of Lester Thurow's paper is also relevant here. How far should we go in setting not only an overall target rate for total unemployment—whether 2, 3, or 4 per cent—but also specific unemployment rates for the various parts of the labor force? We would do well to heed Bowen's warning that we cannot expect, nor should we try, to equalize unemployment rates for all age, sex, color, or occupational groups. Nonetheless, should we not think of the goal of full employment in *structural* as well as *aggregative* terms? It is not enough to say that, by a combination of monetary-fiscal and manpower policies, we hope to bring down the overall unemployment rate to 3 per cent (or some other figure) and maintain it there. Do we want a national rate of 3 per cent with the unemployment rate for nonwhites continuing to be twice that for whites—and the teenage rate three times that for adults? How much of the nonwhite, teenage, and unskilled unemployment differentials can we hope to eliminate in two or five years or over a longer period—and by what means and at what cost? And given an adequate level of aggregate demand, what will these reduced differentials mean in terms of an overall unemployment rate that can be maintained without inflationary consequences that we are not prepared to accept?

What can manpower policy contribute to our aggregative goals in addition to that of full employment? This is the specific question dealt with by Lester Thurow in his excellent paper. As this is being written, the aggregative goal most in the public mind is price stability. Thurow considers not only what manpower policy can contribute to price stability but also what manpower policy can do both to achieve and to raise the targets with respect to economic growth, full employment, and equalization of incomes. His efforts to quantify the relevant relationships are a welcome contribution to the literature on manpower policy.

In his review of Swedish experience, Bertil Olsson emphasizes the contribution which a comprehensive and vigorous labor-market policy can make to rapid economic growth and a liberal foreign trade policy as well as to full employment and price stability. It is obvious that not only does Sweden have a much more comprehensive labor-market program than the United States but that she has also more successfully integrated the instruments of manpower policy with monetary and fiscal tools.

Sweden is generally considered to have the most effective manpower program of any of the advanced economies in the Western world. This success is measured along a number of dimensions, for example, the scale of the program relative to the size of the labor force and the national income of the country, the range of authority given to the Labor Market Board, the degree of integration of manpower with other economic policies, and the extent to which manpower programs are tailored to the needs of all parts of the labor force (including the needs of those, such as elderly persons or the handicapped, who can be brought into the labor force).

In what direction should American policy now move? Mr. Olsson, not surprisingly, believes that we might consider moving further in the Swedish direction. But another alternative is suggested by Levitan and Dunlop. As Levitan puts it, the "urgent need in the United States is not for further proliferation and expansion of manpower programs but for consolidation and more effective administration of existing programs." Dunlop offers substantially the same advice when he cautions that: "Manpower policy has reached a time for reflection, administrative review, and consolidation."

What sort of manpower program does the United States need in the years ahead? As the Secretary of Labor stated in the 1966 *Manpower Report of the President*, "Manpower policy, it is now evident, is as important in periods of high employment as when jobs are hard to find. It is an adjustable instrument which must be directed continually toward the changing manpower problems that attend changing economic conditions." [2] At the same time, in line with the quotations from Levitan and Dunlop, it seems clear that "More attention needs to be given to fitting the diverse elements [of American manpower policy] into a rational, over-all framework." [3] Hopefully, the chapters that follow will be of some help to those who are and will be concerned with the further development and improvement of American manpower policy.

## NOTES

1. See R. A. and M. S. Gordon, editors, *Prosperity and Unemployment* (New York: Wiley, 1966).
2. *Manpower Report of the President and A Report on Manpower Requirements, Resources, Utilization, and Training,* March, 1966, p. 2.
3. Richard A. Lester, *Manpower Planning in a Free Society* (Princeton: Princeton University Press, 1966), p. 170.

# CHAPTER 2

# The Emergence of
# a National Manpower Program

## BY GARTH L. MANGUM [1]

The years 1961–1965 were impressive years of social and economic experimentation in the United States. At the public policy level, most of those experiments could be described as either employment policy or manpower policy—on the one hand, fiscal and monetary measures to speed economic growth and raise the general level of employment; on the other, programs and policies concerned with skill development, the creation or development of job opportunities for disadvantaged groups, and the matching of men and jobs. The atmosphere of 1966 impends a lessening in this thrust; but whether this means a brief respite for consolidation of gains or a loss of the necessary dynamics for change can only be determined with time. Whichever it proves to be, this appears a useful juncture for evaluation: Where are we now? How did we get here? What has been accomplished? How much further do we have to go? This paper attempts to answer these questions by placing present manpower programs in historical perspective, assessing their contributions to recent unemployment declines, and suggesting some present challenges for future action.

## A Brief History of United States Manpower Policy

Manpower is a key economic resource. It is also people, most of whom are dependent upon employment for their livelihood. The dual threads of concern for manpower as an economic resource and for the welfare of workers and their families have long histories. Because so much of the action prior to the last three decades was at the private and state and local levels, those histories are difficult to trace. It is sufficient to note a few legislative manifestations: manpower as an economic resource paramount in slavery, immigration, the Morrill Act, and the Smith-Hughes Act; the welfare of workers in the abolition of slavery and child labor and in wage-and-hour, safety, and income-maintenance legislation. Both threads have coexisted historically but dominance of the social-welfare orientation is a development of recent decades.

**The Great Depression.** The overwhelming influence on the present stage of American manpower policy has been unemployment. The depression of the 1930's was a traumatic experience which provided a "continental divide" not only in the economic policies of the United States but in those of most Western democracies. The contribution was not in terms of real solutions; the success of the policies of the time was meager, but so were the efforts relative to the magnitude of the problems. Rather, the contribution was to force us to recognize that the insecurities of an industrial society imposed new public responsibilities, and to demonstrate that when the insecure became a large enough proportion of the total their political power was sufficient to bring public action.

The impact of the Great Depression was similar in Western European nations, but the contrasting experiences following the Second World War provide useful insights into United States manpower policies. In Europe as in the United States, the war's end was marked by public assumption of responsibility for maintaining full employment. Western Europeans followed their declarations of employment policy with aggressive fiscal actions. Then when these proved inadequate to eliminate the insecurities of industrial life, and when labor shortages exerted heavy pressures on price levels, they developed manpower policies designed to ease adjustment and increase labor-market efficiency. Only now, as labor shortages and the demands of more sophisticated technologies threaten to throttle economic growth for lack of highly educated and trained manpower, is the development of labor as an economic resource receiving attention in those countries.

**Employment policy, 1946–1960.** In contrast, and in the light of subsequent economic developments, immediate postwar policies in the United States appear as a detour. The Second World War temporarily turned attention to allocation of scarce manpower, but the fear of a return of serious unemployment was a constant policy goad. The major manifestation of that fear was the Full Employment Bill of 1945, which after passage by the Senate and emasculation by the House became the Employment Act of 1946. Rather than the dawn of a new day in employment and manpower policy, however, the Employment Act turned out to be the twilight of the depression decade. The postwar boom quieted fears of unemployment, while the frustrations of the Korean conflict, following hard upon global war, brought demands for a recess from public exertion. There followed seven years during which private enterprise, budget balance, international balance-of-payments equilibrium, and price stability took priority over economic growth; and inflation, mild though it was, appeared a greater threat than unemployment.

In the massive unemployment of the 1930's, job creation was the almost total concern. Training people for jobs which did not exist received little attention. Education had historically been considered important to democracy but was not a federal responsibility. The federal role gradually changed in the postwar years, but at first this was for demographic rather than economic reasons when the schools were overwhelmed by a rising flood of children.

The G. I. Bill, following the Second World War, was one of the most far-reaching social decisions ever made in the United States. Yet manpower development seems to have had little, if anything, to do with its goals. The economic returns on that investment have never been adequately assessed; the social returns were imposing. A quiet social revolution was purchased as men whose backgrounds made higher education improbable were lifted into totally unexpected positions in life. But the education and training provisions of the G. I. Bill must probably be listed as a fortunate accident built upon a desire to make up lost years to veterans and to slow their return to the labor market. We have the Soviet Union to thank for awakening public opinion to the importance of developing manpower resources. The main theme of postwar policy in the international sphere became competition with communism, while anti-inflation dominated domestic policy. Russian development of nuclear weapons and the launching of the first space satellite plunged us into a race to produce scientific and technical manpower marked by the National Defense Education Act three years before we returned to welfare-oriented manpower policies.

## The Rebuilding of Consensus

The 1946–1960 recess in employment and manpower policy does not indicate a loss of interest by the country, but a loss of consensus. Continued concern was manifested in each recession, but at a subliminal level. Too few were affected for too short a time, and the nation was resting from its past exertions. Legislation was introduced during the 1949 recession to supplement and effectuate the Employment Act but was forgotten when the downturn proved shortlived. The 1954 recession was marked by proposals for tax reduction, public works, and "depressed areas" legislation, by demands from organized labor for a "conference on unemployment," and by criticisms from liberals and academics of public inaction. The proposals, criticisms, and arguments were repeated in 1958 with increasing support, reflected in the Congressional elections of that year. Notable, in light of subsequent events, was the strong advocacy of tax cuts by some businessmen and bankers.

The gradual rebuilding of consensus on unemployment is illustrated by the 1960 presidential campaign. "Get America Moving Again" was a slogan, and the major domestic issue was unemployment. It is an oversimplification, but probably not a contradiction of fact, to say that 49.7 per cent of the people agreed.

## The Causes of Unemployment

When the path charted during the Depression was resumed, we again pursued employment and manpower policy in reverse order to European developments. In Western Europe, governments had endorsed aggressive fiscal policies, following them with labor-market programs to ease inflationary pressures and the plight of individual workers. We chose to place the structural cart before the job-creating horse. In part this was evidence of the slow buildup of consensus. It was also an indication of the level of economic sophistication among the public and their representatives. As a result, several years of experimentation, education, and political realignments were required before substantial gains against unemployment were made.

In retrospect, the explanation of the unemployment which rose persistently following the Korean conflict is readily apparent. The Gross National Product, which grew at an average rate of 4.9 per cent per year between 1947 and 1953, rose by only 2.4 per cent per year during 1953-1960. The fiscal exertions necessary to have prevented unemployment from rising above its 1953 level of 2.9 per cent of the labor force would have been slight.[2] Lacking this narrow margin, labor-force growth and productivity increases exceeded economic growth, and unemployment rose to an average of 5 per cent during the post-Korean decade and 6 per cent from 1958 to 1963.

With inadequate economic growth the primary source of unemployment, the economically rational solution would have been immediate adoption of aggressive fiscal policies. Politically, the nation was not prepared to step so far so fast. Even in the new Administration, forces advocating fiscal stimulus were few and muted. The location and characteristics of the unemployed were readily observable, but the solutions to general unemployment required more sophistication among the populace and flexibility among their representatives than in fact existed. Therefore the first experimental efforts were directed at the structural impacts rather than the basic causes of unemployment.

**The structural attack.** With the legislature organized along geographical lines, the attack upon unemployment began with federal aid to depressed areas. Such legislation had been introduced
as early as 1955 but had met repeated Administration rebuffs.
The next consensus reached was on the need for a training program. This, too, had been presaged at the state level in Pennsylvania and in a bill introduced by Senator Joseph S. Clark in
1959. The concentration of unemployment among the unskilled
and uneducated was noted and accepted by many as an explanation of unemployment. The fiscally conservative blamed lack
of salable skills rather than the lack of jobs. Others, noting the
unabsorbed victims of technological change and overly impressed
by a few early examples of automation, hypothesized that a
new technological revolution was twisting the demand for labor,
eliminating jobs for the unskilled, and creating unfillable demands for workers with higher education and skills. Those who
would have given first priority to aggressive fiscal policies advocated education, training, and expenditure increases as good in
and of themselves. Accordingly, the Manpower Development and
Training Act (MDTA) of 1962 and the Vocational Education
Act of 1963 received overwhelming bipartisan support. When
experience demonstrated that many unemployed lacked the basic
literacy skills required for successful retraining, MDTA was
amended in 1963 to add basic education to skill training for
the unemployed. With continued unemployment, relocation allowances—once political anathema—were written into the law
on an experimental basis. Each of these amendments, and others
in 1963 and 1965, enjoyed bipartisan endorsement and minimal
opposition.

Just as unemployment was concentrated by education, skill,
and location, it was also concentrated by age and race. The unemployment rate among youth, persisting at nearly three times
the high general unemployment rate, was described as "social
dynamite," and a Youth Employment Act, first introduced in
1957, was passed by the Senate in 1959 and again in 1963 as
a rescue operation. Essentially, the Act was modeled upon the
Civilian Conservation Corps of the 1930's and provided for: (1)
a conservation corps to employ youth in rural conservation
camps, and (2) a home-town youth corps to employ youth in

socially desirable activities in their home environments. Once again, the proposal appeared to have predominant support, but it foundered in the House Rules Committee upon the integration issue.

Negro unemployment, persistently double the overall rate, was an important element in the civil rights struggle occurring at the same time. Concern for the two related issues, youth and Negro unemployment, was a primary impetus to the Economic Opportunity Act passed in 1964. The Act was an enlargement and a repackaging of several existing and proposed programs but still marked a new departure in manpower programs. The Area Redevelopment Act, the Accelerated Public Works Act, the MDTA, and the Vocational Education Act were all directed at the mainstream of employment in the private, profit-making sector of the economy. In contrast the Youth Employment Bill had proposed public and nonprofit employment for youth. Under the 1962 Social Security Amendments, designed to promote "rehabilitation rather than relief," a token program had been inaugurated to allow parents of dependent children to work for benefits they would have received without working. The Juvenile Delinquency and Youth Offenses Control Act had underwritten local experiments with an emphasis upon employment. All of these were picked up, enlarged, and repackaged as the heart of the new "War on Poverty." These programs are now incorporated in the Job Corps, the Neighborhood Youth Corps, the Work Experience Program, and the Community Action Program. For the first time since the 1930's, direct public employment is being provided upon a substantial scale to the unemployed.

Also inspired by concern for youth and Negro unemployment was a new look at the schools from which, along with home environments, the disadvantages of many stemmed. The fruits of this recognition came the following year with the Primary and Secondary Education Act and Operation Head Start.

**The aggregative solution.** But all of these developments, dramatic though they were, were largely of long-run significance. Though they were primarily aimed at unemployment, they had relatively little to offer in the short run. At the end of 1963, unemployment still stood at 5.6 per cent. A year later it had dropped to 5 per cent and the following year to 4 per cent, falling below that long-sought goal in the spring of 1966. But the reason was not the accumulated impact of the impressive package of manpower tools which had been developed. The combination of the manpower programs and the increased draft calls may account for as much as 0.2 of a percentage point in the unemployment decline. The rest of the reduction in unemployment came through aggressive fiscal policies. The commitment made in 1946 was debated in 1949, 1954, 1958, and throughout 1961–1963, but not until the tax cut of February 1964 was the consensus equal to action rather than exhortation. Whether the consensus is permanent remains to be seen. The unfortunate co-existence of international conflict has made further test of the commitment to "maximum employment" currently unnecessary.

**The Status of Manpower Policy**

In the development of manpower policy, the United States, as said earlier, put the cart before the horse. But, since horsepower was soon furnished, the ordering of priorities is of more academic than practical interest. A more rational approach would have simultaneously supplied jobs through fiscal policies, provided skills through education and training, and matched them through labor-market programs. If a choice was necessary, the measures to stimulate demand merited top priority. But the structural experimentation was necessary for public education. Some element of mythology is probably inherent in the policy-making process, and policy-makers must be more concerned with the practicality of results than the rationality of approach.

Despite the haphazardness of approach, the United States now has the basic elements of an "active" manpower policy. The 1946 commitment to "maximum" employment was given under duress —the fear of resumption of the Depression. There is reason to hope a new commitment may have been made, based upon understanding of the effectiveness of the tools and the implications of their use. The tax cut of 1964 is likely to stand out as the most important economic act of a generation; however, the success of fiscal policy does not diminish the importance of the manpower programs. Rather, it has only created the environment within which the manpower tools can be used effectively.

**The size of the manpower program.** The experiences of 1961–

1965 were probably a necessary experimental prelude. The Area Redevelopment Administration made little imprint, but the Appalachian Commission and the Economic Development Administration hope to learn from its experience. Training the unemployed under MDTA did not create jobs, but the experimental size of the program reduced the significance of that fact. The 200,000 persons who had completed MDTA retraining programs by the end of 1965 did not exhaust the inevitable mismatches in a labor force of 75 million. Seventy per cent of the trainees found training-related jobs, but the extent to which they did so in preference to others who would have filled the same jobs cannot be known. The implementation of the relocation experiments was at first blocked by the absence of labor-shortage areas in which the unemployed could be relocated. With the resumption of rapid growth, 1200 persons were assisted by relocation grants and loans between late 1964 and the close of 1965.

The manpower elements of the Economic Opportunity Act were more rationally related to their targets. The Neighborhood Youth Corps was employing 150,000 a month in early 1966, but three-fourths were in school and employed only part-time on NYC projects; approximately 25,000 were enlisted in the Job Corps, and 46,000 adults were enrolled in the Work Experience Program in March 1966. But these totals are small compared to a 75 million labor force, the 3½ million unemployed at the beginning of 1965, and the 2½ million jobs created by the ordinary workings of the economy during the same year. By contrast, the least publicized but most complete of all federally supported manpower programs, Vocational Rehabilitation, placed 135,000 handicapped persons in productive jobs in 1965.

Inability to solve unemployment does not, however, imply criticism of any of the programs. The mating of strange bedfellows and the dramatization of the prosaic are central to the art of politics. In 1961, 1962, or 1963 aggressive fiscal policies were not yet politically salable, but manpower programs were. Appeals that, for instance, manpower training would enable the unskilled to compete more effectively for the few existing jobs, or that it might be wise to tool up for possible future periods of labor shortage, would have attracted little support. Combining the carrot and the stick—the suggestion of an easy solution to unemployment through matching supposedly nearly equal numbers of unemployed and job vacancies and the fears of automation gobbling up unskilled jobs and spawning only skilled ones—was highly effective.

Each of the 1961–1965 manpower programs, though limited in overall impact, was helpful to thousands of individuals. Compared to a $16 billion tax cut and the magnitude of defense expenditure increases, the less than $2 billion per year presently spent on the manpower programs introduced between 1961 and 1965 is minor. Yet one has no way of knowing whether a larger expenditure on manpower programs would have brought a notably larger impact. The manpower programs have their own manpower shortages which may impede effective expansion.

**The relative impact of employment policies and manpower programs.** The relative impact of fiscal policies and manpower programs can be illustrated by conceiving of the labor market as a nationwide "shape-up" confronting a single aggregate employer. The members of the labor force are queued in order of

TABLE 1.   ESTIMATED FEDERAL EXPENDITURES ON MAJOR
MANPOWER PROGRAMS, FISCAL 1966[a]
(millions)

| | |
|---|---:|
| MDTA | $ 279 |
| Neighborhood Youth Corps | 245 |
| Job Corps | 240 |
| Community Action Program | 344 |
| Work Experience Program | 130 |
| Adult Basic Education | 20 |
| Vocational Education Act of 1963 | 182 |
| Total | $1440 |

Source: Figures are from U.S. Budget for Fiscal 1967.

[a] Does not include general education, income maintenance programs, or specialized training programs which could be considered as manpower programs, nor vocational rehabilitation which is clearly a manpower program but which predates, though it has been augmented substantially during, the period under discussion here. The Community Action Program is only in part a manpower program, but information is not available to separate its manpower components.

attractiveness to the employer, whether that attractiveness is determined by rational factors of education, skill, and experience, or less savory ones of age or race. The "shape-up" is a dynamic one with constant entrances and exits, with rising educational attainment feeding the front of the line, and the influx of inexperienced youth, refugees from agricultural technology, and high Negro birthrates feeding the rear. The employer reaches as deeply down the line as required by the demands of his customers and the prevailing technology. Increasing aggregate demand can cause the employer to reach further back in the queue. Manpower programs can increase the ability of those at the rear to compete for jobs with the more favorably situated or can offer employment tailored to the needs of those left behind.

The employed portion of the line increased 3.5 million between February 1964 and the same month in 1966. The unemployed portion declined by 1.4 million. MDTA training was absorbing an average of 100,000 persons in the spring of 1966, most of whom would probably have otherwise been unemployed. It had also probably improved the competitive position of the 200,000 who had completed training in 1963–1965. A 300,000 net increase in the size of the armed forces doubtless removed some from the employed and some from the unemployed portion of the queue, as well as some who were not in the job market. Many of the 85,000 students getting work-study assistance during fiscal 1966 under the Vocational Education Act of 1963 might have been unemployed in its absence. The increased availability of general educational support may have removed others from the labor force, though this was offset to a substantial degree by the additional 76,000 16- and 17-year-olds who seem to have been encouraged by the availability of jobs to drop out of school between 1963–1964 and 1964–1965.[3] The combination of the Neighborhood Youth Corps, the Job Corps, and the Work Experience Program account for perhaps 130,000 full-time and nearly that many part-time jobs for people, most of whom would probably otherwise be unemployed or out of the labor force. Those aided by the Vocational Rehabilitation Program are, almost by definition, brought from outside the labor force into employment. The total numbers affected by all these programs are difficult to fix. A guess that nine-tenths of the progress was made by the employer reaching back from the front of the line and one-tenth by the programs operating on the rear of the queue does not seem unreasonable.

Both approaches aided more than proportionately those who had been disproportionately burdened by unemployment (see Table 2). The others already had jobs. But still left unemployed at the back of the line were others in the same categories. The intent of most of the manpower programs is to aid those "left behind" directly, though most, like the aggregate approach, tend to help the best situated of the competitively disadvantaged.

**Current status.** The number of major labor markets with substantial and persistent unemployment fell from 41 to 17 between February 1964 and March 1966. Many labor markets found themselves with 2 per cent unemployment and below. Occupational shortages varied from engineers, tool-and-die makers, and construction craftsmen to unskilled help in low-wage industries. Labor shortages, however, were not sufficient to prevent growth in employment and production. The interim 4 per cent unemployment target was broken, and the fall of unemployment to 3.7 per cent in April 1966 was accompanied by no evidence that unemployment could not fall further without serious difficulties. Prices and wages rose, but there was little indication that labor shortage was a direct cause. Clearly, however, the time has arrived when the European philosophy of manpower programs as a hedge against inflation in tight labor markets is applicable to the United States as well. The difference between those at the front and those at the rear of the line is probably greater in the United States than anywhere else. Rapidly rising educational attainment inevitably puts age at a disadvantage. High educational attainment puts the school dropout further behind. Race, accompanied by prejudice, adds an additional competitive burden. And employers do have alternatives. They can bid with their fellow employers for the more attractive workers at the front of the line. They can increase their substitution of machines for labor, thus raising even higher the aggregate demand required for full employment. The environment is ripe for manpower policy to demonstrate its effectiveness in the United States. Unfortunately, there is no reason to believe that the manpower programs are large enough to make a significant difference.

TABLE 2.  DISTRIBUTION OF INCREASED EMPLOYMENT, 1964–1966

| Labor Market Category | Percentage Distribution of Total Employed Labor Force | Percentage of New Jobs |
|---|---|---|
| Sex | | |
| Male | 65 | 47 |
| Female | 35 | 53 |
| Age | | |
| 14–19 | 7 | 29 |
| 20–24 | 10 | 22 |
| 25–34 | 19 | 13 |
| 35–64 | 60 | 36 |
| 65 and over | 4 | 1 |
| Race | | |
| Nonwhite | 11 | 16 |
| White | 90 | 85 |
| Occupation | | |
| Blue collar | 36 | 53 |
| White collar | 46 | 43 |
| Service | 13 | 13 |
| Farm | 5 | −9 |
| Education[a] | | |
| Grammar school | | |
| 0–8 years | 23 | −15 |
| High school | | |
| 1–3 years | 19 | 10 |
| 4 years | 35 | 72 |
| College | | |
| 1–3 years | 11 | 7 |
| 4 years | 7 | 22 |
| 5 years and over | 5 | 5 |

[a] Education comparisons are for March 1964 to March 1965; all others, for February 1964 to February 1966. The less than proportionate share of employment going to grade school, high school, and college dropouts requires further analysis. Part of the explanation is tautological. Since graduates got most of the jobs, they must have been available. If they were available, it is not surprising that they were hired in preference to nongraduates. Components may not add to totals because of rounding.

## The Unfinished Business of Manpower Policy

Despite the $2 billion price tag, the manpower programs of 1961–1965 are better analyzed as experiments than as action programs. There have been successes and failures, but only the easier problems, if any, have been solved. As a result of these experimental efforts, the United States now has a varied kit of manpower tools, considerable experience in their use, and the basis for further improvements. The time may not be propitious for new departures, but the lessons are there when the politically ripe moment comes to profit from them. There is no lack of challenge.

1. Unemployment has declined encouragingly, but full employment has not yet arrived. To use analogy, the jet transport of economic growth has not yet touched down at the haven of full employment where it needs to reverse its engines to taxi more slowly to the terminal. It is still in the air but approaching the field. The crew are arguing among themselves whether the rate of approach is too rapid and whether more flap is needed to slow the rate of descent, and the situation is sufficiently marginal for a case to be made for either course but not for slowing to stalling speed while still in midair.

The Senate Subcommittee on Employment and Manpower in early 1964 recommended a fiscal program to bring unemployment to 3 per cent by the beginning of 1968.[4] Some thought the goal unrealistic. The Subcommittee had no unchallengeable reason for choosing 3 per cent rather than, say, 2.7 per cent or 3.4 per cent. The 3 per cent levels of the Korean period had been accomplished during partial mobilization accompanied by wage and price controls. However, it was the Subcommittee's conviction—an act of faith really—that, with the aid of the manpower programs it recommended and with adequate time for adjustment, 3 per cent unemployment without unacceptable price increases was possible. Subsequent events have not disproved this premise. Two years of growth of GNP at above 5.5 per cent have created no manpower shortages but have left manpower reserves adequate for further expansion. The rise in the unemployment rate in May 1966 from 3.7 to 4 per cent reflected the return of school-age youth to the summer labor market and the influence of weather on farm employment. However, it also demonstrated the unchallengeable fact that, with present rates of productivity and labor-force growth, the economy must continue to grow rapidly to prevent rising unemployment. The reverse of that coin is the ability to grow rapidly without the restraints of labor shortage. The landing place of full employment is buried in a fog of inexperience, but we have sufficient statistical radar to reduce the danger of feeling our way toward it.

2. The manpower programs have proved their usefulness in general while demonstrating the need for modification in many specifics. Also demonstrated, in an economy where employment can increase by over 2 million in one year and the labor force by 1.6 million, is the inability of manpower programs of the present sizes to have a significant impact on the total economy.

More rapid growth has brought the economy within shooting distance of solving the problem of general unemployment. This only places in more stark relief the places where unemployment persists by age, by sex, by race, or by location. A truly structural situation has been defined which can only be solved by individualized and localized actions, although continued rapid economic growth can still help. The May 1966 increase in unemployment again demonstrated the phenomenon described by the analogy of the labor market to a shape-up. Those at the back of the line were the last in and the first out. The overall unemployment rate jumped from 3.7 to 4 per cent: Unemployment of males over 20 years of age and of married men remained at 2.4 per cent and 1.8 per cent, respectively; white male unemployment rose from 3.4 per cent to 3.5 per cent; teenage unemployment rose from 12 to 13.4 per cent; and nonwhite unemployment rose from 7 to 7.6 per cent.

In addition to economic growth to assure sufficient job opportunities, the deficiencies which place members of these groups at the back of the queue must be attacked either by improving their ability to compete with those at the front of the line or by providing jobs tailored to their needs. Both approaches have been undertaken experimentally. The Neighborhood Youth Corps, the Job Corps Conservation Centers, and the Work Experience Program are small-scale attempts to create such tailored employment. Pressure will continue for the "public service employment as the 'employer of last resort' concept" proposed by the Automation Commission and endorsed by the Office of Economic Opportunity, the Democratic Study Group in the House of Representatives, and the recent White House Conference on Civil Rights.[5]

Such employment opportunities are a tool, but their effective use depends upon successful diagnosis of individual need. Current experimental and demonstration projects jointly pursued by the Department of Labor and the Office of Economic Opportunity point the way. In a human-resource development project in three Chicago slums, indigenous interviewers were sent out to "knock on every door" to discover persons who could profit by training or jobs and encourage them to come to a neighborhood center for help. The process proved expensive but effective. Between December 1965 and April 1966, 2671 households containing over 6000 persons were contacted in order to bring 600 persons in to be interviewed, tested, and counseled, and in Chicago's tight labor market it was possible to place nearly all of them in training or in jobs. The failures were primarily due to scarcity of day-care centers. The "customers" proved to be 95 per cent women. The approach is being extended to other cities but still on an experimental basis.

Vocational Rehabilitation remains the one comprehensive manpower program with substantial experience in tailoring assistance to individual need. The individual counselor can provide or buy—at his discretion—services ranging from orthopedic equipment through psychological help to a college education. The program is not without its problems, but both the concept and its accomplishments are impressive. It is also expensive.

3. Though small in size relative to the problems confronting them, the manpower programs have helped people who needed help. But that does not mean they have done so in the most efficient manner. The programs will have value as experiments only as their experience is objectively evaluated. What are the goals of manpower policy? What are the goals of each program? To what extent are the programs consistent with and to what extent do they contribute to the accomplishment of the goals? Which are the most efficient in accomplishing what goals, and are there other approaches potentially more efficient? How can education, occupational preparation, and job creation be most

effectively linked? We have experienced both labor surplus and labor stringency; and, with a legislative lull likely, the time is propitious for such evaluation.

4. Competitively disadvantaged communities, as well as competitively disadvantaged individuals, find themselves at the back of the queue and in need of specialized approaches. In many ways it is a misnomer to speak of federal manpower programs. In most cases only the funds and guidelines are federal. The initiative and administration are state or local. MDTA institutional training courses come into existence only as a local Employment Service office identifies unemployed workers and potential employment opportunities, seeks the cooperation of local educators to design training courses, and the two groups together approach federal agencies for funds. Neighborhood Youth Corps projects are designed by state and local governments or nonprofit private institutions, which then seek federal funding. Work Experience Programs are financed in part by federal matching grants but run by local welfare agencies. Vocational rehabilitation and vocational and general education are completely state and local operations assisted by federal matching grants.

Every community differs in need and can best be assisted by approaches tailored to those needs. That tailoring is difficult for federal agencies to do. But communities lack more than finances. They are not well structured to recognize and attack their manpower problems and too often lack initiative and competence. For example, in one metropolitan area, federal manpower officials found themselves lost in a morass of 9 counties, 18 unified school districts, 11 Community Action Agencies, and 9 Departments of Social Welfare, "each with its own peculiar way of dealing with manpower problems, each with its own sphere of influence, and each sensitive to 'outside interference.'" In another city, 31 different state, city, and private agencies were conducting manpower programs for out-of-school persons with no connecting links. There are problems of duplication. For instance, in the latter case, three separate courses for secretarial training were established within a few blocks of each other, each funded by different federal agencies and all with excess capacity. One had idle electric typewriters while another was seeking donations of obsolete manual typewriters. But much more important is the failure to identify the community's manpower problems and undertake a concerted effort to solve them in the light of long-term prospects.

A community with a good educational system and a relatively well-trained labor force but with numbers of persons who have fallen behind the rest in preparation for employment has a different set of problems and should have different priorities and remedies than one where the educational system is poor and the entire work force suffers in comparison with other communities. In both cases a concerted identification of short-run and long-run problems, inventory of resources, exploration of alternatives, and establishment of goals are prerequisites to reasonable solutions. Such a unified effort would require both a different structure and greater competency. The structure should be attuned to local needs and could range from a committee representing all relevant interests to a metropolitan human resources administration. The crucial elements are initiative and ability. In addition to the provision of financial resources, the federal manpower agencies will, at some point, find it necessary to foster and provide technical assistance to state or local manpower planning agencies. And, if the latter are to be successful, some type of internship program will have to be undertaken to provide competent manpower for tasks which, for the present at least, can be learned only in practice.

5. To adequately serve local labor market needs, the federal government will have to put its own manpower house in order. It is a long way from the halls of Congress or the desk of the federal administrator to the home, the workplace, the classroom, and the local community. The federal manpower programs were put together piecemeal. They often function more as competitors for the privilege of serving the unemployed or the unsatisfactorily employed than as a carefully honed and polished set of tools available to the social and economic mechanic for application in the appropriate combination. Instead each tool tends to belong to a separate mechanic who has only that tool and insists on applying it regardless of fit. Federal, state, and local officials are both aware of and working at the problem of improved coordination at the Washington and local levels, but solutions are elusive.

Jurisdictional agreements which almost take on the nature of treaties have been signed between federal agencies. Three-man teams representing the Departments of Labor and of Health, Education, and Welfare and the Office of Economic Opportunity have been assigned to bring about coordination among federal agencies at the local level. In a best of all possible worlds, one might opt for a single Department of Human Resource Development to handle all of the manpower, poverty, social welfare, and education programs. The future may yet make it necessary.

More important than the delays and jurisdictional problems among the federal agencies is the problem the fragmented federal structure presents to communities seeking assistance with their manpower problems. A few sophisticated communities have become experts in grantsmanship. They follow every Act of Congress and influence legislation on their own behalf. They study the eligibility rules and application procedures of every program and maintain personal contacts in every agency. On these bases, they are able to select packages which fit their needs from among the available programs and resources. But these are the minority. The communities with the greatest need are also those with the least leadership and sophistication. Those who have, receive; too often, those who have not fail even to find the handles which turn on the spigots of federal help. Short of a single manpower agency, a single designated federal agent at the community level could provide a "one-stop shopping center" for available federal help. The minimum—presently unavailable— would be a handbook listing and describing all programs with their eligibility rules and procedures and providing simple instructions for accessibility.

6. As long as the problem has been to create enough jobs to go around, the quality of the jobs created has been of little concern. Various levels of government have prescribed certain minimum conditions of employment in terms of wages, working hours, and safety. As time goes on, these conditions may be raised and others added, but the potential contribution of government regulation to quality is always limited. Public policy, however, need not rest only on government fiat. Positive incentives can be provided, and social norms can be favorably modified. The most potent factors in the quality of employment are technological progress and educational attainment. Despite recent fears of

"automation," technology has been the factor primarily responsible for gradually freeing man from slavery to his own
physical needs. The trick is not to prevent technological change
from relieving man from the strain, dangers, and tedium of the
farms, mines, and factories but to see that he is prepared for
more "human" work and that more human work is available.

7. Wage and income policies have been almost totally absent
from the manpower policy developments of the past few years.
As far as policies of wage restraint are concerned, the neglect
in a period of slack demand, stable prices, and concentration
upon welfare-oriented manpower programs has been wise. In the
long run, low wages might encourage the employment of labor
relative to the employment of machines. However, the effect
would only be long run, and the price would be lower levels of
productivity and lower standards of living. Fortunately, better
alternatives are available. Higher levels of demand, fostered
by appropriate fiscal policies, can generate employment for both
men and machines at higher levels of productivity and income.

But this is true only with respect to maintaining wage levels
in periods of unemployment and relatively stable prices. Full employment creates product- and labor-market environments which
all participants, if not restrained, will exploit to their advantage.
It may also include shortages of labor and capacity which push
costs and prices upward. Theoretically, more widespread and
better education and training and improvements in labor-market
efficiency should reduce the latter pressures, but this has yet to
be proved. The advantages, both economic and philosophical,
of free markets make us reluctant to adopt wage and price controls. So far there is no apparent alternative to some considered
compromise among full employment, stable prices, and economic
freedom. Whether it be called manpower policy, wage-price
policy, or economic policy, achievement of the "best" wage-price-
employment relationship remains an open challenge.

Income policy, on the other hand, is not only a matter of
price stability. Increased sensitivity to the injustices of poverty
has been one of the great social accomplishments of this impressive half-decade. The War on Poverty has only defined
poverty incomes. None of the programs has really launched an
attack. Minimum wages, wage-related social insurance benefits,

and public assistance have not met the need. The degree of consensus that some form of a guaranteed minimum family income is needed is remarkable. But the methods of providing it have yet to receive serious legislative study.

8. The heart of manpower policy is on the supply side. The solutions to unemployment will allow us to turn our attention more appropriately to preparing the labor force for employment and matching available manpower with vacant jobs. We really know little about the relative effectiveness of alternative ways of preparing people for employment. In reaction to the concentration of unemployment among the uneducated, there have been demands for more specific occupational preparation within the schools. In a calmer atmosphere, there now appears to be a drawing back from this position. Education as a major answer to general unemployment, it is generally conceded, can guarantee only better educated unemployed. Education can affect who becomes employed and unemployed, but, at least in the short run, not how many. But education is for more than employment; it is for life, of which employment is only an important part. The optimum combination of general education and occupational training, the appropriate locus of each within the educational system, the relative responsibility of school and employer, the extent of adaptability and the transferability of skills —these are all questions which can best be studied and answered in a climate of adequate employment opportunity. Problems of motivation and social and psychological handicaps are also relatively unplumbed.

9. The matching of men and jobs has primarily geographical and occupational dimensions. Throughout the five years of active assault on unemployment, a few students have continued to maintain that skill shortage rather than job shortage is the problem. As they appear right in 1966, and hopefully in 1967 and beyond, they seem likely to claim retroactive confirmation for 1961–1965 as well. But the problem is nevertheless real. The gap between the "hard core" unemployed in a central city slum or an Appalachian hollow and the vacant tool-and-die job in the suburb of another city is a wide one. Having to bridge this gap is a relatively pleasant, though challenging, task.

The Area Redevelopment Act, the Accelerated Public Works

Act, the Public Works and Economic Development Act, and the Appalachian Regional Development Act all had as their assignment the attraction of jobs to areas of surplus labor. The desirability of protecting investments in private and public facilities and maintaining the stable values of homes and communities is clear. The effective means for reversing long-term regional economic decline are still elusive. Unassisted outmigration has historically been the most effective answer, but it weakens communities even further. In the relatively small and immobile societies of Western Europe, relocation assistance has proved its value as one of a kit of manpower tools. Only further experience can determine its effectiveness here.

10. Throughout all of the manpower policy developments of the past five years, the U.S. Employment Service, despite constant criticism, has neither enjoyed nor suffered legislative attention. With nearly 1900 affiliated state Employment Service offices scattered throughout the country, the federally financed but state-administered public employment service is inevitably the front-line arm of any locally oriented manpower policy. Each new manpower program has increased the workload of the employment service offices without corresponding increases in budgets. National economic developments have buffeted the completely locally oriented agencies. State salary structures have prevented the recruitment of sufficient competent personnel to handle the involved problems of the unemployed. The public Employment Service has been simultaneously criticized for weakness and inability to aid the unemployed and for attempting to monopolize the labor markets of the nation. Only now, as unemployment is declining as a general problem, is Congress turning its attention to strengthening this vital arm of manpower policy. The results of current legislative efforts remain to be seen.

## The Emergence of Manpower Programs:
## A Summary Statement

Considered in the perspective of the historical pace at which public policy progresses, the developments of the past five years are impressive. The ability of fiscal and monetary tools to control the levels of economic growth and employment have been convincingly demonstrated. Controversy will continue over marginal choices between employment and price stability, but the 1953–1960 slack is unlikely to recur. Fortunately so, because the growth requirements of full employment are higher than ever before.

The manpower programs were developed in response to high unemployment, but unemployment is not the sum and substance of manpower problems. In fact, only as general unemployment ends can manpower programs work effectively.

Though the manpower programs preceded the adoption of aggressive fiscal policy, they have not been recipients of the same degree of consensus. Politically, they are likely to undergo increasing criticism. The apparent lack of success from which the criticism arises is inherent in the unrealistic expectations with which the programs were launched. As solutions to general unemployment, they had little to offer. As solutions to the problems of individuals competitively disadvantaged in favorable labor markets, their contributions have been and can be considerable. Looking to the past, the major justification must be the need for experimentation. The future of the manpower programs should depend upon the flexibility with which they learn from experience and adjust to new realities. To end on a note of pessimism, both patience and consensus suffer as the proportion threatened by unemployment declines and other claims for public concern demand priority.

## NOTES

1. Director of the Manpower Policy Evaluation Project, financed by the Ford Foundation, at the W. E. Upjohn Institute for Employment Research. The author's views do not necessarily represent those of the Ford Foundation or the Upjohn Institute.

2. Assuming that the rates of labor force growth and productivity increase which actually occurred would have been no greater, an addition to GNP growth rates of another 0.4 per cent per year would have been adequate to prevent the rise of unemployment between 1953 and 1960. Given faster economic growth, however, both the labor force and productivity would probably have experienced somewhat more rapid increases. Even so, it is doubtful that more than the postwar average growth rate of 3.5 per cent would then have been necessary to restrain unemployment.

3. I will name this the "Kellogg effect" after my colleague Frazier Kel-

logg, who predicted this phenomenon in 1963 and modestly pointed out
to me this evidence of his prophetic vision.

4. *Toward Full Employment: A Comprehensive Employment and Manpower Program for the United States,* Subcommittee on Employment and
Manpower of Senate Committee on Labor and Public Welfare, 88th Cong.,
2d sess. (Washington, D.C.: 1964), p. 90.

5. *Technology and the American Economy, Report to the President and
Congress by the National Commission on Technology, Automation, and
Economic Progress* (Washington, D.C.: Government Printing Office, 1966),
pp. 35–37; "An Action Program for Full Employment", *Congressional Rec-
ord,* 89th Cong., 2d sess., Vol. 112, No. 7 (January 19, 1966), p. A-212;
*To Fulfill These Rights,* Council's Report and Recommendations to the
White House Conference on Civil Rights (Washington, D.C.: June 1–2,
1966), p. 20.

# Discussion

## BY JACK STIEBER

Garth Mangum has presented a comprehensive and lucid account of the development of manpower programs in the United States. I am in general agreement with most of his paper, but, fulfilling what I believe to be the proper role of a discussant, I shall direct my remarks at areas of disagreement and points which might profit from further discussion.

In assessing the role of manpower programs in reducing unemployment, Mangum comes to the following conclusions:

1. In the United States we were able to obtain political consensus on manpower measures before there was agreement on fiscal policies to combat the high unemployment of the early 1960's. This was putting the cart before the horse. We should have relied on fiscal policies to create jobs and followed them up with manpower programs when unemployment had been brought closer to the full employment level.

2. Manpower programs are most effective under conditions approaching full employment, to help meet labor shortages, increase labor-market efficiency, and train unemployed and especially disadvantaged workers for jobs.

3. As full employment is reached, or even approached, it becomes more and more difficult to obtain political support for manpower programs of the magnitude necessary to be effective.

### European Experience

I think Mangum has overstated his case on the relative roles of fiscal and manpower policies in achieving and maintaining full employment in the United States and has misread the Western European experience in this regard. I agree with his evaluation that manpower programs are most effective in a full or near-full employment economy, but I believe they also have an important role to play before this period is reached. Finally, I suspect that he is right, but hope that he is wrong, in his pessimistic conclusion regarding the unwillingness of the American people to support a really effective manpower program once the specter of general unemployment has been exorcised.

Mangum's comparison of the U.S. and Western European approaches to achieving the proper relationship between fiscal policy and manpower programs is not entirely accurate. While fiscal and monetary policies may have been used more rationally and aggressively, European countries did not wait for full employment before instituting manpower programs. Margaret Gordon's study of retraining in Western Europe notes that, with the exception of Sweden and West Germany, legislation providing for retraining programs was passed immediately after, or shortly before, the end of the Second World War.[1] A major purpose of these programs was to meet the problem of unemployment, along with facilitating the return of veterans and war workers to civilian employment and relieving anticipated shortages in certain occupations. West Germany started to emphasize retraining after the end of the Allied occupation, when unemployment was a major problem, and sharply decreased its programs when full employment was reached. Even Sweden, which comes closest to the Mangum model of putting manpower policy in its proper place, started to expand its previously limited retraining effort in 1958, when unemployment was at 2.5 per cent, which is considered an unacceptable level for most Western European countries.

Though considered as a permanent part of a broader labor-market policy in all countries, retraining programs were cut back sharply as unemployment decreased in some countries. In others, most notably Sweden, they were maintained and even stepped up. In Belgium retraining was opened to employed workers in 1961, as had been the case in France from the outset.

In all these countries, as in the United States, it was found that it takes considerable time to develop courses, recruit instructors, and iron out all the problems that crop up in any sizeable retraining program. The experience in Western Europe certainly does not support the view that retraining programs in the United States were started too soon and should have waited until fiscal policy had reduced the manpower job to manageable proportions. On the contrary, had the United States started its retraining activities earlier, it would undoubtedly have been geared to do a much better job during the 1960's.

## Combining Aggregative and Manpower Measures

The important question regarding the proper relationship between aggregative and manpower measures is not which should come first but rather what is the best combination between the two. In the United States we were too slow to use fiscal policy to reduce the high unemployment rates of the late 1950's and early 1960's. We were also dilatory in developing manpower programs which could be adjusted to the needs of the economy in periods of full or less than full employment.

I agree with Mangum that full employment can only be achieved and sustained by maintaining high levels of economic growth and by making effective use of fiscal and monetary policies. However, I believe that he has exaggerated the success of the 1964 tax cut and underrated the contribution of manpower programs when he says that "the solution to unemployment came through aggressive fiscal policies." As Mangum himself recognizes elsewhere in his paper, with some 3 million unemployed and a 4 per cent unemployment rate (as of June 1966) we can hardly claim to have solved our unemployment problem. Furthermore, while fiscal policies deserve almost the entire credit for the reduction in unemployment in 1964 and perhaps the beginning of 1965, they must share the credit for the equally sizeable decrease in 1965 and early 1966 with the manpower programs contained in the Economic Opportunity Act and the Manpower Development and Training Act, not to mention the impact of Selective Service. Mangum's own figures for the Neighborhood Youth Corps, the Job Corps, and the WEP, plus the 100,000 students enrolled under the Work-Study Program which he does not mention, add up to more than 300,000, most of whom would probably be numbered among the unemployed in the absence of these programs. Instead of measuring this total against the total labor force, the total number of unemployed, and the new jobs created during 1965, as Mangum does, it should be compared with the decrease in the number of unemployed—about 700,000—in 1965 in order to assess the contribution of manpower programs to reducing the level of unemployment.

## The Need for Relocation Programs

The United States has made rapid progress in developing a variety of manpower programs. However, it still lacks, except on a demonstration basis, a program to assist workers in depressed areas to move in order to accept jobs in other parts of the country. The 1200 who were assisted by relocation grants and loans in 1965 compare most unfavorably with the same number who were assisted in 1962 in France, a country with one-fourth of our population, not to mention the 26,000 who received relocation help amounting to a maximum of $1200 in Sweden in 1964. Other Western European countries also have comprehensive worker-relocation programs.

The view that worker-relocation programs are more important in Western Europe because the people are relatively immobile is not borne out by a recent ILO study.[2] It found that the frequency of moves between counties and states in the United States was not markedly different from mobility patterns between local authorities and *Länder* in West Germany, though people in both of these countries were about twice as mobile as those in France and Italy during the 1950's and early 1960's. Even in the latter two countries—each of which has a population of about 50 million—an average of 1½ million people moved to a different commune every year, including some 500,000 who moved to another region.

A case can be made that financial assistance to encourage geographical labor mobility is even more necessary in the United States than in other countries because of the greater distances and the higher costs of moving. The major obstacle to including worker-relocation assistance as a regular part of our manpower program is more political than economic, which bodes ill for the future of such a program in the United States.

## Reconciling Full Employment and other Goals

Mangum notes the conviction of the Senate Subcommittee on Employment and Manpower—a conviction which he apparently shares—that a 3 per cent unemployment rate can be achieved in the United States without unacceptable price increases. He does not give the Committee's or his own definition of what would constitute an unacceptable rate of price increase.

Recent events would seem to indicate that most economists and even the Administration would put the unacceptable rate too low to permit unemployment to go down to 3 per cent. In April 1966, a majority of 560 university and business economists, responding to a questionnaire survey by the Chase Manhattan Bank, indicated that they considered inflation the "most pressing economic problem now facing the United States." And about 90 per cent thought that inflation was already under way. They advocated higher taxes, reduced federal spending, and tighter money to stem inflation. At the time of the survey the Consumer Price Index had risen by 2.8 per cent during the previous 12 months (March 1965 to March 1966) and was rising at an annual rate of 4 per cent based on the first quarter of 1966. It continued to rise at a somewhat slower rate during the next two months. Wholesale prices rose by 3.3 per cent from May 1965 to May 1966 after holding virtually steady for several years. During this period (May 1965–May 1966) the unemployment rate declined from 4.6 to 4.0 per cent after having reached a low of 3.7 per cent in February and again in April 1966.

There is little question that fiscal and monetary measures designed to stem the ascent of prices would also arrest the decline in unemployment. It is to the Administration's credit that (as of June 1966) it had not accepted the advice of most professional economists to increase taxes. However, it is doubtful whether Congress and the Administration are prepared to accept price increases on the order of 3 per cent or more per year in order to attain a 3 per cent unemployment rate.

We have tended to look with envy at Western European countries which have consistently maintained unemployment rates of less than 2 per cent. But this record has been accompanied, in most countries, by price increases far greater than those experienced by the United States. In addition some of these countries have had restraints on wages and prices, imposed either by the government or through labor-management agreements, which go far beyond the wage-price guideposts in the United States. In short, our European neighbors have not solved the dilemma of achieving the triple objectives of full employment, price stability, and economic freedom any more than the United States. But they differ from us mainly in having achieved a consensus on priorities which puts full employment ahead of the other two objectives. We, on the other hand, want all three and are likely to end up without fully achieving any.

The high value placed on full employment has led most Western European countries to put restrictions on the freedom of employers to lay off or dismiss workers, requiring substantial advance notice or even government approval in a few countries. Such policies probably result in some overmanning, inefficiencies in the production process, and higher unit labor costs. Whatever their social value, it is doubtful whether they are desirable or appropriate from an economic point of view. However, if we opt for having economic decisions in the firm made solely on economic grounds, as we have in the United States, we should recognize that workers who accept lay-off or dismissal with little or no advance notice are contributing indirectly to the increased efficiency of our firms. This recognition would indicate a policy of relatively liberal unemployment insurance benefits, generous retraining allowances, and other measures to ease the plight of the unemployed. In fact, however, we are less liberal in the treatment of our unemployed and of retraining workers than are most Western European countries. And, to close on the same pessimistic note as Garth Mangum, the vote in the House of Representatives, turning down the provision calling for federal benefit standards in the Administration's Unemployment Insurance Bill of 1966, holds little promise that our record in this regard will improve in the foreseeable future.

## NOTES

1. Margaret S. Gordon, *Retraining and Labor Market Adjustment in Western Europe* (Washington, D.C.: U.S. Government Printing Office, 1965), Chapter 3.

2. *International Differences in Factors Affecting Labour Mobility* (Geneva: International Labour Office, 1965).

CHAPTER 3

# What Are Our Manpower Goals?

## BY PHILIP ARNOW [1]

Dr. Garth Mangum, in his paper, has in a broad way touched
upon the major goals of manpower policy. He has started, as
everyone must, with the three major goals that have become the
cornerstones of manpower policy as presented in the annual manpower reports of the President: creating jobs, training people for
jobs, and matching people and jobs.

The setting of goals is part of the logical process of planning
any activity. It is one of the key steps taken in developing policies and action programs. In the new era of policy planning and
cost-benefit analysis, it helps those administering programs to
keep all eyes on the ball and is supposed to aid in evaluating
performance. As we develop more conscious (and self-conscious)
planning and programming in both the private and public segments of the economy, the conscious establishment of goals becomes more and more commonplace. And with it goes the com-

panion emphasis on the question: Are the goals addressed to the right problems?

## Manpower and Other Goals

There are various kinds of goals: goals that are broadly stated and those that are narrow, those that are very long range and those that are immediate in their application, those that are general and those that are so specific that they are virtually programmatic. The last are sometimes called objectives rather than goals, but in practical operating terms it is usually not worthwhile to make this distinction.

One question that arises in formulating manpower goals is whether they are designed to help achieve other (more primary?) goals such as certain specific industrial, developmental, or economic objectives, or whether we are—or should be—dealing with manpower goals *per se*.

Both approaches are in fact a part of our tradition. Immigration policy, for example, has helped us toward the goal of manning our industry. In this sense the manpower policy that was implicitly involved in immigration policy was subsidiary to the policy of building industry, but immigration policy also had the goal of providing opportunity for self-advancement for those who came to our shores; in fact, the latter goal was perhaps as important as the first. Similarly, educational policy has helped us toward the goal of manning our industrial establishment, but it has also helped toward the goal of rounded achievement and the advancement of individuals. There are some key differences between the two approaches. The approach which views a manpower goal as a goal to achieve other economic objectives is indifferent as to which part of the manpower force is affected. Immigration and educational policies can help fill job opportunities with no regard to the question, "Who does this policy let in and who does this policy keep out?"

The approach that starts with manpower and tries to develop whatever it takes to achieve a satisfactory distribution or utilization of manpower (however that might be defined) can give a more direct answer to the question, but it seems to be a more difficult approach—perhaps only because we have not tried it too often. It is an approach that may involve more action by government and may even involve more "intervention"; it will, therefore, necessarily call for great care concerning the form and appropriateness of action. For example, to insure maximum benefit to individuals and to society,—in a sense to achieve manpower goals—some aspects of educational policy have in fact led to mandatory actions, such as the mandatory school attendance requirements, and the draft is, of course, a mandatory system. If we were to embark upon manpower programs designed to reach all, as we reach all for some levels of education, to what extent would mandatory screening or participation be necessary and acceptable?

The approach that starts with manpower is also an approach which is likely to concentrate on specific groups of people and in a sense discriminate in their favor. Yet this apparent discrimination may in fact be necessary to secure reasonably equal results and to overcome several kinds of handicaps which exist in the labor market. Governmental social policy has always made such distinctions in developing specific programs; yet we have sometimes dealt with the unemployed as though each unit had an equal claim on society's efforts to do something about his or her unemployment. On the basis of what we know about the unemployed, the point is that it will perhaps take unequal action to bring about, from one or another point of view, equal results.

Both approaches to manpower goals—those which adjust manpower to meet the needs of industrial society and those which start from the point of view of the needs of the individual—in fact wind up looking at the individual, but they may not come up with the same answers for a great many individuals. An obvious illustration is the experience under various government public works programs, which have found it difficult to design activities that meet normal project tests for public works and at the same time offer substantial help to the hard core unemployment groups. The latter have usually benefited only indirectly, if at all, as a consequence.

Nonetheless, more knowledge of employment possibilities that arise from anticipated trends and needs and from nonmanpower "goals" will be very important to the achievement of manpower objectives.

Some new tools which should help to fit manpower goals into

other goals are provided by the new economic projections made by the Bureau of Labor Statistics (BLS) in its growth-studies project and by the projections of national "needs," beyond the BLS projection levels, provided by the National Planning Association studies. Use of these should certainly bring us nearer to the achievement of our three basic manpower goals.

The BLS Growth Project—starting with projections of consumer, government, and investment demand for output and their translation into industrial employment by the use of input-output relationships—offers a picture of the economy in the years ahead, toward which vocational guidance, counseling, and training efforts can be directed. These are projections of what is expected as a practical matter, rather than projections of "need" which go beyond such expectations. When these industrial projections are translated into detailed occupational projections by use of the BLS occupational matrix, and when the occupational projections, in turn, are translated into educational needs, by further use of the pioneer work on educational requirements done in connection with the recent revision of the Dictionary of Occupational Titles, we will have even more useful tools.

The projections of the National Planning Association (NPA) start with an analysis of "national needs"—which are realistic as individual needs but are not all likely to be realized in combination—as they were developed by the Commission on National Goals and supplemented by actions taken in the early days of the Kennedy Administration. These have been "priced out" in terms of resource needs and translated into manpower in broad terms, although not yet in terms of manpower needs as reflected by educational levels, specific skills, etc. Techniques for these conversions are still in an embryonic state.

The goals used by the NPA are not official government goals. Government officials are often reluctant to establish goals for their action programs that go too far beyond immediate legislative possibilities. At what point in the process of Administration announcement, development of a proposal, and enactment of a program is one to say that we have now settled upon a "goal"? Government projections, such as the BLS Growth Study projections, are usually made on the basis of foreseeable and, in the case of the public sector, practicable legislative and fiscal achievements. It was precisely because of these limitations upon government that the NPA, as a private organization, undertook to add a new dimension of "needs" to the goal-setting process.

The upshot of the NPA goal-analyzing exercise has been to establish the economic implications of needs that are based on the reasonable judgment of experts—judgment imaginative to a degree but hardly "pie in the sky" theorizing. What has emerged is a set of requirements for manpower that in total is substantially beyond our present resources, for a considerable number of years ahead, on the basis of the way we operate our economy. The conclusion one would draw is that we have to decide what things we want to do, and the task of manpower policy after these choices have been made is to help people along lines which fit into the evolving trends. These findings undercut the views of the apocalyptic forecasters of doom, those who have repeatedly argued that we are running out of jobs. Of course, there is a time limit on the NPA projections, and the field is still open as to whether human needs—hitherto assumed to be insatiable—would yield the same job results if projected into the next century.

If I may make a parenthetical comment at this point, it would be to distinguish such goal-setting and projection from the setting of output goals as part of economic or "indicative" planning of the sort found in several countries of Western Europe. While the latter type of planning is often justified by its adherents on the basis of its social or even manpower consequences, there is yet considerable uncertainty about its contribution to manpower objectives. Its origins in Western Europe were really nonmanpower in character: (a) the planning of the Marshall Plan days, (b) a cartel philosophy, (c) remnants of a Marxist view that the only way to use resources properly for human ends is to plan them in detail, and (d) a devotion to planning as such, or a view that planning is the surest way to full employment. Specific industry or commodity goals, whatever their own merits, are set with little or only marginal planning of manpower considerations. Whenever the relationship of these goal-setting activities to specific human or manpower goals is raised, answers within the countries themselves seem to come in nationwide rather than specific industry or commodity terms, whether the matters be questions of redundancy, training, movement, etc. Thus there seems to be a real question whether the degree of product planning that takes place is really necessary to the achievement of human and manpower goals. Whether and how the two can or should be meshed is a subject which needs more attention.

**Specific Manpower Goals**

Let us turn now to goal-setting that starts with manpower as a point of departure.

It is clear that there are specific and different program implications that flow from this type of goal-setting. For example, current emphasis on youth and minority-group unemployment rates and on specific programs which could bring these two rates down as a key part of the process of reducing the overall unemployment rate, clearly yield different programs—and different results—than activity directed only at the overall rate without regard to which group of unemployed persons is affected.

Let us develop this approach on a systematic basis by looking at the detailed composition of the unemployed and see what goal and program implications result—a process that has in fact been carried on by government manpower-program analysts. What goals does such analysis lead to? What specific programs might be most appropriate for specific groups of the unemployed?

If we do this, we of course find at the outset unusually high rates for minority-group workers, teen-agers, persons in their early twenties, and older workers. If we make the same kind of analysis on an industry basis, we find the highest rates among construction and farm workers, including migrant workers, with some feeling that a large volume of the unemployed is really unattached to any industry group. Analysis by duration of unemployment invariably produces some portion of the long-term unemployed as a target group.

Looking at these categories from a program viewpoint, we find a considerable overlap between the distribution of unemployment by industry and the concentration of unemployment among youth and minority groups, which suggests that programs directed at young people and minority groups might have a significant payoff. But not entirely, among other reasons because serious seasonal unemployment, which constitutes perhaps one-fifth of our total unemployment, is still left, especially for workers who remain attached to the seasonal industries.

Obviously, target groups can be selected in some detail. There are arguments for both broad and narrow groupings, and I have used only broad groupings here. One can then fashion, for the primary target groups that one selects from such a detailed analysis of unemployment rates, manpower programs specifically directed at the groups. The programs could be designed to reduce unemployment in a specific group to a certain point, or to bring it down a certain degree, or to equalize certain rates.[2]

The specific programs can be designed on the basis of practical experience with various operating and experimental programs already undertaken under the Manpower Development and Training Act, the Economic Opportunity Act, the education statutes, and other federal and state legislation. Planning and operational judgments can be made as to the numbers that can be handled and the probable effect on specific unemployment rates resulting from various programs of institutional training, expanded on-the-job training, bonding assistance, special training for armed forces rejectees, adult-worker upgrading, special private job development efforts, special public service employment, new types of Employment Service activity, and other efforts directed at the specific target groups. It is now practicable to design such a structure, calculated to bring the volume of unemployment down by at least a million, on the basis of current experience and knowledge, and work along these lines has been in progress. Financing, of course, is another question.

## A Numerical Illustration

Tables 1 and 2 illustrate this approach, using 1 million as an arbitrary (but practicable) overall goal and applying the approach to those manpower programs for which the Department of Labor is responsible.[3] The tables show the estimated effect of selected types of manpower action on unemployment among specific target groups: youth, nonwhite adults, white adult long-term unemployed, and 20- to 24-year-old whites.

These calculations were originally made when there was a

TABLE 1. ILLUSTRATION OF A STRUCTURE OF MANPOWER PROGRAMS TO REDUCE ANNUAL AVERAGE UNEMPLOYMENT BY 1 MILLION OVER A 2-YEAR PERIOD USING FISCAL 1966 PROGRAM LEVELS AS A STARTING POINT

(Table shows only those program activities for which the direct quantitative effects on average unemployment levels can be approximated)

| Action Program | Ratio Program Level to Decline in Unemployment | 1966 Program Levels[a] (individuals) | Illustrative Program Levels and Unemployment Reductions | | | | | | Total Decline in Unemployment by End of Second Year[b] |
| --- | --- | --- | --- | --- | --- | --- | --- | --- | --- |
| | | | First Fiscal Year | | | Second Fiscal Year | | | |
| | | | Total Program Level | Program Increase Over 1966 | Resulting Decline in Unemployment | Total Program Level | Program Increase Over 1966 | Resulting Decline in Unemployment | |
| Total | — | 685,000 | 1,320,000 | 635,000 | 360,000 | 1,940,000 | 1,255,000 | 751,000 | 1,007,000 |
| *Activities contributing directly to employment* | — | *240,000* | *470,000* | *230,000* | *227,000* | *795,000* | *555,000* | *524,000* | *551,000* |
| Neighborhood Youth Corps—out-of-school | 1–1[a] | 120,000 | 220,000 | 100,000 | 100,000[c] | 300,000 | 180,000 | 180,000 | 180,000 |
| Adult work experience | 1–1[a] | 0 | 100,000 | 100,000 | 100,000[c] | 150,000 | 150,000 | 150,000 | 150,000 |
| Job development | 1.1–1[d] | 120,000 | 150,000 | 30,000 | 27,000 | 180,000 | 60,000 | 54,000 | 81,000 |
| Labor mobility | 1.2–1[e] | 0 | NA | NA | NA | 100,000 | 100,000 | 85,000 | 85,000 |
| Bonding assistance | 1.2–1[e] | 0 | NA | NA | NA | 65,000 | 65,000 | 55,000 | 55,000 |
| *Improvement in matching of workers and jobs* | — | | | | | | | | |
| ES improvements[f] | — | NA | NA | NA | — | NA | NA | NA | *96,000* / 96,000[f] |
| *Improvement of workers' skills* | — | *445,000* | *850,000* | *405,000* | *133,000* | *1,145,000* | *700,000* | *227,000* | *360,000* |
| MDTA Title II[g] | 3–1[h] | 205,000 | 350,000 | 145,000 | 48,000 | 405,000 | 200,000 | 67,000 | 115,000 |
| MDTA youth program | 3–1[h] | 70,000 | 220,000 | 150,000 | 50,000 | 335,000 | 265,000 | 88,000 | 138,000 |
| New program for disadvantaged | 4–1[i] | 0 | 100,000 | 100,000 | 25,000 | 150,000 | 150,000 | 37,500 | 62,500 |
| Apprenticeship | 1–1 | 170,000 | 180,000 | 10,000 | 10,000 | 205,000 | 35,000 | 25,000 | 35,000 |
| Decasualization of jobs[j] | NA | 0 | NA | NA | NA | 50,000 | 50,000 | 9,500 | 9,500 |

a Assumes average duration of enrollment of 52 weeks per individual; in second year all enrollees will be employed the full year—such time lapse as might occur would be offset by small unemployment reductions stemming from the first year's program.

b Originally calculated when overall average unemployment rate was about 4 per cent, but still regarded by and large as a valid illustration of what is practicable at lower levels, in the light of the composition and growth of the labor force.

c Unemployment decline not cumulative.

d Assumes 10 per cent time lapse.

e Assumes 85 per cent of workers relocated or assisted by bonding stay employed.

f Represents only direct impact on unemployment of *speeded placement* due to modernizing of communication techniques; other Employment Service improvements which have long-run impacts on unemployment and on maintaining higher employment levels cannot presently be quantified. Assumes improvements in ES efficiency will reduce unemployment by 1 week below current experience for each nonagricultural placement made, other than casual placements: 7,500,000 placements $\times$ 0.67 (not casual) = 5,000,000 weeks of unemployment eliminated = 96,000 reduction in average unemployment.

g Includes program as presently authorized in Title II, less special youth program.

h Assumes (1) equal distribution of reemployment throughout the year; *ergo*, reduction in *average* unemployment is only one-half the number of persons placed in jobs; (2) 20 per cent dropout rate; (3) 75 per cent placement rate.

i Assumes (1) same as in footnote h; (2) 22 per cent dropout rate; (3) 64 per cent placement rate.

j Assumes an average of 10 weeks per year is added to the work experience of those able to find only intermittent work and a corresponding reduction in unemployment, or 500,000 weeks = 9,600 decline in average unemployment.

TABLE 2. Distribution of Unemployment Reductions by End of Second Year Among Selected Labor Force Groups, by Program[a]

| Action Program | Total Reduction in Unemployment by End of Second Year | Reduction in Unemployment among | | | |
|---|---|---|---|---|---|
| | | Youth | Nonwhite Adults | White Adult Long-term | White, Aged 20-24 |
| *Total* | *1,007,000* | | | | |
| *Total distributed* | *955,000* | *400,000* | *205,000* | *200,000* | *150,000* |
| Activities contributing directly to employment | *551,000* | *222,000* | *123,000* | *155,000* | *50,000* |
| Neighborhood Youth Corps—out-of-school | 180,000 | 165,000 | — | — | 15,000 |
| Adult work experience | 150,000 | — | 60,500 | 89,500 | — |
| Job development | 81,000 | 37,000 | 15,000 | 18,000 | 10,000 |
| Labor mobility | 85,000 | — | 37,500 | 37,500 | 10,000 |
| Bonding assistance | 55,000 | 20,000 | 10,000 | 10,000 | 15,000 |
| Improvement in matching workers and jobs | *96,000* | *2,500* | *7,500* | *2,500* | *32,500* |
| ES improvement | 96,000 | 2,500 | 7,500 | 2,500 | 32,500 |

| Improvement of workers' skills | *360,000* | *175,500* | *74,500* | *42,500* | *67,500* |
|---|---|---|---|---|---|
| MDTA Title II | 115,000 | — | 40,000 | 25,000 | 50,000 |
| New MDTA youth title | 138,000 | 128,000 | — | — | 10,000 |
| New MDTA title for disadvantaged | 62,500 | 22,500 | 25,000 | 15,000 | — |
| Apprenticeship | 35,000 | 25,000 | 2,500 | — | 7,500 |
| Decasualization | 9,500 | — | 7,000 | 2,500 | — |

[a] See Table 1 for assumptions and for program levels required to reduce average unemployment by the amounts shown.

higher overall level of unemployment than exists today. Yet they are still, by and large, a valid illustration of what is practicable at the present level. Obviously there are many variations that can be envisaged. Obviously, too, the effect of a given program level on unemployment rates—both the detailed rates and the overall rate—will depend on a number of things, including the economy's general performance. The illustrative relations between program level and expected effect on unemployment shown in Table 1 are rough judgments based on some degree of operating experience, but a great deal of additional experience is needed. The development of new types of cost-benefit analysis in the Department of Labor, now under way, will help to focus on this point.

These programs, directed at specific targets, would, of course, also generate additional effects on the unemployment of nontarget groups (adult married white males, for example), and computations concerning these and other multiplier effects can be made.

## Some Related Questions

A series of corollary and related questions arises. When we analyze the detailed rates and find some low rates—such as the overall rate for white married adult men—we ask how "low" this rate really is, and conclude that an answer will require much more searching analysis than has been given. But the existence of a low level does raise the question: to what extent will general efforts to reduce the overall rate result in more overtime hours for those in the group with the low unemployment rate, and what are the consequences of and alternatives to such policies?

A look at the detailed unemployment rates raises the question whether the terms full employment, over-full employment, unemployment, and underemployment, which have historically been applied to the overall rate, do not take on additional significance when applied to specific groups, and whether it is now the task of manpower specialists to see what these terms do mean when applied to specific groups. What conclusions do we draw from a situation in which a key part of the labor force is appropriately designated by each of these terms when looked at separately, regardless of the term that characterizes the overall rate?

Should we have specific separate goals for each part of the whole, as part of our manpower policy? How official should these goals be? And what should they be? The tables presented above do not reflect goals in any ultimate sense. In part, this is because there is still much work to be done to develop specific goals, and in part perhaps because we usually deal with next steps rather than with ultimate goals. Our concept of goal in the field of employment is a dynamic one, and new horizons emerge as we reach successive partial or interim goals.

A goal, even as an interim matter, is usually developed with an eye to the best performance of the past. But once one begins to develop detailed goals for subgroups of the labor force, one also begins to question some of the factors underlying past unemployment rates that were regarded as "normal." Let me take just two examples.

First, higher youth-unemployment rates and lower proportions of youth participating in the labor force have been accepted because they existed even in past periods of prosperity. Are these inevitable characteristics of youth or simply a reflection of the fact that we still have a lot to do to organize our labor market to bridge the gap between youth coming out of school and getting a job? To what extent will higher levels of preparation before young people come into the market result in firmer and quicker attachment and therefore less unemployment between the first few jobs? What are the real limits here?

Second, a significant part of our unemployment reflects time in transit from one job to another. It has been calculated that a reduction of one week in the average duration of unemployment by improved Employment Service methods would cut overall unemployment by about 100,000. Suppose, for example, that we were able to achieve the instant communications system, with the use of computers, recommended by the Automation Commission as part of a total process of improving the Employment Service, and that this step also had the effect of reducing overall unemployment rates. We should certainly have then another new dimension to the concept of "minimal irreducible" unemployment.

Similar questions can be raised about our assumptions of normality regarding unemployment rates of older workers and about the still-untackled problem of seasonality. The latter accounts for about one-fifth of all our unemployment and is responsible for a substantial part of the total cost of the unemployment insurance system.

The goals we have talked about are invariably expressed in terms of quantities—numbers of workers to be brought into jobs and unemployment to be reduced to an acceptable numerical low level. How about the quality of work and life? It is interesting to note that in the 1966 President's Manpower Report the following is stated in italics: *"Our goal is not just a job for every worker. Our goal is to place every worker in a job where he utilizes his full productive potential for his own and for society's benefit."* What are the full implications of these words? Some of the needed steps are outlined in the Manpower Report. Others, to give full meaning to this concept, will evolve as we learn more about quality of work that people will expect or desire from a society that may increasingly think in these terms. We have already seen major steps during the past 20 years in the provision of new forms of fringe benefits and new forms of security, but other forms of security that affect productive effort are still evolving, particularly in situations where work rules have impeded productive advances in the absence of arrangements for security. We have hardly tackled the restrictions that seasonality place upon the use of full productive potential. We have not yet begun to consider programs that will enable people to apply their abilities better by changing jobs without loss of security or by improving their productive potential by refreshment gained through sabbaticals and adult education.

What much of the foregoing means to me is that our manpower goals are dynamic goals, perhaps fixed in the broadest conception but certainly changing in their application. Perhaps this is partly because the whole matter of setting manpower goals is relatively new. The essence of their dynamic quality, I think, is shown by what has been happening: as new methods used to achieve full utilization of manpower have been found to leave some people still stranded, we have gone on to try to reach these people.

Sometimes it has almost seemed as if there were a kind of universal law, holding that whatever was started would have a 30 per cent dropout rate, whether it was a school program or a training program to pick up dropouts, a counseling program to pick up training dropouts, a program to reach those resisting counseling, and so on. What this seems to mean is that no single program can be applied to any group of people and be expected to meet the needs of all of them.

Certainly it has been the case that even where manpower programs have been successful, people who needed a program the most were often the last to consider that it could be meant for them. Realization of this fact has led to a variety of "outreach" programs designed to get to individuals who have been left out, to try to bring them into the kind of programs that will enable them to develop their abilities and get and maintain productive employment.

The approach that starts with reaching the individual is under way on an experimental basis under Labor Department auspices, under some educational jurisdictions, and under OEO programs. These activities are also leading to efforts which go beyond what we often think of as manpower activities in the traditional sense, but which are necessary if we are to bring the individuals involved into the main stream of society: health services, both physical and mental; remedial education; attention to the problems that inhibit the hiring of older workers, including the restrictive effects of some pension plans; coping with the general reluctance to hire part-time workers; attention to the special problems of the prison population, including steps to overcome discrimination and steps to train while in prison. (If our goal is rehabilitation rather than revenge, we have thus far drawn away only from the Biblical version of the latter.)

What I have essentially talked about are the kinds of goals that loom large in the consideration of those concerned with government manpower programs, but they are challenges for labor, management, and academic persons as well. Since the role of government is often to pick up the pieces left by others, it is only natural that manpower policy as operated by government concentrate on the most effective means of picking up pieces, as well as on means of ensuring that the economy operates in a manner designed to leave as few pieces as possible that need picking up.

**Conclusions**

I would conclude by noting that the setting of specific man-power goals becomes more and more significant not only to deal with specific human problems, such as those which were the subject of the very recent White House Conference on Civil Rights, but as a means of reaching our overall employment goals as well. This is especially the case as fears concerning inflation and balance-of-payments problems place inhibitions on some of the dimensions of overall action. Indeed, pinpointed manpower programs have fiscal implications too, but these implications are relatively low per unit of unemployment reduction, and the way in which they improve the work force should enable the economy to cope better with the "inflationary" factors. This in turn can lead to rather new views concerning what our employment goals should be and the manner in which they can be reached.

So long as there are inhibitions on overall action by the government to spur the general level of the economy because of fears concerning inflation—whether these fears arise from domestic or offshore considerations, whether or not they are justified, whether or not overall measures can in fact lower unemployment rates "if only given a chance"—pinpointed manpower programs can be a significant addition to the measures we use to reach full employment. They should enable us to reach lower and lower levels of unemployment with increased comfort and less strain—whether real or fancied—on the economy, and they should enable us to achieve other social objectives more surely than might otherwise be the case.

**NOTES**

1. This paper represents the views of the author, who is on leave from the U.S. Department of Labor, but draws upon work which has been under way in the Department of Labor—especially in the field of overall program planning in which the author has been involved, i.e., analysis of unemployment rates, under the leadership of Harold Goldstein, and the planning of specific manpower programs, under William B. Hewitt.

2. R. A. Gordon has presented an illustrative set of full-employment

targets in "Full Employment as a Policy Goal," in A. M. Ross, editor, *Employment Policy and the Labor Market* (Berkeley: University of California Press, 1965). The paper now being presented in a sense illustrates the program developments which might be undertaken to reach targets of this type, although not precisely the targets in Dr. Gordon's paper.

3. Similar additional calculations can also be made, of course, showing the effects of education and other programs upon unemployment rates of specific groups.

# Discussion

## BY WILLIAM G. BOWEN [1]

It is a brave man who writes a paper on manpower goals—or who discusses one. Platitudes are hard to avoid, because so often they seem appropriate—indeed, are appropriate. And I want to plead guilty at the outset of my brief comments to having fallen prey to the temptation to retreat to what I would like to think of as "first principles," but which may also be regarded as somewhat banal generalities.

At the highest level of conceptualization, all of our various sets of proximate goals, ranging from manpower goals to foreign policy goals, ought to be derived from a single set of notions concerning the nature and characteristics of the good life. However, while manpower policies clearly do, in various ways, affect our ability to attain such goals as peace, freedom, and the dignity of the individual, our present discussion will be facilitated if we quickly take a giant step down to a second level of goals, to a set of macroeconomic and social goals which are more immediately related to manpower policies and which can be viewed as means to the attainment of our ultimate goals.

Here we might list low unemployment, reasonable price stability, an efficient allocation of resources, a satisfactory rate of economic growth, concern for the economic security of the individual and his family, and the promotion of social welfare—this latter rubric encompassing equality of opportunity, fair treatment of minority groups, and the elimination of concentrations of poverty. So, in a very general sense, I should argue that the task of manpower policy is to contribute to the attainment of this broad set of goals. The fact that these goals often conflict implies a special need to pursue policies which make the trade-offs among them as palatable as possible, as well as policies aimed solely at a particular goal.

## Specific Manpower Goals

The next stage in the goal-setting process should consist of the identification of a still more proximate set of goals particularly susceptible to the blandishments of manpower policies. At this level of discourse, three goals seem to me to be paramount:

1. *Improving the effectiveness with which our system of labor markets performs its allocative function.* Matching the preferences of employers and workers is the most important aspect of this task, but it is not all that is involved. Facilitating movement into and out of the labor force is an increasingly important function, and it is by no means unrelated to the problem of seasonal unemployment which Mr. Arnow discusses in his paper.

2. *Making it possible for each person to receive the optimal amount and kind of education, training, and health care.* Some people might describe this goal as "improving the quality of the labor force." While, more often than not, this is what is required, it is important to recognize that a society can overinvest in education, training, and health care as well as underinvest. Phrasing the goal in terms of the "optimal" provision, while having the undesirable attribute of sounding like jargon, has the more than offsetting advantage of suggesting that incremental costs must be weighed against the likely benefits.

3. *Improving the job opportunities of disadvantaged groups.* What constitutes a "disadvantaged group" is a question worth more discussion than it can be given here. However, this difficult question can perhaps be passably fuzzed over for the moment by including within the disadvantaged category not only minorities of various kinds who encounter discrimination but also families in certain geographic and occupational categories, children from certain family situations, and people who suffer from various mental and physical handicaps.

It is, I hope, plain from what has been said so far that I believe strongly in treating manpower goals as "derived goals," in Mr. Arnow's terminology, and that I disagree with the view that approaching manpower goals in this fashion is tantamount to being indifferent as to the part of the manpower force that is affected. Indeed, it is because one of our national goals is increased equality of opportunity and treatment that we are concerned about the composition of the unemployed.

It must be at least equally plain that the goals stated above are nonoperational, in the sense that no specific set of program implications flows from them. This is as it should be and is no cause for apology. There is at least a rough and ready distinction to be drawn between goals which describe what we want to see come about and programs meant to accomplish those ends. Our broad goals ought to be clear, shining targets, largely impervious to the shifting circumstances of the day (which is not to say that the relative importance of pursuing various goals ought to be unaffected by changing circumstances). Operational programs, on the other hand, must have a much more pragmatic cast.

Perhaps the most important general point to recognize is that there is no possibility of moving to the operational level without doing a lot of hard analysis. Alternative ways of accomplishing the same (or similar) objectives have to be specified, and the benefits and costs of each have to be evaluated. Of course, there is a point at which the cost-benefit ratio of additional cost-benefit analysis is itself so unfavorable as to suggest the desirability of making up our minds. And since we cannot constantly be restudying all problems, we are surely well advised to search for rules of thumb which will work more often than not. But rules of thumb can be harmful as well as helpful, especially if we forget that they are only rules of thumb.

## Some Other Matters

In the light of the above observations, I should now like to comment briefly on a few specific matters raised in Mr. Arnow's paper.

While sharing the general enthusiasm of others for the BLS Growth Project and the new work on educational requirements, I worry about the interpretation which will be given to the resulting set of occupational and educational projections. Both the input-output matrix and the educational-requirements data are of the fixed coefficient genre; and, since we know that coefficients do change, projections based on instruments of this kind are bound to miss the mark.

But it is not the likelihood of error itself which bothers me; it is the systematic tendency for such projections to exaggerate "needs" (for, say, dentists) by failing to allow for the factor and product substitutions which can be expected to accompany changes in relative prices. Just as a fixed-weight price index exaggerates the extent of increases in the cost of living by failing to allow for the tendency of consumers to substitute items whose relative prices are falling for items becoming relatively more expensive, so projections of the excess demand for dentists will be exaggerated if they fail to allow for both the partial substitution of other factors of production (more nurses, better equipment, cavity-preventing medications, and even new forms of organization in the industry) and some substitution of other consumer goods for the purchase of dental services. In short, beware any forecast which assumes that demands for factors and products are completely price inelastic.

Next, at the risk of reopening a general subject all of us are sick of discussing, I feel impelled to object to the basic premise underlying Arnow's Table 1 and much of the accompanying discussion. I do not think that manpower policies *per se* should have as one of their main goals a reduction in the overall level of unemployment by 1 million or any other number. In the short run, at any rate, the primary determinant of the level of unemployment is the level of aggregate demand. As Garth Mangum stated so well in 1965, "It is a trite but often overlooked principle that jobs are created only by the spending of money. Education does not create jobs; retraining does not create jobs; placement does not create jobs." [2] This is why "reducing the aggregate level of unemployment" appears among my list of macrogoals but not among the set of goals which I regard as particularly susceptible to manpower policies.

To be sure, by pursuing the first two of the three goals on my list—improving the functioning of labor markets and helping to train the labor force—manpower policies play a significant role in determining the extent to which increases in aggregate demand result in increased employment and not just higher prices, which in turn is an important determinant of the desirability of increasing aggregate demand in the first place. Similarly, overtime provisions affect the trade-off between longer hours and more jobs. In addition, those concerned with manpower policies are especially likely to be aware of the human as well as the economic costs of high unemployment, and thus have a valuable perspective to bring to bear on discussions within the government of the arguments for and against additional monetary-fiscal expansion. All of these roles do seem, however, to be essentially supportive in character, and I think that the essential objectives of manpower policies are most likely to be kept clearly in focus if only modest claims are made on behalf of the ability of manpower policies alone to affect the total volume of unemployment.

At a time when there is a general excess of demand over supply, retraining programs and related measures may lead directly to increases in employment, though even in such circumstances manpower policies are likely to make their most important mark by increasing the qualitative contributions which individuals who benefit from additional training will make over their lifetimes. The experience during the Second World War is still the best evidence for the proposition that when demand is very strong almost anyone can find a job. The really challenging task for manpower policies is to see to it that the job prospects of certain segments of the community are not limited to "a" job but that those groups of people, who through no fault of their own now find themselves at the end of every job queue, have a fairer crack at securing not just a job now but *good* jobs throughout their *lifetimes*. Unfortunately, programs aimed at improvements in the overall quality of the labor force, and especially of the long-run job prospects of chronically disadvantaged groups, may be harder to sell both within the Executive branch and to Congress than policies which promise to reduce unemployment by "x" number of people next month. Nevertheless, I remain convinced that the former line of argument is the one which is consistent with using manpower policies to their best advantage.

Responsibility for the amount of frictional unemployment is an entirely different matter. Here manpower policies have a direct role to play. Policies which improve the quality of labor-

market information, and the speed with which it can be trans-
mitted from place to place, tend to reduce the amount of frictional unemployment by lessening the time it takes a particular
worker to find a suitable job.

Caution is called for in estimating the effects of such improvements on the overall amount of frictional unemployment,
however—which is why "tend to reduce" is inserted in the above
sentence. The provision of better labor-market information might
well increase the total number of voluntary job changes, and, if
this effect were strong enough, the overall amount of frictional
unemployment could conceivably increase even though the time
lost per job-changer declined. An increase in the amount of frictional unemployment that was attributable to increased voluntary mobility would not, of course, be a bad thing. My point is
not that a higher level of frictional unemployment is, in fact,
likely to accompany improved labor-market information but that
there is the possibility of such an association—and the possibility
warns against excessive allegiance to the unqualified goal of reducing frictional unemployment.[3]

## Composition of the Unemployed

Now, just a few words about the composition of the unemployed. As already stated, I regard concern for the social and
family consequences of the incidence of unemployment as a
prime area of responsibility for manpower policies. I would
underscore what Mr. Arnow has already said concerning the
importance of this area of concern and add the assertion that
until very recently it has received insufficient emphasis within
our hierarchy of goals.

The purist in me, however, worries a bit about viewing particular unemployment rates above the average as *ipso facto*
evidence that something is wrong. It is, no doubt, a good rule
of thumb to concentrate attention on those groups with abnor-
mally high unemployment rates, but it is only a rule of thumb.
After all, we would expect some differences in unemployment
rates to be associated with such factors as a person's age, family
status, occupation, and industry affiliation, all of which affect the
likelihood that a person will be moving into or out of the labor
force, moving from one job to another, or waiting for his regular

employer to recall him. The market does produce some compensating adjustments for the degree of uncertainty characteristic of employment prospects in different fields (which presumably explains, in part, the relatively high pay scales in construction), and to the extent this occurs it is wrong to view workers in the high unemployment areas as necessarily worse off than other workers.

It is no part of my purpose to suggest that the prevailing distribution of unemployment rates can be rationalized as reflecting the workings of an ever-present and ever-beneficent invisible hand. What I am arguing is that *some* differences in unemployment rates serve proper economic functions while others are evidence of our continuing failures to provide equal opportunities and to find more efficient ways to organize certain labor markets.

The trick is to determine which are which, and this, in a way, summarizes the general tenor of my comments. The setting of explicit goals is plainly a valuable undertaking, but it must not be viewed as a substitute for the hard job of analysis.

## NOTES

1. I am indebted to my colleague, Professor Joseph Mooney, for a number of helpful suggestions.
2. "The Role of 'Job Creation' Programs," in W. G. Bowen and F. H. Harbison, editors, *Unemployment in a Prosperous Economy* (Princeton, N.J.: Industrial Relations Section, Princeton University, 1965), p. 108.
3. In countries where workers are much more closely tied to jobs, whether by law or custom, the amount of cyclical unemployment, as well as frictional unemployment, tends to be lower than in the United States, since there is more reluctance to lay off workers when demand declines. But this simply amounts to converting measured unemployment to hidden unemployment, while simultaneously adding a dose of rigidity to the economic system and can hardly be construed as evidence of superior economic performance.

# Discussion

## BY ARNOLD R. WEBER

As any time-study man will attest, setting goals for other people can be a difficult task. This process is no less frustrating for the manpower specialist than the industrial engineer. In his discussion, Philip Arnow enumerates, directly or by implication, at least 12 generic categories of goals available to the apprentice goal-setter. These include intermediate and ultimate goals, specific and general, social and individual, dynamic and static, long-run and short-run, and qualitative and quantitative goals. If, like Arnow, we accept Garth Mangum's threefold classification of substantive objectives in the area of manpower policy, i.e., creating jobs, training people for jobs, and matching people and jobs, we immediately have 36 possible goals from which to choose. By developing more elegant combinations of generic types and substantive objectives, the number of choices rapidly approaches infinity or outruns the technical competence of the labor economist trained in the precomputer era.

This statistical note is not introduced to bedevil Mr. Arnow. If that were the case, it is clear that the wrong knight is on the wrong horse. However, such an exercise does indicate the range of options and problems that await the policy-maker who is commissioned to formulate manpower goals on an Olympian level. In fact, the goals of manpower policy, like the policy objectives in other areas of social and economic activity, cannot be formulated *in vacuo*. Instead, these goals must reflect the context and technical constraints that will affect their implementation. Although Arnow's paper gives a comprehensive view of manpower policy options, it neglects those factors that should or will determine the effective policy choices. My comments will be directed to a brief specification of those considerations.

**Conditions for Setting Manpower Goals**

First, national manpower goals and programs must be related to other, private activities concerned with the process of manpower development, allocation, and utilization. In this respect, there is ample evidence that most manpower issues have been and will continue to be resolved by private individuals and institutions. The labor market has been a durable and generally effective instrument for the allocation of labor. Management has developed extensive corporate programs for the development of required skills. Union policies have had a direct impact on manpower issues. And an increasing number of private, charitable institutions have manifested a growing interest in what might be identified as manpower questions.

Obviously, Mr. Arnow and other members of the Department of Labor have given considerable thought to this issue. However, there is little indication in his paper of the relationship of public goals to the wide range of activities in the private sector. Instead, we can only infer that some *ad hoc* experimentation between public and private agencies has been taking place, as indicated by the increased emphasis on on-the-job training under the Manpower Development and Training Act (MDTA), the enlisting of private agencies in the "outreach" programs, and the use of private corporations to administer the Job Corps camps.

Second, Arnow's paper is marked by a general neglect of what might be called "the economics of manpower policies." This point may be best illustrated by reference to Table 1 of his paper. That is, if the ratio of program level to the projected decline in unemployment is one to one for the Neighborhood Youth Corps (NYC) and three to one for MDTA Youth Programs, it is difficult to understand why all the available public resources to aid unemployed youth are not shifted from MDTA to the NYC. The answer may lie in differences in the cost of the respective programs, differences in the clientele served, or old-fashioned, bureaucratic empire-building. Similarly, it is difficult to understand why, within the framework of MDTA, more emphasis has not been given to on-the-job training (OJT) as contrasted to institutional training. The average cost per trainee in OJT programs is about one-third the cost for trainees in institutional courses. In addition, OJT trainees enjoy a higher ratio of "success" measured in terms of both completions and subsequent employment. Recognition of the economics of manpower policies also implies that some attention should be given to the complementary relationships between different elements of manpower programs. Thus, to what extent does a program to promote labor mobility improve the success of retraining efforts? And how will the programs for labor mobility benefit from the investment in resources to improve the operation of the Employment Service? In this manner, the simple categorization of manpower goals and programs may overlook important considerations of substitutability and complementarity. By relating manpower goals to the context of total manpower activities and by applying standards of efficiency, a clearer idea may be obtained of the comparative advantage of public activities and the appropriate combination of measures that may be used to achieve these goals.

Third, it is probably redundant, but necessary, to state that the formulation of manpower goals cannot be insulated from short-term political pressures and must be flexible enough to accommodate them. In this respect, the short history of explicit manpower policies in the United States, like geological strata, bears the clear imprint of contemporary events. The initial manpower goals and policies largely reflect the Great Automation Scare of the late 1950's and an attempt to grapple with structural unemployment. The second layer of goals and policies reveals the scorch marks caused by the civil rights revolution and gives the greatest attention to youth and to minority groups. And most recently, we can only conjecture how many drafts of the President's Manpower Report were rewritten to give prominence to the problems of skill shortages induced by full employment—albeit "interim" full employment.

It is clear that one of the major problems of goal-setting in the manpower area is defining objectives that will be durable enough to permit the implementation of the related programs. In the United States we have seen a shift of goals from ameliorating the consequences of automation, to expanding the economic and social opportunities of minorities, to relieving skill shortages. The three goals are not incompatible, but the attainment of each will require modified strategies and tactics. As I read Mr. Arnow's paper, he appreciates these factors when he says that manpower goals must be "dynamic" and that the government must be prepared to "pick up the pieces." Nonetheless, I am hard pressed to reconcile these characterizations with the discussion of manpower needs based on an input-output matrix and the static specification of programs presented in Table 1.

## A Suggested Dichotomy

This discussion leads me to establish my own dichotomy of national manpower goals. My preference is to simplify the task by specifying two types of programs: those that are client-oriented and those that are institution-building and improving. (If you should say that these distinctions represent short-run goals and long-run goals or intermediate or ultimate goals, I would wince but would accept these characterizations with humility.) That is, there are those manpower programs that will have as their objective the alleviation of the economic plight of identifiable groups that, at any particular time, suffer special disabilities in the labor market. Such programs would be responsive to the short-term consequences of economic change and immediate political pressures that inevitably will play on the government in this area. At this time, the focus of our concern is members of minority groups and young people. In the next few years it may be white, Protestant, middle-aged, middle managers who have been displaced by IBM 360. In Mr. Arnow's terms the government should be prepared to "pick up the pieces" for both economic and compassionate reasons.

On the other hand, there are those programs whose goal will be to build or improve those institutions that are directly concerned with the quality and allocation of the nation's manpower. This means programs to improve the educational system, to develop effective systems of labor market information, to remove barriers to entry, and to stimulate individual and corporate investment in human resources.

Obviously, the significance of client-oriented goals and programs will diminish to the extent that the goal of developing improved manpower institutions is realized. Moreover, the benefits of improved manpower institutions will extend beyond the immediate needs and pressures generated by particular client groups. To date, most of our public manpower efforts have been of the short-term, client-oriented variety. Mr. Arnow's exposition of alternative goals and current legislative activities indicate that long-range, institution-building goals will be given greater prominence in the future. Such a change in emphasis should be welcomed for it will provide the occasion for more clearly defining the government's role vis-à-vis private institutions and for subjecting public programs to more demanding tests of social efficiency.

CHAPTER 4

# The Role of Manpower Policy in Achieving Aggregate Goals

## BY LESTER C. THUROW

The general framework for public manpower programs is furnished by society's qualitative and quantitative choice of aggregate goals and the time constraints placed on their achievement. Goals and time constraints have to be specified since manpower programs needed to reach 3 per cent unemployment in one year are not necessarily optimal to eliminate poverty in ten years. Analyzing linkages between manpower programs and aggregate goals can show how targets might be achieved and improved, but the role of public programs cannot be specified until the extent of private programs has been delineated. How will private programs respond to aggregate changes in the economy, and what part will they play in providing labor skills? Present data make a precise answer impossible, but the question needs to be posed since the role of public manpower programs emerges as the difference between programs needed to reach postulated goals and those the private sector will automatically provide. If private programs are not adequate, policy-makers still have two major alternatives. They can design policies to change the nature and magnitudes of private manpower decisions, or they can institute direct public programs.

Manpower programs can be broadly defined to include any economic policy which affects labor; but since most economic policies would fall within this definition, manpower policies are here defined as *programs designed to improve the matching of skills demanded and supplied in the labor market.* Some programs would increase the size or skills of the labor force, others would improve the allocative efficiency of the labor market, and still others would alter the size or skill content of labor demands.

This paper examines using manpower policies to achieve and improve targets in four areas. The four goals are: (1) high growth, (2) low unemployment, (3) income equalization, and (4) stable prices; but each of these goals will be more explicitly quantified later. After we investigate each goal and the areas in which manpower policies might have an impact, the determinants of private manpower decisions are analyzed to see how public policies might be used to change private decisions. Since private programs provide the overwhelming bulk of manpower training after formal education, these private decisions have to be a central concern of aggregate policy.

Section I presents a method for calculating the potential rate of growth and analyzes the potential impact of manpower policies. Section II examines minimum levels of frictional unemployment and methods for reducing it. Section III outlines the interaction between aggregate growth and manpower policies in eliminating poverty and Negro-white income differences. Section IV compares manpower and incomes policies as tools for reducing inflation. Section V examines the determinants of private training decisions in a dynamic economy. Section VI offers a short conclusion.

## I. High Growth

Are public manpower policies necessary to accelerate the potential rate of growth? To answer this question the policy-maker needs to know the magnitude of the present potential rate of growth so that he can judge its adequacy or inadequacy. Using an aggregate production function provides a simple yet flexible tool for calculating the potential growth of output and productivity, but, more importantly, it has the advantage of making explicit the sources of growth and the places where public and private policies can have an impact.

In a modified version of a production function derived by Solow, there are five general sources of growth (see equation 1).[1]

$$(1) \qquad Y(t) = e^{a+bU+cU^2}A e^{\alpha t}[K_{X_1}(t)^{1-\lambda}L_{X_2}(t)^{\lambda}]^{\gamma}$$

where $Y$ = private GNP
$\quad\ \ U$ = unemployment
$\quad\ \ t$ = time
$\quad\ \ X_1$ = rate of embodied technical progress in capital
$\quad\ \ X_2$ = rate of embodied technical progress in labor
$\quad\ \ K_{X_1}$ = capital stock measured in efficiency units
$\quad\ \ L_{X_2}$ = labor stock measured in efficiency units

They are (1) the growth of disembodied technical progress $(\alpha)$, (2) the growth of capital and labor stocks ($K$ and $L$), (3) the rates of embodied technical progress in capital and labor ($X_1$ and $X_2$), (4) any economies or diseconomies of scale $(\gamma - 1)$, and (5) favorable or unfavorable utilization adjustments $(a + bU + cU^2)$. Disembodied technical progress is caused by improvements in organization; embodied technical progress in labor is a function of education and training; embodied technical progress in capital results from the development of more efficient types of capital equipment; and the utilization factor accounts for the cyclical impact of utilization on the average level of productivity. Given estimates of the parameters of equation (1) and the growth of capital, labor, and embodied technical progress, the production function can be used to estimate potential growth.

The same production function used to calculate the potential growth of output can be transformed into a function giving the determinants of the potential growth of productivity per manhour. This is done by dividing equation (1) by observed manhours and then differentiating the resulting expression with respect to time (see equation 2).[2]

$$(2) \qquad \frac{\dot{P}}{P} = b(\dot{U}) + \alpha + \gamma\lambda \frac{\dot{L}_{X_2}}{L_{X_2}} + \gamma(1 - \lambda) \frac{\dot{K}_{X_1}}{K_{X_1}} - \frac{\dot{L}}{L}$$

where a dot over a variable indicates the change in the variable with respect to a change in time, and $P =$ output per observed manhour, $L_{X_2} =$ embodied manhours, $K_{X_1} =$ embodied capital stock, and $L =$ observed manhours.

In equation (2) the potential growth of productivity is a positive function of the rate of disembodied technical progress $(\alpha)$, the growth of the embodied labor stock $\frac{\dot{L}_{X_2}}{L_{X_2}}$, and the growth of the embodied capital stock $\frac{\dot{K}_{X_1}}{K_{X_1}}$, but a negative function of the growth of physical manhours $\frac{\dot{L}}{L}$.

Using parameters statistically estimated by fitting equation (1) to annual data from 1929 to 1965,[3] and combining a potential growth of labor manhours of 1.5 per cent[4] with the assumption that the capital stock grows at the rate projected for 1966 by the U.S. Department of Commerce's survey of investment intentions,[5] the potential rate of growth from 1965 to 1970 would be 4.4 per cent. Lacking an adequate investment function, however, several alternative assumptions could be made about the growth of the capital stock. A representative sample of these assumptions is presented in Table 1. Depending on the growth of the capital stock, the potential growth of productivity ranges from 2.5 to 3.3 per cent, and the growth of output ranges from 4.0 to 4.9 per cent. The lower estimates are the most relevant since they correspond to the more reasonable assumptions about the growth of the capital stock. Because investment was low in the Depression and the Second World War, nearly all of gross investment was a net addition to the capital stock in the immediate postwar period. By 1965, the capital stock was much larger, and therefore so were depreciation charges as a result of the high investment of the previous twenty years. If the capital stock $(K)$ is to grow from 1966 to 1970 at its average postwar rate, private investment will have to rise to 12.4 per cent of private GNP. This is substantially above the high levels of 1965 (11.6 per cent) and far above the average level of 10.6 per cent from 1957 to 1964. And for the capital-labor ratio to grow from

TABLE 1.  POTENTIAL GROWTH RATE OF OUTPUT
AND PRODUCTIVITY, 1965–1970
(per cent per year)

| Capital Growth Hypothesis | Productivity | Private GNP |
|---|---|---|
| 1946–1965 Growth of capital | 3.1 | 4.7 |
| 1946–1965 Growth of capital-labor ratio | 3.3 | 4.9 |
| 1965 Growth of capital-labor ratio | 2.5 | 4.0 |
| 1966 (estimated) Growth of capital stock | 2.9 | 4.4 |

1965 to 1970 at its postwar trend would require an investment ratio of 15.9 per cent and thus a major shift from consumption to investment.

Using equation (2), Table 2 presents the estimated and actual growth of productivity for three postwar periods: (1) the first postwar cycle and the period of growth during the Korean War, (2) the stagnation of the mid- and late fifties, and (3) the current expansion. Analysis of the past five or six years reveals that there is little justification for concluding that the growth of productivity has accelerated since the 1960–1961 recession. Productivity gains have been good, but this is to be expected because of favorable utilization adjustments. The productivity function somewhat underestimates productivity since 1960, but this is due to a large underestimate in 1962 when the economy was coming out of a recession. Productivity actually rose 5.3 per cent in 1962, but the predicted increase was only 3.9 per cent. Part of the overestimate is offset by 1965, when productivity did not rise as much as predicted. The difference between the estimated and actual gains from productivity in 1965 results essentially from misestimates of the size of the gains from improvements in utilization. For some reason this improvement did not materialize. It would be imprudent to conclude that productivity has autonomously increased when the dominant ob-

servation was a strong recovery year several years in the past and
particularly when the most recent year was below expectations.

TABLE 2.  ESTIMATED AND ACTUAL PRODUCTIVITY GROWTH IN
THE POSTWAR PERIOD
(per cent per year)

| Year | Rate of Growth of Productivity | |
|------|-------------|--------|
|      | Estimated   | Actual |
| 1948–1953 | 4.2 | 4.5 |
| 1954–1959 | 2.9 | 2.8 |
| 1960–1965 | 2.7 | 3.0 |
| 1962–1964 | 3.1 | 3.9 |
| 1964–1965 | 3.2 | 2.6 |

**Accelerating potential growth.** If the potential growth of output and productivity are unacceptable, many methods can be
used to alter them. The capital stock could be expanded faster
by investing more and consuming less; research expenditures
for improving capital equipment could be enlarged. From a manpower point of view, manhours could be increased by increasing
participation rates or by lengthening hours of work. Any manpower programs which resulted in a lower minimum level of unemployment (see below) would increase potential output directly
by increasing labor supplies and indirectly through the coefficients of a favorable utilization adjustment. A program which
reduced the nominal full employment level of unemployment by
0.5 percentage point would increase the level of potential output
by 1.2 per cent by virtue of induced increases in the labor force,
voluntary lengthening of hours of work, and a favorable utilization adjustment, in addition to the direct increase in employment. Since embodied technical progress in labor is a function
of education and on-the-job training (OJT), changes in these
variables could influence the productivity of labor. In the estimating equation (footnote 3) embodied technical progress in
labor occurs at 1 per cent per year since this is the rate of
growth of median school years completed. If expenditures on
formal education and OJT were equally productive and if there

were no diseconomies of scale in these expenditures, a 10 per cent increase in current expenditures on education and OJT would cause the embodied rate of technical progress in labor to rise to 1.1 per cent and the potential rate of growth of output to rise by 0.08 percentage points. Since OJT is specifically designed to increase productivity while education is partially a consumption good, the same increase might be achievable with a smaller investment in OJT alone. On the other hand, a more highly educated labor force might also have an impact on the rate of embodied technical progress in capital since this is ultimately a function of human skills.

In equation (1) disembodied technical progress ($\alpha$) is a function of time and independent of actual changes in the economy. This may be a bad assumption. Business pressures to reorganize might increase during periods of rapid growth when additional labor cannot be hired and when capital expansion is already occurring at capacity rates. During periods of rapid growth and low unemployment, labor mobility increases and labor's resistance to reorganization and innovation decreases. An economy which is continually at full employment might cause changes in the behavior of both labor and business which would result in a faster introduction of new organizational techniques. Government programs to provide technical assistance to the private sector (such as those in the Departments of Agriculture and Commerce) might also accelerate disembodied technical progress, as well as embodied technical progress in capital and labor.

## II. Low Unemployment

Given present institutions, what is the minimum level of unemployment that can be achieved by expanding aggregate demand? This level of frictional unemployment is not reached at the point at which the labor market is forced to adjust to a different composition of age, sex, race, and skill characteristics among the newly employed. Early in 1965 employers started to find experienced adult white males in short supply and had to shift employment standards so that young workers, females, and Negroes accounted for a much larger proportion of total employment gains. Nor is frictional unemployment to be defined in terms of the point at which prices start to rise or at which price increases become intolerable. It is simply the point at which unemployment will stop falling regardless of the expansion of aggregate demand. But this is probably not invariant with respect to the time period under consideration. For example 3 per cent unemployment might be frictional unemployment in the short run, but not in the long run. Thus as aggregate demand expanded the economy would reach 3 per cent unemployment. Unemployment would stop falling in the short run, but if the economy remained at this level for a period of several years, changes in expectations, training decisions, and other relevant parameters might allow the economy to proceed to lower levels of unemployment. With the experience of several years of full employment, the economy might very well be able to proceed to European levels of frictional unemployment. Since the American economy has had no experience of a long period of peacetime full employment, the rest of this section will be devoted to examining short-run frictional unemployment.

Frictional unemployment is principally determined by four factors: (1) seasonal unemployment, (2) the number of workers who are unemployable due to personal handicaps or habits, (3) unemployment from volutary or involuntary mobility between jobs, and (4) unemployment from movements into or out of the labor force. Several methods of isolating frictional unemployment are possible,[7] but one method is to go back to a past period in which only frictional unemployment existed and try to determine what changes have taken place in the intervening period.

Unemployment of 2.6 per cent is used as the starting point since three consecutive years of rapidly expanding output were able to bring unemployment to this level for five months in 1953, but the economy was never able to reach lower levels. Lower rates were reached during the Second Word War, but labor controls were in operation. Since 1953 the number of females and young workers has risen relative to the number of adult males, but this factor is counterbalanced by higher education levels. According to analysis presented in the Economic Report of the President, a rising proportion of female and young workers has led to an increase in unemployment of 0.1 percentage point since 1957, but this was more than offset by increased levels of education which would have reduced unemployment by 0.4 percentage point (*ceteris paribus*).[8]

The analysis of the Council of Economic Advisers implicitly assumes that unemployment within each component of the labor force has not changed. Only the relative weights are different. The difference between supply- and demand-induced changes in educational requirements are difficult to distinguish, but the level of education demanded in the labor market can be rising just as well as the level of education supplied. What was a frictional level of unemployment for eighth-grade graduates in 1953 might be a frictional level of unemployment for high school graduates in 1966.

No direct observations exist on within-group frictional unemployment, but indirect methods can be used. Since current unemployment reflects the pressures of demand and supply changes by age, sex, education, and other relevant variables, it provides the best source of information about any changes that may have occurred. By picking two periods of equal national unemployment and investigating alterations in the component unemployment rates, actual rates might be used to give a rough indication of possible changes in frictional unemployment.

In the quarter composed of December 1950 and January and February 1951 and in the first quarter of 1966, national unemployment was 3.8 per cent. These two quarters occurred in very similar situations. Unemployment was falling at about the same rate, and a war was taking young men out of the civilian labor force. Since 1950–1951, there has been a sharp increase in unemployment for teenagers and females 20–24, a small increase for males 20–24, and a sharp decline for both males and females over 25 years of age according to the age-sex unemployment vectors (see Table 3).

Table 3 also presents the corresponding vector of unemployment for the five months of 1953 when unemployment was 2.6 per cent. If these rates are applied to the labor force in the first quarter of 1966, changes in the relative importance of different age-sex groups increase frictional unemployment from 2.6 to 2.7 per cent. But age-sex unemployment rates that have risen between 1950–1951 and 1966 furnish evidence that frictional unemployment for the same groups may have also risen. Where unemployment is higher in 1966, two assumption are made. Frictional unemployment for these groups is assumed to have risen above 1953 levels by the same proportion as actual unemployment increased from 1950–1951 to 1966, or it is assumed to have risen by the same absolute amount (see Table 3). For those age-sex groups for which 1966 unemployment is lower than in 1950–1951, frictional unemployment is assumed to remain at 1953 levels. If the unemployment vector based on the proportional assumption is applied to the 1966 labor force, frictional unemployment rises to 3.1 per cent; if the vector based on the

TABLE 3. CALCULATIONS OF FRICTIONAL UNEMPLOYMENT RATE (per cent)

| Sex and Age | Recorded Unemployment 1966[a] | Recorded Unemployment 1950–1951[b] | Frictional Unemployment 1953[c] | Projected Frictional Unemployment Rates Proportional Assumption[d] | Projected Frictional Unemployment Rates Absolute Assumption[e] |
|---|---|---|---|---|---|
| Men | | | | | |
| 20–24 | 4.5 | 4.3 | 4.0 | 4.2 | 4.2 |
| 25 and over | 2.4 | 2.9 | 2.0 | 2.0 | 2.0 |
| Women | | | | | |
| 20–24 | 6.2 | 4.8 | 3.8 | 4.9 | 5.2 |
| 25 and over | 3.3 | 4.1 | 2.3 | 2.3 | 2.3 |
| Both Sexes | | | | | |
| 14–19 | 11.6 | 7.7 | 6.3 | 9.5 | 10.2 |
| Total | 3.8 | 3.8 | 2.6 | 3.1 | 3.2 |

[a] Based on January, February, and March 1966.
[b] Based on December 1950, and January and February 1951.
[c] Based on February, March, May, June, and July, 1953.
[d] Based on assumption that 1953 rates for teenagers and for men and woman from 20–24 are increased by same proportion as increase from 1950–1951 to 1966.
[e] Based on assumption that 1953 rates for teenagers and for men and women from 20–24 are increased by the same absolute amount as increase from 1950–1951 to 1966.

absolute assumption is used, frictional unemployment rises to 3.2 per cent. While 2.7 per cent probably represents a minimum estimate of frictional unemployment in 1966, 3.1 or 3.2 per cent probably represents an upper bound for estimates. Higher rates can only result from two factors. First, frictional unemployment for age-sex groups whose actual rates have fallen relative to national unemployment in the past fifteen years may have risen. If something occurred which increased the number of unemployed due to seasonal, mobility, turnover, or unemployability factors, frictional unemployment rates for adult males (20 and up) and adult females (25 and up) may have risen. While this is a logical possibility, there is as yet no evidence to support the conclusion. At the same time it is hard to think of factors that would cause the frictional rates for these groups to fall. Second, the differential applied to 1953 rates may widen in either relative or absolute terms as the economy moves to lower rates of unemployment. The experience of the past two years contradicts this hypothesis. Since 1963 there has been a slight narrowing in proportional terms and a large narrowing in absolute terms. To the extent that the queue theory of the labor market is correct, the differentials could be expected to narrow since the most disadvantaged workers are absorbed last. Thus the relative rates for young workers would not be expected to fall until the rates for adult workers had reached frictional levels.

**Altering frictional unemployment.** Frictional unemployment of between 2.7 and 3.2 per cent may or may not be satisfactory as a national total, but the impetus for lowering it and the direction of manpower programs are specified by dissatisfaction with the distribution of unemployment. Even returning to the 3 per cent distributions of the Korean War (1951–1953) would no longer be satisfactory since Negro unemployment was still 5.0 per cent (vs. 2.9 per cent for whites), and unemployment among young workers (14–24) was still 6.1 per cent although the relative number of young workers was at an all-time low. By both industry and occupation, the highest unemployment rates were over twice the national average. Since then there is very little evidence that the dispersion has either widened or closed.

Part of the dispersion could be eliminated by progress designed to reduce seasonal unemployability, mobility, or turnover unemployment since the impact of each of these factors is not equally distributed among different unemployment categories. If seasonal unemployment could have been eliminated, national unemployment would have fallen by 24 per cent in 1965, but unemployment in the 14–19 age group would have fallen by 53 per cent.[9] This same differential impact is visible for construction workers, agricultural workers, the unskilled, and Negroes.

As the federal government's seasonal adjustment programs recognize, part of what now appears as seasonal unemployment is a function of the general level of unemployment. When seasonal workers can find alternative jobs, the probability of being able to hire seasonal labor is reduced, and the profitability of seasonal scheduling procedures is consequently less. In February 1953, seasonal factors contributed 0.7 percentage point to unemployment among males 25 and over, but in February 1961, seasonal adjustment factors contributed 1.7 percentage points. But even at low unemployment levels, substantial amounts of seasonal unemployment still exist.

To the extent that seasonal unemployment is discounted in the labor market and workers choose to go into fields with high seasonal unemployment because of a compensating wage structure (a situation which may exist in some types of construction), society is not concerned with seasonal unemployment except as it influences other goals such as growth. To the extent that labor is forced to accept seasonal jobs because of a lack of viable alternatives, society has a direct concern. Three general methods exist for creating alternatives. Public or private training programs can be designed to train workers for nonseasonal jobs, programs can be designed to eliminate seasonal labor demands (such as Canada's contra-seasonal subsidy for housing starts), or the government can directly provide contra-seasonal jobs. Among young people, public job-creation has to be used. Since training programs cannot provide the answer for seasonal unemployment due to the desire for jobs during school (training) vacations, and since the private labor market probably will never be able to adjust efficiently to the influx of several million teenagers all looking for short-term jobs at exactly the same time, programs like those already started will have to be expanded if society decides that summer employment for students is socially important.

Turnover and mobility factors also have differential impacts. If the mean period of unemployment could have been reduced from 11.8 weeks to 10.8 weeks in 1965, national unemployment would have been 0.4 percentage point lower, and specific groups, such as Negroes, would have experienced even larger unemployment reductions. Reducing the time necessary to find a job is partially a function of the efficiency of the labor market and partially a function of the productivity of individual workers.

Given that employers are rational and attempt to hire the most productive workers first and the least productive workers last, the lower the average level of productivity the higher a group's unemployment. Lower potential productivity could be caused by less native ability, lower past investment in training, or the expectation that the group would provide lower potential returns on training investments. If abilities and past training investments were equally distributed, an employer might still find it more profitable to go farther down the queue of males than of females since their attachment to the labor force and to a particular employer tends to be stronger. Thus any employer's probability of being able to recoup his training investment will be correspondingly higher. Since this situation existed in the past, past training will probably not be equally distributed either. The same handicaps face young workers. By definition they have little past investment in OJT, and their proclivities for mobility mean that an investment in an 18-year-old may be a much less profitable private investment than one in the same individual at age 24. By 24 he is likely to be married, permanently in the labor force, and anxious to obtain career skills. These factors make it rational for any individual employer to avoid training women or young people, but the same factors do not apply to society. Society could certainly gain if training occurred at 18 instead of 24 unless skills depreciate very rapidly; and even though returns from training women may be less than for men, training may still be a good social investment, especially as the proportion of women who return to the labor market after the childrearing ages is rapidly rising.

This means that a very good case may exist for financing train-

ing expenditures socially. Training subsidies could differ according to the age, sex, race, or education of the worker involved—
the greater the handicaps, the larger the subsidy. An alternative
is to accept lower actual productivities but to offset the unemployment effects through guaranteed job programs. The choice
between these alternatives has to depend on an analysis of the
relative costs and benefits of lowering unemployment by making
training investments or by providing guaranteed jobs.

### III. Income Equalization

The elimination of poverty and Negro-white income differences
are both currently part of the goals of aggregate policy. The
second goal is usually formulated in terms of equal opportunity,
but this is merely the desired method for solving the problem.

**The war on poverty.** The relationships between poverty and
aggregate growth are usually shown by making poverty a function of median family incomes.[10] Differences in median family incomes explain over 90 per cent of the variance in the incidence of
poverty (both over time and across geographic areas), but
median incomes and poverty are partially measuring the same
phenomenon. To explain poverty by median incomes is to introduce a near tautology. The two variables undoubtedly move together and can be used in forecasting, but this occurs because
the same causes influence the behavior of both.

Some of the factors influencing poverty (and median incomes)
can be isolated in an econometric model. To increase the number
of observations and to provide greater variation in the incidence
of poverty, the 50 states and the District of Columbia are used
as units of observation. In 1960, 21.4 per cent of the nation's
families were living in poverty (incomes of less than $3000),
but the average masked a dispersion ranging from a high of
51.6 per cent in Mississippi to a low of 9.8 per cent in Connec-
ticut (see Table 4).

The independent variables used in the model are: (1) the
percentage of families living on farms, (2) the percentage of
families headed by a Negro,[11] (3) the percentage of families
with no one in the labor force, (4) the education of the family
head, (5) the percentage of the population working full time,

(6) the industrial structure of the state, and (7) a dummy variable necessary to correct for the particular circumstances of Alaska and Hawaii (see equation 3).

TABLE 4. RANGE OF DATA USED IN POVERTY REGRESSION
(per cent)

|  | United States | High | Low |
|---|---|---|---|
| Percentage of families living on farms | 7.4 | 31.3 | 0.0 |
| Percentage of families headed by a nonwhite | 9.4 | 64.2 | 0.1 |
| Percentage of families with no one in the labor force | 10.7 | 24.7 | 7.5 |
| Percentage of family heads with 0–7 years of school completed | 21.9 | 45.0 | 8.0 |
| Percentage of population 14 and above who worked 50–52 weeks per year | 34.8 | 47.4 | 28.2 |
| Index of industrial structure | 98.9 | 103.1 | 83.9 |
| Incidence of poverty | 21.4 | 51.6 | 9.8 |

Source: U.S. Census, 1960.

Given our current theoretical and empirical knowledge of poverty, equation (3) cannot be considered a structural model since causation presumably does not move solely from independent to dependent variables. Low education levels and a poor industrial structure lead to a high incidence of poverty, but poverty also leads to low education levels and to a poor industrial structure. Eliminating this circle is difficult, both conceptually and from a policy standpoint.

Using these variables in a weighted regression gives the following results:[12]

$$(3) \quad P = 96.5125 + 0.2978F + 0.1133N + 0.5410L$$
$$\quad\quad\quad (23.1516) \quad (0.0978) \quad (0.0544) \quad (0.1677)$$
$$\quad\quad\quad\quad ** \quad\quad\quad ** \quad\quad\quad * \quad\quad\quad **$$
$$\quad\quad + 0.4345E - 0.5368W - 0.7600I - 10.3777D + u$$
$$\quad\quad\quad (0.0480) \quad (0.1117) \quad (0.1978) \quad (4.8210)$$
$$\quad\quad\quad\quad ** \quad\quad\quad ** \quad\quad\quad ** \quad\quad\quad **$$

* = significant at 5 per cent level    d.f. = 43
** = significant at 1 per cent level    $S_e$ = 2.3
                                             $\bar{R}^2$ = 0.98

where $P$ = percentage of families in poverty (income less than $3000)
   $F$ = percentage of families living on farms
   $N$ = percentage of families headed by a nonwhite
   $L$ = percentage of families with no one in the labor force
   $E$ = percentage of family heads with less than eight years of school completed
   $W$ = percentage of population 14 and above who worked 50–52 weeks per year
   $I$ = an index of the industrial structure of the state [13]
   $D$ = dummy variable for Alaska and Hawaii
   $u$ = error term

The poverty regression indicates that most of the variance in the incidence of poverty from state to state can be explained in terms of the 7 variables.[14] All but one of the explanatory variables are significant at the 1 per cent level, and that one is significant at the 5 per cent level. All of the coefficients have the signs that would be expected theoretically.

In equation (3) there are 5 variables through which manpower programs can potentially have an impact on the incidence of poverty. For each 1 percentage point reduction that manpower programs are able to make in the independent variables, our regression suggests that facilitating farm migration would reduce the prevalence of poverty by 0.3 percentage point, attracting families into the labor force would reduce poverty by 0.5 percentage point, lowering the number of family heads with less than an eighth-grade education would reduce poverty by 0.4 percentage point, and shifting workers from part-time jobs to full-time jobs would reduce poverty by 0.5 percentage point. The fifth way to reduce the incidence of poverty is by a set of programs which affect nonwhites. Here the goal is not to change the independent variable but to reduce the regression coefficient to zero. If eliminating discrimination and increasing investment in nonwhites could bring this coefficient to zero, poverty would fall by 1.0 percentage point (see below).

**Equalization of Negro and white incomes.** Median Negro family income rose from 51 to 57 per cent of median white family income between 1947 and 1952, but by 1958 all of the gains were lost, and median Negro income was back to 51 per cent. With high unemployment and fewer job opportunities, Negroes found jobs increasingly difficult to find, and increases in their incomes fell behind those for whites. During every recession in the postwar period, the ratio of Negro to white income dropped sharply. With improving employment opportunities in 1964, median Negro income rose from 53 to 56 per cent of median white income, but this was still below the 1952 level.

What factors determine the growth of white and nonwhite family incomes? Over time the growth of output per worker resulting from gains in productivity is the major source of higher family incomes for the entire economy. In addition to secular growth, explanations of changes in family incomes have to consider cyclical variations in the share of output going to persons and the level of utilization of the available labor force. If median family incomes are made a function of gains in output per employee, the level of utilization of the labor force, and the share of total output going to personal income, we can write:

$$(4) \qquad \ln M_t = a + b \ln P_t + c \ln E_t + d \ln S_t + u_t$$

where $M_t$ = median family income
$\quad\;\; P_t$ = GNP/employee
$\quad\;\; E_t$ = percentage of labor force employed
$\quad\;\; S_t$ = personal income/GNP

The elasticity of median family income with respect to output per employee is approximately 1.15 for both nonwhites and whites (see Table 5). The elasticity of family income with respect to the personal income share and the level of labor utilization differ sharply, however.

TABLE 5.  REGRESSIONS FOR MEDIAN FAMILY INCOME,
BY COLOR, 1947–1964

|                         |   a    |   b    |   c    |   d   | $\overline{R}^2$ | d.w. | d.f. | $S_e$ |
|-------------------------|--------|--------|--------|-------|------|------|------|------|
| Median white family income | −0.882 | 1.140 (0.031) | 1.209 (0.520) | 2.353 (0.462) | 0.998 | 0.78 | 14 | 0.02 |
| Median nonwhite family income | −1.967 | 1.172 (0.070) | 2.285 (1.157) | 1.603 (1.023) | 0.990 | 0.70 | 14 | 0.04 |

The elasticity of the personal income share is 1.6 for non-whites and is not statistically different from 0, but for whites it is 2.4 and highly significant. Since the share going to personal income rises in recessions and falls in expansions, the much larger positive elasticity for whites means that their incomes rise relative to Negroes during recessions and fall during expansions. During a recession the income of both whites and Negroes can fall due to a decline in the utilization of the labor force (see below), but a larger part of this decline is offset for whites than for Negroes by the variable for the share of personal income in GNP. Unemployment insurance, the consistency of dividends, lower tax payments, and other factors contributing to the shift to personal income in recessions are of much more cyclical importance to whites and lead to a relative decline in nonwhite income during recessions.

The cyclical income shift is exacerbated by different coefficients for the utilization of the labor force. The results show that a fall in the level of employment has almost twice as much effect on Negro as on white incomes (the elasticities are 2.29 vs. 1.21). Negro incomes fall almost twice as fast as white since Negro unemployment rises twice as fast as white. In expansions the relations are reversed and Negroes make larger relative income gains. When these two cyclical factors are combined, non-white incomes can be falling in recessions while white incomes are still rising. This phenomenon occurred in both 1958 and 1961.

Equation (4) indicates that Negro incomes would approach 60 per cent of white incomes if the economy were operating at a 3 per cent level of unemployment. After full employment is reached, there is no tendency for general economic growth to narrow the gap in relative terms, and it widens in absolute terms.[15] Accelerating potential growth will not eliminate the gap between white and Negro incomes (though it will make training programs and the elimination of discrimination easier and more effective), but this seems to be a poor reason to sacrifice the large (and equal) gains that would accrue to both whites and Negroes from a faster growth rate.

To eliminate income differences, specific programs have to be developed to supplement the effects of aggregate growth. The poverty model (equation 3) can be used to examine some of the factors which cause a higher incidence of poverty among non-whites. The coefficient for the percentage of families headed by a nonwhite is relatively small in equation (3). If this variable were the only factor in the equation which was responsible for nonwhite poverty, the variable should account for 4.3 percentage points of the total incidence of poverty, yet it actually accounts for only 1.0 percentage point. Since many of the other regression coefficients are also important determinants of Negro poverty, the coefficient for Negroes primarily represents the sheer handicap of being a Negro. Negroes are poor in part because they suffer from direct discrimination when they cannot get jobs commensurate with their abilities, but they are also poor because they have low education levels, are more apt to be out of the labor force, and are crowded into part-time jobs and into the lowest occupations. Because of this, the coefficients of the other variables in the regressions include many of the long-run effects of discrimination that would have to be eliminated before Negroes could achieve true equality.

The hypothesis that the different variables in the poverty regression have a homogeneous effect across race as well as across states could be tested by estimating the same poverty model with data for Negroes and then for whites. If the regression coefficients were the same, the hypothesis would be substantiated. Lacking this test because the data are not available, an alternative is to insert national data for Negroes and whites into the poverty regression and compare the actual and the predicted values. The two could be similar due to offsetting errors among the different explanatory factors, but agreement between the predicted and the actual values for both whites and nonwhites would create a presumption that the effects were similar. Most of the explanatory variables have very different values for Negroes and whites (see Table 6), but the equation does a very good job of projecting the incidence of both Negro and white poverty. The projected and actual rates are identical for whites and differ by only 0.1 percentage point for Negroes (48.0 per cent vs. 47.9 per cent), although the incidence of Negro poverty is more than twice that for whites. Both qualitatively and quantitatively the same variables seem to explain Negro and white poverty.

The major sources of inequality are education and the factors embodied in the discrimination coefficient. Programs which equalize nonwhite educational attainments would lower nonwhite poverty by 12.7 percentage points, and eliminating the set of factors embodied in the coefficient for nonwhites would lower their incidence of poverty by an additional 11.3 percentage points (see Table 6).

**IV. Stable Prices**

Prices can be stable in at least three senses. First, prices are stable if the relevant price indexes are constant. Second, prices are stable if they are rising at a rate which is slow enough not to induce public interest in measures to achieve even lower rates of increase. Given the general satisfaction with the price performance from 1958 to 1964, a stable Wholesale Price Index and a rise in the Consumer's Price Index of less than 1½ per cent per year can serve as a good approximation of price stability in this second sense. Third, prices are stable if they are rising no faster than that rate which society is willing to tolerate as the price for full employment. This point depends on society's trade-off between inflation and full employment. In the short run, programs designed to reduce inflation are aiming for price stability of the third type, and in the long run the goal is price stability of the second type. The costs of inflationary programs will determine whether it is worth achieving price stability of either type three or type two, but price stability of the first type will not be a social goal unless anti-inflationary programs are completely costless.

TABLE 6.  POVERTY REGRESSION FOR WHITES AND NONWHITES

| Variable | Data (per cent) | | Contributions to Difference Between White and Nonwhite Poverty (Nonwhite minus white) |
| --- | --- | --- | --- |
| | Whites | Nonwhites | |
| Percentage of families living on farms | 7.5 | 6.6 | −0.3 |
| Percentage of families headed by nonwhite | 0.0 | 100.0 | 11.3 |
| Percentage of families with no one in the labor force | 10.5 | 12.9 | 1.3 |
| Percentage of family heads with 0–7 years of school completed | 19.2 | 48.5 | 12.7 |
| Percentage of population 14 and above who worked 50–52 weeks per year | 35.5 | 28.9 | 3.6 |
| Index of industrial structure[a] | 98.8 | 97.8 | 0.8 |
| Incidence of poverty | | | |
| Projected | 18.6 | 48.0 | 29.4 |
| Actual | 18.6 | 47.9 | 29.3 |

Source: U.S. Census, 1960.

[a] The index of industrial structure is calculated by weighting the index of each state by the number of white and nonwhite families living in that state.

If I could report having found an equation which would adequately explain price changes, the logical procedure would be to analyze how manpower policies might be used to shift the parameters of the equation or how they might be used to make new variables relevant to price determination. Lacking the lodestone of inflationary analysis, the examination proceeds by investigating inflation due to: (1) demand-pull in the labor market, (2) demand-pull in the product market, (3) cost-push in the labor market, and (4 cost-push in the product market. Either general or sectorial inflation can occur in either of these markets or as a result of either of these causes, but sectorial inflation has always appeared long before general inflation in American experience.

Since manpower policies and incomes policies such as the guideposts are sometimes complementary, sometimes substitutes, and sometimes in conflict as methods of controlling inflation, the two policies are examined together. By generally or specifically increasing labor supplies, manpower programs can have a direct effect on potential output and thus on inflation. Guideposts present a set of rules which, if followed, would result in a noninflationary economy that would approximate the results of a perfectly competitive economy without excess demand. They can be used as general standards of where inflation is occurring and with a minimum of supplementary analysis to determine who or what is causing the problems. This is not to say that the guideposts are devoid of analytical problems. The whole problem of the second-best (when prices are not constant or when wages are rising faster than productivity) has not been solved. But the more sophisticated approach that they bring to the public discussion of inflation is necessary since the causes of inflation are not necessarily in those sectors where prices are visibly rising (automobiles provide a vivid illustration). A second and not necessarily related part of the guideposts is enforcement. According to the editorial page of the *New York Times* and perhaps too frequently in government, enforcement means direct wage or price confrontations. Alternative enforcement provisions exist. Anti-trust actions, manpower programs, breaking down institutional constraints where the market is unable to respond to demand, efforts to lower government or private demands, increasing supplies from government stockpiles, guaranteeing the long-run demand for a particular product or type of labor to encourage private expansion of supplies, and a whole host of other actions can all provide indirect methods of enforcement.

**Demand-pull in the labor market.** Excess demand in the labor market is certainly derived from demand in the product market, but it occurs when the constraints on increasing output are labor constraints. Labor constraints on output have led to some of the most pressing and persistent inflationary problems in fields such as construction and medical services. Increases in the construction deflator accounted for 27 per cent of the total increase in the GNP deflator from 1964 to the fourth quarter of 1965; increases in the cost of medical care accounted for 31 per cent of the increase in the prices of nonfood items in the Consumer Price Index from 1964 to February 1966. Some of the increase may be due to inadequate measures of quality improvements, but in both areas labor supply constraints resulting in local shortages or in local monopolies have led to significant price increases. Projections of demand indicate that the problems will increase in both areas in the near future.

Manpower programs designed to expand labor supplies have to provide the necessary anti-inflationary weapons since direct enforcement of the guideposts is almost unworkable in these particular areas. Institutional limitations make effective isolation, investigation, adjudication, and persuasion impossible before wage and price decisions have already been made. Even if the institutional limitations could be overcome, the constant pressure of excess demand for labor would probably cause wage drifting. Since manpower progress involve a time lag, they will have to be combined with a system of projecting problem sectors several years in advance before they can be an effective tool against inflation.

**Demand-pull in the product market.** Demand-pull in the product market results from nonlabor capacity constraints. Currently, nonlabor constraints on output account for a large part of inflation. Nonferrous metals and foods account for 68 per cent of the total increase in the Wholesale Price Index of 4.8 percentage points from 1964 to February 1966 (food alone accounts for 60 per cent), but labor constraints are not important in either sector. Neither manpower policies nor direct enforcement of the guideposts can do very much about these areas. In the competitive food markets guideposts cannot be enforced, and in nonferrous metals the present policy of encouraging private producers to hold prices below market levels just results in some very questionable private rationing schemes. By the very nature of private rationing, copper supplies are frozen into the more traditional markets and not necessarily into the most productive uses. Shortages just as well as price increases cause substitution of alternative materials, but an inefficient distribution of shortages probably results in inefficient substitutions in the wrong sectors of the economy. The proper guidepost response is releasing stockpiles, guaranteeing future demand to increase investment in conditions of uncertainty, encouraging the substitution of alternative products, or letting prices rise to conserve scarce materials.

**Cost-push in the labor market.** Equations which have been developed to explain wage changes implicitly consider both demand-pull and cost-push elements in wage determination. Some of the cost-push effects are visible in the variables found to be significant, and some of the effects are buried in the size of the coefficients of demand variables. Unfortunately, there is no way to separate the demand-pull and cost-push effects which are mixed up in the coefficients. Unemployment, changes in unemployment, profit rates, changes in profit rates, and price indexes are all variables which have been found to be significant.[16] Roughly speaking, the cost-push elements show up in the magnitude of the coefficients for unemployment and changes in unemployment and in the selection of profits, changes in profits, and price indexes as explanatory variables.

Consider the Eckstein-Wilson model, where a 1 percentage point decrease in unemployment adds 0.6 percentage point to the increase of money wages, and a 1 percentage point increase in the profit rate adds 0.7 percentage point. According to the mechanisms postulated by Eckstein and Wilson, companies do not wish to lose sales and profits because of strikes in periods with high-profit rates, and their willingness to share high or rising profits with labor are much greater than their willingness to share low or falling profits. At low levels of unemployment, union members expect large increases, job losses resulting from high settlements are less since employment is expanding and since work cannot be easily shifted to nonunion areas or plants, the striking workers' probability of finding other jobs is higher, and nonwage fringe benefits such as job security become less important.

Perhaps other explanations exist, but an examination of this postulated list of causal mechanisms does not indicate that manpower policies could have much of an impact on any of the mechanisms. Potentially, incomes policies might have an effect, but this probably requires labor-management agreement on the content of the policy rather than present methods of enforcing an incomes policy on a hostile private sector.

**Cost-push in the product market.** An effective incomes policy requires agreement in the product market as well as in the labor market, but in neither case does it excuse the government from the responsibility to limit the area where cost-push elements can operate. Efforts to stimulate competition through anti-trust actions, not providing import protection, or by attempts to change industry beliefs about the relevant price elasticities have to be made regardless of incomes policies. In the short run, negotiated guideposts might shift cost-push propensities, but in the long run real factors will dominate. Pressures from substitute products and falling employment opportunities have to supply the long-run forces to shift the relationships. In the case of steel, the reality of Japanese steel imports has probably done more to shift the wage and price relationships than the Federal government's highly publicized interventions in wage and price decisions.

## V. Private Manpower Policies

What factors determine private investment in manpower programs? The profit-maximizing firm provides training programs until the marginal returns and costs have been equalized. If marginal returns are greater than marginal costs, more training is undertaken; if the reverse is true, less training is undertaken. In Becker's notation, equilibrium can be expressed as:[17]

$$(5) \qquad \frac{MP_o + \sum_{i=t}^{n} (MP_i - W_i)}{(1 + r)^n} = \frac{W_o + \sum_{i=t}^{n} C_i}{(1 + r)^n}$$

where:    $MP_o$ = marginal product before training

$W_o$ = wage before training

$\sum_{i=t}^{n} MP_i$ = marginal product stream after training

$$\sum_{i=t}^{n} W_i = \text{wage stream after training}$$

$$\sum_{i=t}^{n} C_i = \text{time stream of opportunity costs and outlays on training}$$

$$r = \text{rate of discount}$$

As Becker points out, marginal returns to the firm $\left[\sum_{i=t}^{n} (MP_i - W_i)\right]$ will be larger, and therefore training more extensive, the more specific the training ($W_i$ will not rise with an increasing $MP_i$), the greater the monopsony power of the employer (the larger the difference between $MP_i$ and $W_i$), and the longer the labor contract that can be negotiated ($n$).

In Becker's analysis, firms never provide general training, since the returns can only be appropriated by the individual worker, and always provide specific training since the returns can only be appropriated by the firm. General and specific training are convenient analytic terms, but they actually represent two poles of a continuum. Very few types of training are completely specific to one company, and very little OJT could really be considered completely general. Firms have to decide how far they are going to move along the continuum between specific and general training rather than just deciding to provide no general and all specific training. In some isolated company towns firms provide all training including formal elementary and secondary education; in other situations they provide no training. Public manpower policies need to know what factors influence these decisions and how they can be changed to increase investment in general as well as specific training.

As equation (5) stands, public policies can only affect private manpower decisions through taxes, subsidies, or wage policies. Profit taxes could be cut to raise the after-tax marginal product stream $\left(\sum_{i=t}^{n} MP_i\right)$, subsidies could be given to cut the costs of training $\left(\sum_{i=t}^{n} C_i\right)$, or wage policies could be used to hold down the wage stream $\left(\sum_{i=t}^{n} W_i\right)$.

Before public policies can be designed to change private man-power decisions, the reasons for intervention need to be de-termined. Several possibilities exist. First, private firms may lack knowledge about future or present demands for labor. Indi-vidual firms may not be able to see that real or potential short-ages exist and that competitive bidding for skilled labor will be self-defeating. Second, to the extent that training is a true externality that cannot be appropriated by the private investor but accrues to society in the form of higher wages to labor, higher profits to some other business, or lower prices to the consumer, private training decisions will not be optimal unless there is some mechanism for these groups to finance part of the necessary investment. Both of these reasons lead to a strong case for so-cially financing training programs, but they do not necessarily lead to public investment. Instead the criteria of benefit taxa-tion should be used to distribute the cost of training programs efficiently. Payments from general revenues should only be made if training were thought of as serving broad social goals. If training programs were designed to achieve society's goals of eliminating poverty, equalizing Negro and white incomes, re-ducing the minimum level of unemployment, accelerating the rate of growth, or reducing inflationary pressures, general reven-ues might legitimately be used without violating the general criteria of benefit taxation.

**The dynamic model.** In a static world with perfect labor mar-kets, public influences on private training decisions are limited to taxes, subsidies, and wage controls. The situation is very different, however, in a dynamic world with imperfect labor markets. Imperfect labor markets by themselves move train-ing investments down the continuum from specific to general training. Cost of moving, pension plans, attachments to geo-graphic areas and friends, seniority provisions, inadequate knowl-edge about alternative opportunities, and a host of other factors all lead to a higher probability that training returns can be appropriated by the investing firm.

Internal labor markets which are separated from the external labor market by constraints on hiring, firing, or promotion also serve to increase the likelihood of private training. If skilled positions can only be filled from workers already in the internal labor market, firms are forced to provide training even when trained workers are available in the external labor market or when training is general rather than specific. Most internal labor markets have more than one entry point, but to the extent that workers can enter only at the least skilled jobs, firms are forced to internalize the problem of labor training rather than leaving it to the external labor market.

In a dynamic world, a firm's perception of the stream of benefits gained from training programs is going to be a product of several factors not given in equation (5). Some of these factors are given in equation (6).[18]

$$(6) \quad \sum_{i=t}^{n} (MP_i - W_i) = \gamma[U, E(U), E(G), ES_{KL}, ES_{L_1 L_2}]$$

where:    $U$ = unemployment
            $E(U)$ = expected future unemployment
            $E(G)$ = expected growth of output
            $ES_{KL}$ = elasticity of substitution of capital for labor
            $ES_{L_1 L_2}$ = elasticity of substitution of labor of type 1 for labor of type 2

Unemployment $(U)$ and expectations about future unemployment $[E(U)]$ are important determinants of the stream of benefits from training investments since they are indicators of the probability that a firm will be able to hire desired workers from the pool of unemployment without having to provide training. Expectations that 3 per cent unemployment is normal and that any deviations will be quickly eliminated may lead to very different training decisions than a 5 or 6 per cent expectation.

The expected growth of output $[E(G)]$ is important since it gives an indication of how many workers will be needed. Depending on expected needs and the probabilities of finding the necessary skills in the pool of unemployment, firms will alter their training investments. Long-run private training programs might be very adequate if everyone's expectations were geared to 3 per cent unemployment and the present potential rate of growth, but very inadequate in the current transition period. Expectations may not have completely shifted from a 5 or 6 per cent unemployment level, the potential growth rate is accelerating to accommodate a more rapidly growing labor force, and actual growth is exceeding potential growth as the gap between actual and potential is closed. Private manpower decisions are probably in the process of transition, yet manpower training needs are even higher than they will be when the economy has reached full employment and is growing at its potential rate.

In a dynamic economy, private training expenditures can probably be increased by cutting unemployment to low levels and by letting firms, unions, and individuals know that unemployment is going to be kept there. The firmer this commitment and the more firmly the private sector is convinced of its validity, the greater private training outlays will be. By committing themselves to low unemployment and high growth, government planners will be able to improve private manpower decisions by improving private knowledge. Thus federal policy-makers should seriously consider reversing their present policies of not setting unemployment goals or giving firm long-run growth commitments. These commitments certainly open the policy-maker to charges of failure since deviations from stated objectives are easier to spot when the objectives are known, but failing to make public commitments might necessitate an even larger price in inferior private planning and inadequate investment in private training programs.

In addition to improving private information, consideration might be given to using public guarantees to encourage private manpower programs. A short time ago, newspaper reports indicated that the Federal government was going to guarantee the future demand for copper in order to stimulate the expansion of supplies in a situation in which private interests were not sure that additional copper was needed in the long run. Similar guarantees should be considered to stimulate the supplies of labor in sectors in which different estimates of future demand block expansion of private programs. In an area such as construction, where demographic factors indicate a very large boom in the near future, the procedure should be seriously considered.

The need for training is also a function of the elasticity of substitution between capital and labor ($ES_{KL}$). The higher the elasticity, the less the training needed. In the context of a full employment economy, increasing the capital-labor ratio to increase the growth of productivity and income is certainly a goal worth pursuing. Research expenditures and efforts to speed up the spread of technology might provide viable alternatives to large manpower programs in some cases.

Training expenditures also depend on the elasticity of substitution of unskilled for skilled labor $(ES_{L_1 L_2})$. Simplifying and dividing jobs so that labor with less training can be used in place of more highly skilled workers is important, since some groups are difficult, if not impossible, to train, and since training probably will not be an efficient investment for all types of labor. Wartime experience, such as that in shipyards, indicates that conscious government policies designed to promote the substitution of unskilled for skilled labor through research and technical assistance might have some effect. The elasticity of substitution for on-the-job skills is also probably affected by the general level of education. The higher the formal level of education, the more flexible the labor force.

Methods for influencing private manpower decisions other than those mentioned above undoubtedly exist. With a creative use of the whole range of government policies there seems to be little reason why private programs could not be harnessed to provide some of the training necessary to reach social objectives at a lower cost than may be possible with direct public programs.

## VI. Conclusion

The principal handicap of manpower policies as instruments in the pursuit of aggregative goals is a general lack of knowledge (or skepticism) about their efficiency. As the analysis in this paper indicates, manpower programs are theoretically important, and the potential effects are large enough to make them empirically interesting, but actual returns have yet to be calculated. Actual programs may not achieve potential effects, or costs may lead to a very low return on invested resources. The general efficiency of actual manpower programs needs to be determined, since there is usually a choice between manpower programs and some alternative instrument or within manpower programs between specific policies. Efficient use of manpower programs cannot be made unless general cost-benefit information is available. Increasing capital investment may prove to be the efficient way to raise the potential rate of growth, and guaranteed jobs may prove to be more efficient than training as a way of reducing poverty among older workers. Within training a whole range of potential policies exist. In management techniques alone they stretch from direct public programs to subsidized private programs with intermediate stopping points such as privately managed direct public training programs. *A priori,* there is little reason to assume that any of these is more efficient or that the same type of program would be the most efficient for all problems.

Investment in human capital through training programs may be below optimal levels due to inadequate knowledge, the existence of significant externalities in training, or the lack of consideration for social benefits by private decision-makers. All three of these are testable hypotheses. To the extent that labor bottlenecks are caused by inadequate estimates of present or future labor demand, inadequate knowledge is an important problem. Occupations which require a long period of training and thus need relatively accurate long-run forecasts of demand are apt to be in this category. Most skills with long training periods are acquired in formal education rather than provided by private industry, but some highly skilled trades may be cases in point. If significant externalities exist in training investments and are leading to underinvestment, cost-benefit analysis of additional training programs should indicate a relatively high rate of return even when social benefits are not considered. Of the three reasons for underinvestment, social benefits are probably the most important. Social benefits from eliminating poverty or Negro-white income differences may be large relative to resultant increases in output, but though the social benefits are large compared with the private benefits, there is certainly no reason to think that private decisions will result in optimal human investments. This is especially true if relatively equal investments in human capital or at least relatively equal opportunities for such investment is valued as the labor-market equivalent of political democracy.

## NOTES

1. R. M. Solow, "Technical Progress, Capital Formation, and Economic Growth," *American Economic Review,* LII (May, 1962), 76–86.

2. The $U^2$ term is dropped from this equation since it did not prove to be significant in the postwar period. Variations in unemployment have simply not been large enough to estimate nonlinear effects.

3. Lester C. Thurow and L. D. Taylor, "The Interaction Between the Actual and the Potential Rate of Growth," *Review of Economics and Statistics,* forthcoming.

In the estimating form:

$$\ln \frac{Y}{K_4} = \underset{(0.0284)}{0.5888} - \underset{(0.5417)}{1.1238U} + \underset{(0.0018)}{0.0092T} + \underset{(0.0357)}{0.7744} \ln \frac{L_1}{K_4}$$

$$\bar{R}^2 = 0.995 \quad \text{d.w.} = 1.21 \quad \text{d.f.} = 31 \quad S_e = 2.3$$

Fitted 1929–1965 with utilization adjustment for 1946–1965.

In this function the labor force is improving in quality at the rate of 1 per cent per year, embodied technical progress is occurring at 4 per cent per year in capital, and disembodied technical progress is 0.9 per cent per year. See the above paper for a discussion of problems involved in estimating the potential growth of output and productivity.

4. *Ibid.*

5. This assumption leads to a growth of the net capital stock of 6.7 per cent per year.

6. See Jacob Mincer, "On-the-Job Training: Costs, Returns, and Some Implications," *Journal of Political Economy,* LXX (October, 1962), 50–79.

7. Minimum levels of seasonal, mobility, and turnover unemployment could be estimated. This is essentially the procedure followed by the Bureau of Labor Statistics in Joint Economic Committee, "The Extent and Nature of Frictional Unemployment," Study Paper No. 6, *Study of Employment, Growth, and Price Levels* (Washington, D.C.: November, 1959).

Starting from the present level of unemployment, estimates could be made of how many of the currently unemployed could be employed with existing institutions.

Nonlinear employment functions could be estimated which would set minimum levels of unemployment. Unfortunately history has not provided us with the right kind of data for this approach.

8. *Economic Report of the President,* 1966, p. 75.

9. Calculated according to the methods outlined in "The Extent and Nature of Frictional Unemployment," p. 59.

10. Galloway has shown that changes in poverty are strongly related to changes in median family incomes over time. In his simplest formulation a $100 increase in real median family income reduces poverty by about 0.5 percentage point. L. E. Galloway, "The Foundations of the 'War on Poverty,'" *American Economic Review,* LV (March, 1965), 127.

11. All data in this paper actually refer to the category which is officially

called nonwhite. Since this group is 92 per cent Negro, the text will use Negro and nonwhite interchangeably.

12. A regression using equation (3) needs to be weighted by the population of each state since the dependent variable and most of the independent variables are in percentage terms. Since a large state provides more of the total number of families living in poverty, it needs to have a larger weight in the regression. The large intercept term is a scaling factor in the weighted regression. It does not indicate anything about the incidence of poverty.

13. The index is defined as follows:

$$I = \sum_{i=1}^{n} X_i W_i$$

where $X_i$ = percentage of the state's labor force in industry $i$
$W_i$ = the ratio of the U.S. median income in industry $i$ to the general U.S. median income. The index measures the prevalence of high-wage industries in the state

14. For a discussion of the model and its implications, see Lester C. Thurow, "The Causes of Poverty," *Quarterly Journal of Economics,* forthcoming.

15. This result conflicts with Locke Anderson's evidence that the gap between white and nonwhite family incomes would continue to close after full employment is reached. In his equation family income is simply made a function of per capita personal income. Since the coefficient for nonwhites is much larger than the coefficient for whites, Anderson concludes that general economic growth would reduce the difference between white and nonwhite median family incomes. Anderson's results occur because he fails to distinguish between trend and cycle. When allowance is made for cyclical changes, the coefficients do not differ for whites and nonwhites. If Anderson's coefficients were correct, the postwar growth in per capita income should have led to much higher relative incomes for nonwhites. It clearly has not done so. Locke Anderson, "Trickling Down," *Quarterly Journal of Economics,* LXXVIII (November, 1964), 522.

16. W. G. Bowen and R. A. Berry, "Unemployment Conditions and Movements of Money Wage Level," *Review of Economics and Statistics,* XLV (May, 1963), 163-172; Otto Eckstein and Thomas Wilson, "The Determinants of Money Wages in American Industry," *Quarterly Journal of Economics,* LXXVI (August, 1962), 379-414; and Edwin Kuh, "A Productivity Theory of Wage Levels—An Alternative to the Phillips Curve" (mimeographed).

17. Gary S. Becker, *Human Capital* (New York: National Bureau of Economic Research, 1964), p. 20. This equation can easily be modified to cover training programs undertaken by individuals or unions.

18. Theoretically an equation of this type could be estimated econometrically, but the proper data do not exist. Increases in the trained labor force could be used as a proxy for returns on training, but labor force data are not available in sufficient detail.

# Discussion

## BY NATHANIEL GOLDFINGER

I find myself in the unfortunate position of being assigned to comment on an excellent paper, with which I am largely in agreement. It would be much easier if it were otherwise.

While Thurow places heavy emphasis on the importance of manpower policies—in line with the subject of his paper—I find it interesting to note that few, if any, of these manpower policies have much inherent significance in attempting to achieve and sustain full employment unless they are accompanied by vigorous fiscal and monetary policies aimed at reaching the same objective. Fiscal and monetary policies are the essential underpinning of full employment and should be considered a key part of our national manpower-policy framework.

### Manpower Policy and Full Employment

Both this paper and the actual record of 1963 through the first half of 1966 indicate, it seems to me, that full employment, on the basis of the current labor market and present manpower policies, represents an unemployment rate of about 3 per cent. And with improved public and private manpower policies—to reduce the average duration of unemployment, for example, and directly to create jobs for young people and unskilled workers—I am convinced that within the next several years, we should be able to set a 2½ per cent and then a 2 per cent unemployment rate as the realistic full employment objective.

Moreover, it seems to me that Thurow also indicates rather clearly the intertwined mixture of both demand and structural causes of the unemployment problem of the 1950's and early 1960's, with the dominant cause to be found in the inadequate level of demand—and, I would add, the shift in demand from goods to services, accompanied by technological changes that emphasized indirect labor and cut production and maintenance labor requirements. As Thurow points out, even "part of what now appears as seasonal unemployment is a function of the general level of unemployment." This realistic concern with unemployment and its causes is far more meaningful than the "either/or" argument as to whether excessive uuemployment was entirely due to a deficiency of aggregate demand *or* structural factors that was the fashion only a short time ago.

It was only a few years ago that we heard dire predictions of labor shortages if the unemployment rate were to decline to 5 or 4 per cent. But in the past several months, the unemployment rate did fall to 4 per cent and below without any evidence of widespread manpower shortages. Under the heat of rising demand—with a concentrated increase in demand for durable goods, which require large numbers of unskilled and semi-skilled workers—some parts of the structural-unemployment iceberg actually melted, but not as neatly or completely as the demand idealogues of the either/or debate would have had us believe. Serious problems remain in Appalachia, the Mississippi Delta, Watts, the west-side of Chicago, and other parts of the country. And serious unemployment problems among young people are still with us in mid-1966.

Thurow's paper implies, and the experience of the past three years indicates, that the tough, hard-core structural problems become clearer and more easily delineated as the unemployment rate moves down to 4 per cent and below—as the rise in demand creates enough job opportunities to melt some parts of what are structural problems at higher unemployment levels.

A national commitment to achieve and sustain an unemployment rate of no more than 3 per cent of the labor force is essential at present, as Thurow suggests, along with fiscal, monetary, and manpower policies to live up to the commitment. Moreover, I am convinced that the accompanying improvements in public and private manpower policies, as well as additional manpower-related measures, would soon make it possible to establish new feasible goals of $2\frac{1}{2}$ and 2 per cent unemployment rates. It seems to me that public policy should aim for a sustained unemployment rate of 2 per cent within the near future.

Tight labor markets, for example, are a major incentive to improved private manpower policies. The relatively poor state of employer training programs, in my view, is largely the inheritance of a decade of relative economic stagnation and a rising unemployment trend in 1953–1963. And, as I see it, the beginnings of improvements in employer training since 1963 are clearly related to the rise of economic activity and the decline of unemployment. As Thurow states: "Long-run private training programs might be very adequate if everyone's expectations were geared to 3 per cent unemployment."

Moreover, Thurow indicates the significant decline in the unemployment rate that could occur by reducing the duration of unemployment. He states: "If the mean period of unemployment could have been reduced from 11.8 weeks to 10.8 weeks in 1965, national unemployment would have been 0.4 percentage point lower and specific groups, such as Negroes, would have experienced even larger unemployment reductions." Obviously, such reduction in the duration of unemployment requires the availability of job opportunities. But it also requires an effective, nationwide public employment service as well as relocation measures to enable a much improved matching of workers and jobs.

Thurow also indicates some additional possibilities for the reduction of seasonal unemployment—in an economy of rising economic activity and low unemployment generally—such as government programs to reduce seasonal labor-demand fluctuations and direct government creation of contra-seasonal jobs. There are also other methods that can be used, for example, through the collective bargaining process and the placement of government contracts.

The prodding force of call-in and reporting pay provisions in collective-bargaining agreements have almost completely eliminated the old management practice of laying-off workers after they reported to the job or calling workers to report for a few hours' work. Similarly, the spread of company-paid supplemental unemployment benefits and salaries for production and maintenance workers, under collective bargaining agreements, can and probably will prod companies into improved scheduling of their output. In addition, federal, state, and local governments can place their construction contracts at such times and conditions as to reduce seasonal fluctuations.

Moreover, the skill, education, and age composition of the

present labor force, in relation to technology and the demand for labor, point to the need for direct job-creating programs for young people and unskilled workers, if unemployment is to be driven down to minimum levels and kept there.

Unemployment is much more than an economic problem involving underutilization of manpower and failure to achieve potential levels of output. It is also a social, political, and human problem. In a work-oriented society and culture such as ours, I am firmly convinced that it is a major obligation of the federal government to pursue the necessary fiscal, monetary, and manpower policies that can actually achieve and sustain full employment. This is particularly important in these days of rapid and radical changes in technology, urban growth, and race relations. A solid economic underpinning of job opportunities, at decent wages, for all persons who are willing and able to work is a basic necessity for social peace and orderly progress.

However, I do not believe that a verbal commitment to full employment will be worth very much if economists, political leaders, and the news media start shouting loudly that the economy is becoming "overheated"—and loudly urge restrictive policies—whenever the unemployment rate moves down to 4 or 3½ percent. The essential national goal of adequate employment opportunities for the labor force will be easier to achieve when economists—including some adherents of the "new economics"—lose their trembling fear of full employment.

Moreover, I do not believe, as Thurow apparently does, that "the price performance from 1958 to 1964, a stable Wholesale Price Index, and a rise in the Consumers' Price Index of less than 1½ per cent per year, can serve as a good approximation of price stability. . . ." I do not quarrel with Thurow's apparent intent, but it seems to me that we need a higher price trade-off and an end to the jitters about each month's changes in the price indices. This is particularly true so long as American society, including much of the economics profession, refuses to cope seriously with the social and economic power of giant corporations, the realities of American markets, the outflow of private capital, the private governmental nature of the great multi-national corporations, and the important but apparently unrespectable issue of income distribution. In addition, adequate manpower-related, structural measures can get at part of the price problem and reduce the upward pressure on the price level that may exist at full employment.

## The Underprivileged

But a more-than-verbal national commitment to achieve and sustain a 3 per cent unemployment rate—and, then, 2½ per cent and 2 per cent unemployment-rate objectives—would have to face up to several thorny hard-core problems, such as youth unemployment, the full integration of Negroes into the mainstream of the American economy, and the rapid reduction of poverty. In this regard, I find weakness, as well as strength, in Thurow's paper.

For example, the profile of the poor, based on Mollie Orshansky's work, indicates that somewhat over half of the poor are in families headed by a person in the labor force, while approximately 20 per cent are in families headed by an aged person, and about 30 per cent are in families where the male head of the household is disabled, dead, or absent for other reasons. For almost half of the poor, adequate social security benefits and income-maintenance payments are basic necessities. Such policies are largely outside the manpower area, but not entirely. Social security benefits are related to past earnings, for example, and the levels of social security benefits and income-maintenance payments, as well as public assistance rules, have some effect on labor-force participation rates for various groups in the population.

For more than half of the poor, however, in families headed by a person in the labor force—and for the children of all poor families—the basic necessity is full employment and adequate manpower policies. Although Thurow seems to say something similar, I believe that he omits an essential consideration that all too many academic economists seem to consider disreputable. Thus Orshansky's examination of poverty reveals that approximately one-half of the poor whose family heads are in the labor force—more than a quarter of all poor persons—are in families headed by full-time, year-round workers. In other words, over a quarter of the poor are in families whose breadwinners are employed full-time at miserably low wages. Yet Thurow fails to mention the essential importance of improved minimum wage legislation and the extension of effective trade union organization and collective bargaining. It seems to me that both minimum-wage legislation and collective bargaining are important aspects of manpower policy. This is certainly true in connection with such obvious aspects of manpower issues as quits and turnover. The improvement of wages, working conditions, and fringe benefits is an obviously essential means of reducing the prevalence of poverty. It is also an important means of reducing the menial status of many service occupations and helps to provide a remunerative, meaningful goal for training programs. The fact that about 30 per cent of Manpower Development and Training Act (MDTA) services trainees, in the August 1962–May 1965 period, earned less than $1.25 an hour after completing their training hardly provides much of an incentive for the poor to take training programs—particularly in a society that is so solicitous about incentives for the entrepreneur, corporate enterprise, and wealthy families.

Thurow's discussion of Negro and white incomes points up the importance of both fiscal and monetary policies and manpower policies operating in tandem—along with the essential social insurance and income-maintenance measures that are not mentioned. Sustained full employment is essential if we are to begin to solve the problem of a wide Negro-white income disparity, but traditional aggregative measures would be only a beginning.

As Thurow points out, median Negro family income rose from 51 per cent of median white family income in the recession year, 1958, to 56 per cent in 1964. However, he also indicates that Negro incomes would approach only 60 per cent of white incomes if the economy were operating at a 3 per cent unemployment rate. Thurow's estimate apparently assumes the present labor-force participation rates of Negroes and their present occupational structure. Such an assumption is unrealistic, however, since the occupational structure of Negroes in the labor force is changing, and a sustained 3 per cent unemployment rate would probably increase the labor-force participation rates of Negroes. Nevertheless, even with a more realistic assumption, the rate probably would not move much above 65 or 70 per cent of white incomes in the next decade without "specific programs . . . to supplement the effects of aggregate growth," as Thurow aptly puts it. Even a more realistic assumption, therefore, would still leave a substantial problem.

Thurow's major emphasis on education and other long-run measures, however, would put off any meaningful solution for perhaps a generation or more. But American society cannot afford to wait a generation. Instead of relying on such long-run measures, I believe that we need two different levels of policies simultaneously—policies to get at existing problems immediately and as best we can, while we work on the long-range solutions that may require twenty, thirty, or more years.

An examination of Negro unemployment and poverty points in the direction of several specific measures that are needed now. The substantial decline in the unemployment rate for Negroes— from 12.5 per cent in 1961 to 10.9 per cent in 1963 to 7 per cent in the early months of 1966—was concentrated among adults, mainly adult men, with previous work experience, skills, and seniority. There was practically no improvement in the unemployment rate for Negro teenagers.

Among Negro adult men 20 to 64 years of age the unemployment rate dropped from 11.8 per cent in 1961 to 9.2 per cent in 1963 and 4.4 per cent in January-February 1966. Unemployment among Negro adult women aged 20 to 64 declined more slowly— from 10.6 per cent in 1961 to 9.5 per cent in 1963 and 6.2 per cent in the early months of 1966. This decline of unemployment among Negro adults largely explains the accompanying reduction in the gap between Negro and white family incomes.

The pick-up of economic activity from 1963 through mid-1966 —with a concentrated rise in the demand for durable-goods output and for production and maintenance employment—brought substantial improvements among Negro adults. By the final months of 1965 and early 1966, a large percentage of unemployed workers with previous work experience and seniority rights were recalled or hired in most major industrial centers. All one need do is consider the combined impact of rising production and seniority rights, under collective bargaining agreements, in the steel and auto industries on employment of Negro adult men from 1963 through the early months of 1966. Left out for the most part, however, were the unskilled with little if any formal education, vocational training, and work-experience—a larger group than indicated by the Labor Department's figures, since there is considerable hidden unemployment among the Negro poor.

Disastrous unemployment rates remained, however, for Negro teenagers. Among Negro young men, 14 to 19 years of age, the jobless rate declined from 24.7 per cent in 1961 to 21.8 per cent in the early months of 1966. And among Negro young women, in that same age group, the unemployment rate of 27 per cent in early 1966 was slightly greater than the 26.6 per cent rate of 1961.

A sustained rise of economic activity and further generation of job opportunities could undoubtedly bring some improvement. However, further substantial improvement in the near future, rather than in a generation, clearly points to the need for special measures for young people and the unskilled generally, as well as efforts to lift the incomes of the working poor.

For young people—white as well as Negro—an enlarged and improved Neighborhood Youth Corps (NYC) or similar part-time, work-study programs could be very helpful. It seems to me that such programs for in-school youth—high school and college —should aim primarily at providing young people from low-income families with part-time jobs to enable them to remain in school, combined with personal counseling and vocational training assistance. For out-of-school youth, the employment programs should be enriched with a vocational training and guidance emphasis. The 100,000 to 200,000 young people involved in such programs in 1964 and 1965 could easily be doubled or tripled.

Also, the new GI bill, adopted at long last in early 1966, may provide the basis for a large-scale, youth manpower program. The GI bill after the Second World War was one of the most effective and efficient manpower programs ever adopted by the federal government. The new program should be examined closely as it evolves, with an eye to possible improvements in its effectiveness.

In addition, the federal government should provide financial assistance and encouragement for the development of special employment-qualifying programs, on a local community basis, aimed particularly at young people from low-income families, such as special programs designed to prepare students for civil service examinations, apprenticeship entry tests, and similar job-entry qualifying examinations. Such public efforts are required to compensate for the poor quality of education in many low-income, segregated, and ghetto-area schools and to overcome the cultural deprivation and social alienation of so many low-income families.

For unskilled workers, with little if any regular work experience or education, special MDTA training programs that include literacy training and basic arithmetic should be stepped up. In a rapidly expanding, low-unemployment economy, many of such unskilled workers should be able to find jobs after completing special training programs.

Nevertheless, we have to face the fact that there are a significant number of adult, unskilled people who probably cannot be easily equipped for jobs in the regular labor market. The federal government should provide grants and technical assistance to the states and local governments so that they can provide unskilled public service job opportunities for such people —to supply needed services in public and nonprofit institutions that would not otherwise be performed. These workers should be paid not less than the federal minimum wage. Such public service employment programs should be accompanied by vocational training and guidance, to enable the workers to move into the regular job market as rapidly as possible. The Automation Commission suggested that "an initial sum of perhaps $2 billion be appropriated" for such a program.

Such measures—on a base of a growing private economy and the planned expansion of public investment in the rebuilding of our metropolitan areas—should be able to bring unemployment down to a rate of 2 per cent, with an obvious narrowing of the Negro-white income gap. However, according to Orshansky's findings, in 1963 "73 per cent of the non-white male heads of poor families were currently employed, and more than half of them—42 per cent of all the poor—had been employed full time." Not only are jobs needed; we need also wage increases for the working poor both through the improvement of minimum wage legislation and through the extension of effective collective bargaining.

Higher compensation for low-wage workers in agriculture, hotels and motels, restaurants, hospitals, laundries, the retail trade, and similar industries is required to bring a further narrowing of the Negro-white income disparity. And with the passage of time, improved opportunities for education, training, and upgrading—and enforcement of the fair employment provisions of the Civil Rights Act—should result in changing the occupational structure of Negroes in the labor force. Such a relative rise in the incomes of the working poor generally, and of Negroes in particular, requires a solid foundation of sustained full employment and a fiscal policy firmly based on the concept of equity.

At any point in time, however, there are people who cannot be self-sustaining because of age, disability, or other handicaps. Lifting the incomes of such families—and vastly improving the educational, training, and job opportunities of their children— is essential for the rapid reduction of poverty and narrowing of the Negro-white income gap.

To move meaningfully in this direction requires a substantial improvement of social insurance—the social security, unemployment insurance, and workmen's compensation systems. In addition, ideally, public assistance should be replaced by a system of federal income maintenance payments. Pending the full development of such a program, adequate federal standards and financial grants-in-aid should be established for all welfare payments to which the federal government contributes, and a national general assistance program should be set up for those who do not fit into the categories of federally aided welfare programs. Such measures within the next several years can bring a further significant narrowing of the gap between Negro- and white-family incomes.

### Some Final Comments

We must remember that continued progress toward full employment, the reduction of poverty, and the narrowing of the Negro-white income gap can be halted by slamming on the brakes through generally restrictive fiscal and monetary policies while unemployment rates are still high. Unless we set a clear national goal of a 3 per cent unemployment rate now, in mid-1966, and progressively improve the national target to $2\frac{1}{2}$ per cent and then 2 per cent within the next few years, it will not be possible to achieve and maintain the desired social and economic advances. Moreover, imbalances between soaring business investment and sustainable increases in demand in mid-1966 pose a threat of recession and a reversal of recent progress. Counter-cyclical policy should be an aspect of the discussion of manpower policy. A decline of business investment and leveling-off or decline in military expenditures should be quickly offset by a planned, long-range rise of job-creating, public investment to meet the needs for public facilities and services of a rapidly growing and increasingly urban population.

In this area, I find Thurow's emphasis on aggregates unfortunate. Although he indicates the components in terms of unemployment, his fiscal policy emphasis is on aggregates, with no delineation of alternative fiscal policies and their differential impacts on both the general level and specific categories of employment. Since the transfer of labor from one skill or region to another is neither automatic nor easy, training programs and relocation measures should be accompanied by increased public investment that directly and indirectly creates needed types of job opportunities. This is particularly important at a time when radical technological change is rapidly reducing unskilled and semi-skilled labor requirements in several key parts of the economy. Some selectivity in both fiscal and manpower policies is essential to develop workable solutions for specific problems. And, it seems to me, the need for selectivity in fiscal policy becomes greater as the unemployment level declines.

Emphasis on public investment, I am firmly convinced, is a more direct and efficient means of reducing unemployment in this period of labor-saving and capital-saving technology—directly and indirectly creating needed unskilled and semi-skilled jobs—than is a general tax cut, which is likely to be regressive to boot. But Thurow omits discussion of this important issue and also fails to discuss the possibility of selective public investment in connection with work-study programs for young people, whose unemployment rates are still very high in mid-1966, or public service employment for the poorly educated and unskilled who do not easily fit into the current labor market. It seems to me that Thurow's failure to discuss the differential impacts of varying fiscal-policy alternatives on social groups, economic sectors, and categories of employment is a serious omission.

Manpower policies at present are undergoing reexamination. This is inevitable, and it could be most valuable, since we started so recently to develop a national policy—with very little experience, precedent, and expertise. But I fear that social objectives and national purpose may get lost or pushed aside in the reexamination process, particularly in the emphasis on cost-benefit analysis which frequently ignores or underplays social objectives.

Let us recall the ordinances of the 1780's, which fortunately set aside a great reservation of land in the vast Northwest Territory for the support of elementary and higher education—the foundation for America's investment in human resources which has paid such huge dividends in productivity and economic growth. The Northwest Ordinance of 1787 stood four-square on a base of social objectives, declaring that "religion, morality and knowledge being necessary to good government and the happiness of mankind, schools and the means of education shall be forever encouraged." Styles have changed since 1787, but let us not ignore the essential importance of social objectives in formulating and examining national policies.

CHAPTER **5**

# The Need for Better Planning
# and Coordination

## BY JOSEPH A. KERSHAW [1]

I think it likely that when the topic for my paper was assigned
it was assumed that planning and coordination were more or
less the same thing. After some thought I have decided to treat
them rather differently and indeed to discuss them *seriatim*.
I shall argue unequivocally for planning, but I suspect that
the case for coordination is less clear. This may reflect my
background at the RAND Corporation, where the economics
department on occasion found itself arguing strenuously against
coordination and in favor of what we came to feel was the
opposite side of that coin, namely, competition. Indeed, there
were a number of occasions when we were accused, sometimes
justifiably so, of being strongly in favor not only of duplication
but of wasteful duplication. In any case I will argue that planning and coordination are different things, that the need for
more and better coordination is at least less compelling.

## Defining Terms

At this point I had better define the way I use the terms coordination and planning. For me planning is a future-oriented term while coordination refers to the present operational phase of programs. In developing a plan, one determines objectives, the needs of the population to be served, the means now available for meeting these needs, and possible changes in present means or innovations that may make the delivery of services more effective. Planning, in short, is the drawing board phase of program operations. Coordination involves carrying out the program. Thus, in planning we may structure the Manpower Development and Training Act (MDTA) so that participants in other programs, such as the Job Corps (JC) and the Neighborhood Youth Corps (NYC), are not blocked from moving into MDTA. But in the field diverse agencies must work together (coordinate) to effect the smooth flow of participants.

Further, we can think in terms of a fourfold matrix with the box labeled federal planning, federal coordination, local planning, and local coordination. My talk focuses primarily upon the first and last of these classifications. But, let me comment briefly upon the other two. At the federal level, as I shall mention later, we, in conjunction with the Departments of Labor and of Health, Education, and Welfare, are trying to coordinate our activities. However, at this level, I suspect that coordination and planning tend to merge into an almost inseparable package. As for local planning, I would conjecture that we may be some distance from meaningful planning at that level. Again, our distinction becomes somewhat blurred when we consider the new MDTA state-federal plans in which initial plans have their genesis at the local level. But I feel the real payoff is bringing these diverse needs together at the national level. Hence, in this paper my unmodified usage of planning refers to future-oriented federal action, while coordination implies ongoing local operational activity.

In the establishment of any planning system, we first look for the objective which the system is supposed to achieve. In terms of the manpower-planning system, our objective appears to be fairly simple and straightforward. I should suppose it could be specified as the achievement of employment at its full potential for everyone who has the capacity and desire to work. Like most objectives, of course, this will turn out to be less simple upon examination. For example, it would include help for the already employed who have a high probability of falling into unemployment, as well as the possible establishment of sheltered employment for those who cannot fully meet the needs of the competitive system. Despite these complications I believe our goal is a manageable one.

## The Universe of Need

The first thing we have to ask is what relevant quantification is possible. In the case of manpower this means developing what we at the Office of Economic Opportunity (OEO) have come to call the "universe of need" for each of the programs, as well as for all of them put together. This simply means a specification of the number of persons who need the service that is being provided so that when the system comes to be costed we will know how far the system must extend. We do this in OEO, incidentally, for every program. In Head Start the question is the number of poor children of a given age; for the aged it is the number of poor over 65 who need some kind of program, and so on.

In looking at the universe of need for manpower programs, it is convenient to divide the problem into several parts. The youth manpower problem is different from that of those in the prime working ages. Similarly, a few of those beyond retirement age ought to have an opportunity to work if they want to, and this requires a different kind of program. For each category we are able to make estimates of the number of persons involved. Let me illustrate by detailing the way we derive the universe of need for manpower programs for young people between the ages of 16 and 21. The same exercise can be, and is, followed for each of the other groups that we wish to consider.

We begin with the total number of youths who are classified as poor under our definition. In 1964, the last year for which we have good data, there were about 3 million poor youths between the ages of 16 and 21. Of these almost 60 per cent were out of school. Since the problem of in-school poor youths mainly involves the schools, we include only out-of-school youth in the universe for manpower programs.

To obtain a realistic universe for our present programs (JC, MDTA, and the NYC) we must assume that some of the poor youth will be ineligible or uninterested. Many already have steady jobs paying at least the legal minimum wage. And many, especially young mothers, have no desire to join the labor force. For those poor out-of-school youths in the labor force, we have data indicating whether they worked more or less than 40 weeks in 1964. If a youth worked less than 40 weeks, we assume that he will be interested in our programs. If he worked more than this, we assume that he will not be interested since, especially among youth, steady employment normally means a reasonably well-paying job.

After we obtain the universe estimate for those in the labor force, we add a portion of those outside the labor force since we know that as the job situation improves young people not now in the labor market will begin to look for jobs. This gives us an estimate of all poor out-of-school youths needing manpower programs in 1964. Many of these poor youths will be ineligible for our present OEO programs although not for MDTA training, because the programs rarely accept high school graduates. Therefore, in calculating the universe for these particular programs, we must eliminate high school graduates. In 1964, when we made all these adjustments, our universe was about 500,000. This represented about 30 per cent of all poor out-of-school youths.

Next we take into account changes over time. First, the poverty population has been declining with improvements in the economy. As a result, it is estimated that the universe has declined almost 15 per cent since 1964. Second, there have been changes in the number of dropouts. Although the dropout rate has fallen steadily from 46 per cent in 1948 to 23 per cent in 1964, the total number of youths has been increasing rapidly. Over most time periods, these two factors cancel each other, but between 1964 and 1966 the youth population increase was particularly large. Consequently, the total number of dropouts has increased a little, and we raise our universe estimate correspondingly. Our final estimate for 1966 is 450,000. This represents the number of poor dropouts who we think need the services of manpower programs in the War on Poverty.

## Defining Needs

The next question in planning a manpower system, it seems to me, is to decide what these various groups of individuals need. Let me describe briefly the four main categories of need which these unemployed, underemployed, or nonemployed have. First, is the category called job creation. At some stages of the business cycle there are plenty of jobs generated for all who can handle them; we are at the present time beginning to enter a period of this sort where in many parts of the country it is impossible to find people to fill jobs that are available. A year ago this was not the case, and at that time the problem of job-creation was uppermost in our minds as an essential ingredient of manpower programs for the poor.

I have described elsewhere the public employment program that was worked out in OEO, the purpose of which was to generate jobs for poor people in unskilled occupations. These jobs are largely in the service field and are designed to provide public services which this country needs. Jobs can also be, and are, created in the private sector, and indeed this is one of the purposes of an enlightened fiscal policy. The fact that the unemployment rate is today regarded with such great interest is an indication of the significance of job-creation. In future months, if the unemployment rate continues to fall, job-creation will become less important in our overall manpower system. But I suppose that there will remain pockets of high unemployment where the proportion of nonwhites in the population is high, and where for one reason or another outward mobility has not taken place in response to the increased demand for labor. In such spots there may remain a need for job-creation.

The second class of needs that manpower programs must meet is skill training. This may be the simple preparation of an unskilled worker for a semi-skilled job through training under government or private auspices, either on the job or in an institution. It may also take the form of upgrading already employed people, again either on the job or in an institution, and again either at government or at private expense. In a tight labor market such as is now developing, many people are coming to the conclusion that sensible manpower policy will look to the upgrading of those in semi-skilled or unskilled employment in order that room can be made at the bottom for those who are now not employed at all.

The third set of needs can be said to fall under the general rubric of literacy and what might be called personal training. This is particularly important in the case of youngsters who have never held a job and who have been brought up in disadvantaged areas. They need to learn the simpler skills of reading and calculation and even how to behave when asking for or reporting to a job. Some people who need these services are probably not employable at the time they begin to receive them. To the extent that manpower programs are successful they result in an increase in the supply of labor, which is good for the economy as a whole as well as for the individual involved.

Finally, there is a group of needs which perhaps should be called miscellaneous or "all other." I refer here to services that are needed before people can be put to work and which we customarily do not regard as part of the manpower system. As we come to deal with the hard-core poor, however, we are finding that these needs *should be* regarded as a part of the manpower problem. For example, we have found that poor health is an important element in reducing the employability of a substantial proportion of the population. The health deficiency may be physical or there may be a psychiatric problem. There appear to be a substantial number of people who are simply unable to cope with the complexities of a job in modern society. Another service of this type is the provision of child-care centers where women can leave their children during the day while they are working.

### The Tools Available

The next question is what are the tools available to service these needs, and what is the extent to which these tools can cope with the universe of need described earlier. Let me run over very briefly the programs that OEO now has available and then turn to the question of how planning can help put them together. There is at the present time a heavy emphasis on youth in

American manpower programs, though I am not sure to what extent this is conscious. By definition the young have longer to be productive members of society, and it seems to me proper that this is where our major emphasis should be placed.

The JC now has about 28,000 young men and women receiving basic education, vocational skill training, and some indoctrination in the social graces or what passes for such in this particular slice of the population. It is expected that the JC will grow until about 45,000 slots are available. Given the present nine-month average tenure, this means that about 60,000 to 65,000 youngsters per year will be going through the system. You have all read about the many problems that the JC faces. My own feeling is that these problems are being brought under control; and although we do not yet have definitive evaluation results, there are indications that the JC is achieving a number of quite thrilling successes. There are, of course, also the inevitable failures that come from dealing with youngsters who are at the bottom of the barrel. It will be a while yet before any overall assessment of the JC is possible; and, of course, with the way costs are running, the successes will have to be substantial in order to justify the program. To me the idea still seems a sound one, and I hope we shall be permitted to continue with it to determine whether it is as good in the execution as in conception.

The NYC is a substantially larger program and at present is handling in its out-of-school component about 100,000 youngsters per year. Until now these young men and women have been receiving work training, and that is about all. We are proposing to add a substantial enrichment component to the program so that the young people can be offered basic education and some vocational skills. The wage normally paid to NYC enrollees is the minimum wage, and it is interesting that at the present time, with the tightening labor market, there is greater and greater difficulty in filling the number of slots available. If a program of this sort lacks a considerable element of enrichment, it is not clear what function it can be expected to perform when jobs are generally plentiful. With upgrading built into the program, inability to fill slots will become a matter of real concern.

I should mention that a substantial portion of the MDTA training facilities are now available for young disadvantaged

Americans. MDTA, financed and operated by the Labor Department, is now reorienting its services so that more will be directed toward the poverty group than has been the case in the past. This is essentially a training program designed to give necessary skills to those it serves. It operates both on the job and through institutions of one sort or another, and is administered jointly by the Department of Labor and the Department of Health, Education, and Welfare (HEW), the education component being supplied by HEW. In an expanding economy MDTA can and does supply highly necessary services.

This brings me to the work-experience program, sometimes called the Title V Program because it derives its authority and funds from Title V of the Economic Opportunity Act. The program is aimed at people on some kind of public assistance or who are eligible for public assistance. It is a peculiar amalgam of a welfare program and a manpower program, and, in all candor, it has not worked as well as was expected, at least in the context in which most manpower specialists would like to see the program operate. At the present time the Title V program is operating at its capacity of 58,000 men and women. Many of these are presently unemployable, although by no means all of them, since the prime qualification is welfare eligibility rather than lack of employability. Of the 58,000 participants, about half are male and half female, and about half are white and half nonwhite. The average age is 36, and the average educational level for heads of households is about eight years. More than half of these participants have held one job for six months or more, and of these 55 per cent were employed as service workers or as unskilled laborers.

There is need for a substantial program for adult unemployables that will give them the kind of work experience and training necessary to make them employable in either the private or the public sector. The hope was that Title V would fill this need, but the fact that it has been less of a manpower program than many of us would have liked has militated against its fulfilling this purpose. I should expect that either this year or next the Title V Program will be transferred from HEW to the Department of Labor and made into a genuine manpower program. Congress is even now making motions in this direction.

Next, the government is spending about $60 million on adult literacy training. We think of adult literacy as an integral part of the manpower programs since an illiterate adult is really quite unable to function in the American economic system. There are no adequate data on the extent of illiteracy in the United States, which I find particularly disturbing. We do know that there are about 22 million American adults who have received less than an eighth-grade education; approximately half of these 22 million are in the poverty class. It does not follow that all of these people are illiterate, and it does not follow that this is the total amount of the people who are illiterate. An interesting statistic has come out of our JC experience. The average educational level for an accepted JC applicant is the ninth grade, but his reading and comprehension is at the sixth-grade level. About half of the adult literacy expenditures are made on delegation from OEO to the Office of Education under Title II-B of the Economic Opportunity Act. The other half are made directly through the Community Action Agencies, ordinarily where Title II-B does not have an installation operating.

Finally, Community Action Program (CAP) has a variety of manpower activities too diverse to discuss here. But I shall consider their implications later.

In terms of both the planning and the coordination problems it is noteworthy that some of this total set of manpower programs operate at all levels of government and are joined by many nongovernmental manpower services. This is a situation made to order for both planning—to make sure that the programs are properly designed to fit together—and for coordination—to insure that the agencies and levels of government work together rather than at cross purposes.

There are some programs that the United States does not have that it ought to have, and I should complete this section by a brief reference to one that I consider critical. We do little to increase the mobility of our labor supply. A particularly thorny problem here is movement of unemployed or underemployed labor from rural to urban areas. At the present time, this happens as the spirit moves the individual involved, with consequences that are unpleasant to contemplate. We ought to be doing a good deal more than we now are to train people in

rural areas for jobs that are available in towns or cities and to
make it possible for them to move from one place to another.
Not only are moving allowances necessary following the training,
but it is also essential that potential employers and employees
be able to get together for interviews. I understand that the
Labor Department is working on problems of this sort, and they
bulk large in the minds of those at OEO who are interested in
the manpower problem.

**The Need for Planning**

Let me turn to the role of planning in the heterogeneous, almost random set of programs that I have briefly outlined. Essentially the problem is one of putting the programs together,
of dovetailing them so that an individual who needs training
can progress smoothly and quickly from one program to the
other. This is not an easy thing to do, since there are a number
of federal agencies involved, all dealing with different authorization and appropriation committees in the Congress and with different sorts of people at their heads. There is real scope for
improving the fit of the programs.

Let me cite a couple of examples. At the present time the
NYC pays $1.25 an hour to its enrollees, usually for 32 hours
of work. Upon completion of the NYC experience, many of these
youngsters ought to go on to MDTA for more advanced vocational training. But the youth allowance under MDTA is $20.00
per week. Hence, the more advanced training—which is in the
interest of both the youth and the government—costs the youth
$20.00 per week or a decrease in income of 50 per cent. As a con-
sequence there is very little incentive for a youngster who finishes
his work experience to move on into training at what he regards
as a substantial and intolerable cut in income.

Another area in which better planning is clearly called for is
the division of the youth universe, in particular between the JC
and the NYC. Both of these programs are designed to take disadvantaged youth, give them certain kinds of service, and produce a youngster who is employable in the private sector. Both
are trying to help young people become acclimated to the society
in which they have to live, so that they will be able to earn
more than they otherwise would and, in general, become pro-

ductive members of society. Having stated the basic aims of these two systems, however, it is necessary to go on and point out that they are really very different from each other. One is a resident system, the other nonresident. One places great emphasis on literacy training and other basic education; the other is really little more than a work-training project. One places emphasis on vocational training; the other does very little of this. One has a great deal of individual counseling; the other, a much more modest counseling effort. And so it goes, with the conclusion that the programs, even though they may have the same ultimate objective, are extremely different.

This difference emerges most clearly when one examines the cost of treating a youngster for, say, nine months. It turns out that the JC is perhaps five times as expensive as the NYC. Under these circumstances, it seems to me, appropriate planning would assure that a different sort of raw material entered each of the two programs. It would be nothing short of the most remarkable coincidence if it turned out that two such different systems were equally effective for the same kind of disadvantaged youth. Clearly, we have to regard the JC as a system for the more difficult youngsters while the NYC provides a work experience system for those youngsters who are very nearly employable at the time they enter. It is apparent that the present system, under which young men and women are assigned to these two systems almost by lottery, is unsatisfactory.

There is one other way in which I think planning has a very direct role to play in manpower programs. I am referring to the state of the economy. Manpower programs must be different depending upon whether jobs are plentiful or scarce. Job creation is an important element of manpower policies whenever there is a deficiency of jobs, but as the labor market tightens the emphasis should shift from job-creation to job-training. This is never a black-and-white situation, and some job-creation and job-training are probably always necessary. But certainly job-creation is much more important relatively when unemployment rates are high, and conversely training becomes more important as unemployment rates decline. Indeed, I would urge that, in a tight labor situation like that which is now developing, training, particularly for the disadvantaged, is extremely important. This

is a period in which the jobs are there, and, hence, the incentive
to undergo training ought to be a very real one. We should take
advantage of this situation by doing just as much training as
we possibly can.

## Opportunities for Coordination

Let me turn now to a brief consideration of what kinds of
coordination are needed in operating the manpower programs.
From what has already been said, it should be clear that there
is plenty of scope for coordination. The fact that several different federal agencies are involved, as well as several different
levels of government, means that it is very possible for complete
chaos to set in. And indeed there are those who feel that that
is the best characterization of the manpower programs! There
*have* been cases in which different agencies have been pulling
in different directions, but I think that, on balance, the situation
is not as bad as some believe it to be. In Washington there
have been a number of efforts to bring about improved coordination, one of which I will briefly describe.

During this past winter the agencies primarily concerned—
OEO, the Department of Labor, and HEW—met on a number
of occasions to work out a technique for providing coordination
both at the national and the local level. What resulted was the
establishment of teams of three, one from each agency, which
are being sent to many of the largest cities in the United States.
Inevitably coming to be called the "troikas," these teams spend
a substantial proportion of their time in the cities to which they
are assigned. They work with their local counterparts, making
sure that the city understands where the funding comes from and
how to apply to the various sources for funds, that each program
is aware of the existence of the others, and that efforts are made
on the local level to dovetail these programs. While these teams
have been in operation for only a few weeks, it is already possible to assert that they are achieving a certain amout of success.

The first troikas went to 9 cities during the spring of 1966.
Toward the end of May, these teams met to review their experiences and brief new teams going out to 8 other major-city
areas. The reports of the teams provide some insight into the

problems and possibilities of manpower coordination at the local level.

Perhaps the most frequently mentioned problem is the lack of information. The following quotation was taken from the Chicago report:

One of the most serious deficiencies, even at top agency levels, regional, state, and local, is the lack of information and knowledge about other programs and agencies which have responsibilities in the manpower field . . . and this lack becomes far more serious as one moves down the organizationl scale. When this lack of information is combined with a rather narrow and possessive view of one's program, the effects on coordination are not good.

Aside from such generalizations, the experience of the teams suggests that the particular difficulties in achieving a coordinated manpower program vary considerably from city to city. There was one concrete problem, however, that was shared by all the areas—the issue of achieving a coordinated use of funds. Each agency, and even each program within each agency, seems to have its own set of requirements regarding the matching of federal funds, the kinds of expenditures for which federal funds can be used, the degree of federal, state, or local government control, the criteria for allocation of funds, kinds of application forms, and funding periods and expiration dates. The inevitable horror story is about a training project under $100,000 which was reported as funded from 16 different sources, each with separate criteria, application forms, and expiration dates.

It was dramatically demonstrated by one of the teams that no one in the area had an effective overview of the totality of financial resources available to the area for manpower training and education or of the extent to which such funds could reasonably be expected to be used in commonly funded, joint ventures. As a result, unrealistic expectations about fund availabilities have led to a situation in which actually approved projects in manpower training are almost three times as great as the funds which are likely to be available under present arrangements. It is clear that this very confused funding picture is fostering a creation of hopes both among the potential enrollees and among the potential trainers, including employers, which are going to be unfulfilled and which may make later programs much more difficult to implement.

Related to the common funding problem, at least in my mind, is the attitude toward coordination expressed by manpower agencies at the local level. In some areas, the various governmental and private agencies were hostile to attempts to foster coordination, but in general the response was that the agencies welcomed these attempts because they themselves "don't have time to worry about coordination." To an economist, this is equivalent to saying they have no *incentive* to coordinate. In fact, current funding procedures in the manpower area not only fail to provide positive incentives for coordination but they actually seem to provide strong negative incentives. A minimum effort in this area would seem to require an attempt to remove at least some of the barriers to common funding of manpower training and education.

There are a myriad of other interesting manifestations of bad coordination which were discovered by the teams. For instance, differentials in training allowances which discouraged a proper flow of trainees among programs, with allowances sometimes exceeding the going wage in the occupation being trained for; union resistance to expanded training in certain fields, particularly for the disadvantaged; multiple approaches to employers or potential trainees from competing training agencies; and problems of transporting disadvantaged trainees from home to training site.

The teams were unanimous in endorsing the need for a federal force for coordination in the field, but they differed quite widely in their view as to the form such a force should take. They ranged all the way from those who felt that a one-man, *ad hoc* effort was best, so as to avoid over-institutionalization, to those who felt that a separate federal agency should be created which would be independent of all the operating agencies. I do not think that we are yet in a position to make a decision as to the best form for long-term coordination within the federal system. On the one hand, it would be foolish to say that we must wait for a solution to these more general problems before attempting to settle on a solution for the manpower area. This approach would probably amount to allowing the ideal to be the enemy of the good. On the other hand, we should proceed with caution in creating new federal forms in the manpower area since much of the current confusion arises from the proliferation of new institutions created to deal with problems viewed singly.

While coordination in a sense has a sanctity like motherhood, there are some of us who feel that it can be pressed too far. Or to put it another way, there are some of us who feel that a certain amount of competition in the public sector will bring good results even as it does in the private sector. For example, the Community Action Agencies funded by the OEO have in some areas been doing work that the Employment Service really ought to do. This has been viewed with dismay by some, though not all, in the Labor Department, but I think an objective view of the impact of this competition can only conclude that on balance the results have been beneficial. The Employment Service is better today than it was two years ago, and I think at least some credit can be claimed by the Community Action Agencies, which have been acting as a spur to the Employment Service. No one in OEO wants to replace the Employment Service, though we have been unwilling to agree that the Employment Service should have a monopoly on placement until or unless it can do a better job. This very fact, I think, though it has caused confusion in some areas, has been instrumental in upgrading the Employment Service to the benefit of all.

There is one other system that is supplying some healthy competition, and I should like merely to mention it. I refer to the Opportunities Industrialization Center (OIC), initially begun in Philadelphia by a group of Negroes to provide training for hard-core unemployed Negroes. There have been some real initial successes achieved in the city of Philadelphia by this system, which has some funding from the OEO and some from other sources. It is competing with MDTA and with other training facilities, and competing well. It has recently been extended to a number of other cities, and we are hopeful that we can achieve the same sort of success elsewhere. The existence of this system side by side with other training systems may well have caused some trouble and may be a sign of a lack of coordination. On balance, however, it seems clear that OIC has made a constructive contribution as a manpower program.

In conclusion, I would argue that some coordination in the operation of these programs is clearly necessary, given the federal-state-local situation and the multiplicity of agencies necessarily involved in manpower problems. I would only argue that an excessively tidy administration ought not be the goal; indeed if we were to achieve it—and there is slight danger of this—the effectiveness of our programs might thereby be impaired. To some extent, program effectiveness and tidy administration may be alternatives; where they are, I prefer the former. On the other hand, the need for careful planning seems to me to be clear. Unless we design programs that fit together, are consistent with one another, and are in tune with the external economic conditions under which they must operate, confusion and loss of effectiveness seem the most likely results.

## NOTES

1. The author is Assistant Director, Office of Economic Opportunity, on leave from Williams College. This paper has benefited from the advice and assistance of several OEO staff members, notably Dr. Stanley Masters, Dr. Walter Williams, and Dr. Robinson Hollister. Dr. Robert Levine has been particularly helpful, as he has in everything I have written in the past year while we have been together in OEO.

At the conference, Thayne Robson and Frederick Harbison, who served as discussants, offered a number of thoughtful comments as a result of which I have made several changes in the original manuscript. I am indebted to them for these constructive comments.

# Discussion

## BY R. THAYNE ROBSON

Dr. Kershaw has written an excellent and interesting paper. His major contribution is a description of the approach taken by the OEO in planning for youth between the ages of 16 and 21. The paper highlights the need for more thought in determining methods for ranking present programs in terms of a carefully ordered hierarchy of needs.

The distinction made between planning and coordination is not particularly helpful or valid. Kershaw calls attention to the multiple programs available to serve youth. At present, there are five major pieces of legislation which establish over a dozen separate manpower programs directed in whole or in part to the needs of disadvantaged persons. A careful review of (1) The Manpower Act, (2) The Economic Opportunity Act, (3) The Vocational Education Act, (4) The Vocational Rehabilitation Act, and (5) The Economic Development Act will reveal that each of the dozen of so programs created by this legislation can provide four or more of the generally recognized component parts of a manpower program: (1) recruitment or outreach to locate persons needing assistance, (2) screening, testing, and counseling regarding individual needs and available opportunities for training and jobs, (3) provision of basic education and prevocational training, (4) provision of related services such as minor medical care, tools, or work clothing which may be required to enhance employability, (5) occupational and skill training, (6) development of job vacancies through direct contact with employers, (7) placement in jobs, and (8) follow up to determine the success of those assisted.

The management of this great effort in planning, staffing, and directing, requires coordination in each managerial function and among federal, state, and local agencies. The greatest need is for more coordinated planning among all who manage these efforts.

Given the present structure of manpower programs outlined in his paper, Kershaw's concern about "pressing coordination too far" seems at best a little premature. This brings us to the center of the discussion about the alleged benefits of bureaucratic competition. It would have been helpful if Kershaw had spelled out more clearly the benefits of competition. Government services generally are equated with public utilities; economies of scale, high fixed costs, and other factors tend to reduce the benefits of competition. If the prime purpose of competition is to stimulate one or more agency to do a better job, then one might ask whether building competitive—some say duplicative—efforts is the best or only way to accomplish the goal.

If we agree with Kershaw that the "dovetailing" or "fitting together" of programs is a planning problem only, then the concept of coordination takes on a peculiar meaning.

Kershaw might well have considered more carefully the need to develop better coordinated plans to evaluate manpower programs with a view toward determining the relative merits of each in accomplishing the desired goal. Manpower programs as they presently exist constitute a major part of the Great Society program. In the main, they seek to eliminate some of the competitive disadvantages for those people who have the greatest difficulty in obtaining and retaining good employment opportunities. It is doubtful that each program contributes equally in terms of dollars spent.

The President's Committee on Manpower is presently devoting major emphasis to trying to achieve coordination at the local level of federally supported manpower programs. In my view, this effort will not succeed until local officials, representing a variety of agencies, public and private, are able to coordinate planning, programming, and budgeting at the community level. The total needs of the community must be adequately assessed, and rational policies must be developed for channeling investments into training facilities and faculty and for moving disadvantaged people successfully into the world of work. Overlap and duplication of effort is wasteful and unnecessary. Without adequate and coordinated planning, serious gaps emerge within the community, and some citizens do not receive the service and assistance that these programs are supposed to provide.

The present program of sending three-men teams to 28 metropolitan and 2 rural areas to promote improved coordination of manpower programs should give us a more adequate appreciation of the problems that exist in the present system, and, hopefully, they will point the way to the development of orderly and successful measures to achieve coordination in a way that yields the maximum benefit for the dollars expended.

# Discussion

## BY FREDERICK HARBISON

I am in agreement with the major concepts and conclusions of Dr. Kershaw's paper, as far as they go. His distinction between planning and coordination is sound. I support with enthusiasm his plea for a degree of healthy competition rather than "excessively tidy administration" in coordination of manpower programs. And, of course, I would agree that more careful and comprehensive planning is urgently needed. I should like to *extend* some of the points he made, for, if I have one criticism of his excellent paper, it is perhaps that his concept of manpower policy is too narrow and that, as a consequence, he overlooks some crucial questions for manpower planning and coordination.

### The Scope of Manpower Policy

Dr. Kershaw states that the objective of a manpower planning system is "the achievement of employment for everyone who is or can be made employable at his full potential." This definition of objectives is much too restricted. Kershaw is concerned here primarily with employment and training of disadvantaged persons—those who stand near the end of the "Mangum queue." I think that the scope of manpower policy should be much wider. In the broadest terms, manpower policy should be concerned with *development, maintenance,* and *utilization* of actual or potential members of the labor force, including those who are fully and productively employed as well as those who experience difficulty in getting work.

The *development* of manpower is the process of man's acquiring the skills, knowledge, and capacities for work. For example, vocational education is obviously an instrument of manpower development. But general education is even more important. It is true, as educators and humanists rightly assert, that the

136

broad purpose of education is to prepare people for life rather than simply for employment. Man does not live by bread alone. Yet, as Confucius is reported to have said, "It is not easy to find a man who has studied for three years without aiming at pay." Thus, to the extent that general education is necessary for and oriented toward preparation for gainful activity, it is a central concern of manpower policy. Beyond education, manpower is also developed in the course of employment as persons acquire skill, knowledge, and experience through formal or informal training on the job.

The *maintenance* of manpower is the process of preservation and continuous renewal of man's capacities for work. It could also be thought of as continuous development of manpower. For example, a major objective of unemployment compensation is to maintain a person while he is seeking new employment. The purpose of rehabilitation programs is to restore the capacity for work. The preservation and improvement of health is also important in maintaining the capacity for work. Retraining programs are designed primarily to maintain the ability of persons to participate in the labor force in the face of rapid changes in jobs and required skills. In this age of sweeping innovation, the productivity of the labor force must be maintained by continuous retraining, education, and renewal of human skills and knowledge.

The *utilization* of manpower is the process of matching men and work in accordance with their level of development. Even under conditions of near-full employment, the matching process is imperfect. For example, scientists and engineers may perform tasks which are beneath their knowledge and skills. Unemployment may persist in some localities while vacancies exist in others. Discrimination may favor certain groups in employment. Persons with high potential may not advance as rapidly in an enterprise as their capabilities would permit. Whether because of inadequate information, insufficient mobility, discrimination, or lack of proper incentives, manpower may be and often is used inefficiently. Manpower policy, therefore, is concerned with *improving the utilization* of human resources. It encompasses measures such as the provision of employment and placement services, efficient managerial practices, labor-market information, counseling, encouragement of mobility, and the use of incentives to attract persons into useful and productive activities.

Thus, a *comprehensive* manpower policy would encompass all programs or activities directly related to the *development, maintenance,* and *utilization* of the labor force, and a *cohesive* manpower policy would call for a logical and consistent strategy to guide all activity along these lines. This would be a large order. It would require the combined effort of thousands of policy-makers—private employers, local school boards, community action groups, state education authorities, labor and welfare departments, a wide-ranging group of federal government agencies and institutions, as well as the federal, state, and local governments as direct employers of manpower. In a pluralistic society characterized by decentralized decision-making, manpower policy is almost everybody's business.

## A Comprehensive Policy for the United States

To most people, the very idea of a comprehensive manpower policy of such dimensions is confusing and disturbing. We have not seriously attempted such a planning effort in the United States. But we have been concerned with comprehensive manpower planning for the underdeveloped countries. In other words, we have built manpower planning models *for export only.* Can we develop a comprehensive manpower planning system for home use?

It is much easier to devise a comprehensive and cohesive manpower policy for an underdeveloped country than for the United States—primarily because the manpower problems of the former are so blindingly obvious! In African countries, for example, unemployment in the modern sector is probably over 15 per cent (if one has the statistics to measure it.) Skill shortages and high-level manpower bottlenecks can be readily identified even in the absence of sophisticated labor-force studies. The deficiencies and sources of "power failure" in the education system are apparent even to the untrained observer. Governments are not as yet overdeveloped to the point of being bureaucratic quagmires. And even the lack of statistics is often an advantage, since it enables one to get an almost breathtaking

and crystal-clear view of the essential facts! In an underdeveloped country, it would be unthinkable to limit the scope of
manpower policy *exclusively* to unemployment problems, to
education, to vocational training, to incentive-generation, or any
other single facet of human resource development. One grasps
the idea at once that all of these must be constituent elements
of a manpower policy program. Perhaps we should apply some
of this simple-minded thinking to the manpower situation in the
United States.

In the United States, however, the problems are vastly more
complex. The participants in the manpower planning process are
far more numerous; intragovernment relationships are much
more complicated and cumbersome. And finally, the critical manpower problems do not stand out in such bold relief. In an underdeveloped country, it is easy to identify the critical elements
for a strategy of human-resource development; in this country,
the details and the minutiae becloud our view of the command-
ing heights.

The Kershaw paper identifies a number of manpower problems,
connected for the most part with the War on Poverty. These are
important problems and properly fall within the scope of manpower policy planning. But others are equally if not more critical.
Let me give some examples.

The relationship between general education, training, and
employment lies at the very heart of manpower policy. In preparation of persons for various careers, what are the appropriate
proportions and the costs relative to opportunity of general education, preemployment vocational schooling, and on-the-job development? Should retraining programs be organized primarily
for the disadvantaged, or should a retraining system be a continuing part of in-service development and maintenance of all
employed working forces? To what extent and in what areas
should employing institutions, both public and private, be responsible for training and retraining? What incentives (in the
form of subsidies, tax credits, etc.) would be appropriate to encourage private employers to assume a larger share of the training burden? These and related questions need extensive study.

Manpower policy is also concerned with the *expansion* and
*improvement* of general education. Our economy seems to have

an almost insatiable appetite for highly educated manpower—
for scientists, engineers, teachers, doctors, managers, counselors,
and a wide variety of technicians and subprofessional personnel.
To some extent, the supply of such high-level manpower creates
its own demand, as well as a demand for supporting personnel.
At the other extreme, the economy is rejecting those with less
than a good high school education. Many people argue, therefore,
that in relation to the country's present and expected levels of
economic and technological development, the labor force is
underdeveloped. In other words, the gap between education and
employability is widening because the education system fails to
keep pace with changes in the world of work. What then are the
appropriate remedies? Is a massive, across-the-board increase
in education necessary adequately to develop the nation's manpower? Should free public education include post high school
education, either in technical institutions or in college, for two
or three years, so that fourteen or fifteen years of education
are available to all at public expense? Or, should the expansion
and improvement of education be more selective, giving priority,
as J. Kenneth Galbraith suggests, to improving substandard
schools in the poorest and most disadvantaged areas? Should
more resources be devoted to identification and higher education
of the gifted? What are the appropriate means of financing programs of expansion and improvement of education? And how
will the required teaching personnel be developed?

Another cluster of problems is related to mobility. There is
general agreement that the labor force of the future must be
more flexible and adaptable. But what kinds of mobility are required, and how can they be developed? The first is *occupational.*
Within limits, many persons may have to change their occupations from time to time. The second is *geographical.* Most persons may have to live in several different places during their
working liftime. The third is *internal,* or *movement within the
establishment.* This implies that persons must be prepared to
move upwards or sideways within the career pathways which
an employing establishment (either public or private) may provide. And the fourth is *intellectual.* This requires an attitude
of acceptance of change and a willingness to prepare for new
kinds of employment. Such questions as the following then arise:

Under what conditions is geographical mobility desirable, and how can it be encouraged? What are the respective roles of general education and training in developing intellectual mobility? To what extent is continuous education and retraining necessary for occupational mobility? Under what circumstances should mobility be discouraged rather than encouraged?

These and other problem areas are part of the agenda for manpower-policy development. And there are, I think, three basic steps in the process of policy development.

First, there must be a comprehensive and objective study of the major manpower problem areas, with particular emphasis on analysis of alternative solutions and the relevant opportunity costs involved.

Second, through discussion and education, an attempt must be made to build a nationwide understanding of manpower problems and a feeling of commitment to doing something to solve them. Manpower planning is meaningless without a degree of national consensus.

And third, measures must be devised to *involve* public and private organizations, at the national, state, and local levels, in the development and implementation of manpower programs. The *energetic participation* of people and organizations is certainly just as important as the rational coordination of prescribed activities. We probably have less to fear from duplication of effort than from ignorance, apathy, or complacency.

CHAPTER **6**

# Placement and Counseling:
# The Role of the Employment Service

## Editor's Note

On December 23, 1965, a Task Force headed by Dean George P. Shultz of the University of Chicago submitted to the Secretary of Labor a special report on the Employment Service. This report is here reprinted in full (except for a final section entitled "A Summary of the Task Force Activities," which has not been included).* The report was distributed to all members of the conference and served as a starting point for the prepared comments and for the informal discussion which followed. Following the report of the Task Force, we present the comments prepared for the conference by Dean Shultz, Leonard Adams, and Daniel Kruger.

*As originally submitted to the Secretary of Labor. With some minor changes of wording and also without this last section, the report was published in *Employment Service Review,* III (February, 1966).

## A REPORT TO THE SECRETARY OF LABOR
## FROM THE EMPLOYMENT SERVICE TASK FORCE

### I. Introduction

A new look is being taken at the nation's manpower resources today. The quality and distribution of educational opportunities has never received more attention. The relationship of vocational training and retraining to the adaptability of the labor force is clearly recognized and is reflected in recent Congressional action. Agencies linking the job market with special programs for individuals who have special disabilities have grown in both the public and private sectors of the economy. At the same time skill shortages are appearing and these highlight the need for more effective ways of linking people and jobs.

The growth of programs to deal with manpower problems and opportunities promises better lives for all members of our society. But programs can be no better than the quality of their administration.

This Task Force has reviewed and hereby makes recommendations to improve the quality of management in an Agency that has a major responsibility in the development and administration of programs relating manpower and jobs. The Federal-State Employment Service has offices throughout the country and a great potential for service to job seekers, employers, and other private and public groups seeking improved operations of the labor market. This potential and concomitant responsibility is especially important for members of minority groups, whose needs in this area are most urgent. If the Service can become a more effective center for manpower services in the community, it can contribute much more significantly toward the full and efficient implementation of the public programs dealing with manpower development and utilization.

Thus, while we make recommendations for improved administration, we believe these are intimately related to current or prospective programs under review in the Congress.

Our recommendations fall into seven areas:

1. A statement about the appropriate role and mission of the Employment Service.

2. Further separation of the administration of the Employment Service from the administration of Unemployment Compensation.

3. Improving relations with other groups in the labor market.

4. New provisions for improving the quality and compensation of Employment Service personnel, principally at the state and local levels.

5. Emphasis on the role of the Employment Service in collecting and disseminating information about the job market.

6. Improving the interarea recruitment procedures with the aid of modern information technology.

7. Suggestions for administrative matters designed to improve the quality of management in the Service and strengthening its finances.

A statement describing the activities of the Task Force is attached.

In recent years, Congress has recognized the importance of human resources and of their full development and has made significant legislative break-throughs, establishing ambitious objectives and new programs in the manpower area. A renewed and modernized Employment Service is essential to the effective administration of these programs. Our recommendations are designed to build such a Service and many of them require legislative action. Thus, the Congress is called upon again for affirmative steps toward manpower development.

## II. The Role and Mission of the Public Employment Service

Recent economic events and legislative enactments have created significant opportunities for the public Employment Service to contribute to national welfare. To grasp these opportunities, traditional concepts must be re-examined and existing administrative arrangements profoundly altered. The public Employment Service can no longer be considered a simple labor exchange bringing together job seekers and employers. Rather, it must be established as a comprehensive manpower services agency whose activities provide vital support for a variety of government programs.

The scope and complexity of current developments lend a new note of insistence to the perennial pleas for improving the

Employment Service. On the one hand, the nation's economy is in a period of rapid change requiring new patterns of labor market organization and administration. Dramatic technological advances, the sharp growth in the size of the labor force and changes in its composition, growing skill shortages and changing patterns of consumer demand are imposing severe tests upon the versatility of the nation's manpower institutions. On the other hand, Congress has enacted an amalgam of legislation dealing with manpower, education, and civil rights which is designed to improve the quality of American life and to broaden the distribution of the benefits of economic progress. Clearly, the Employment Service must adjust to these new circumstances in order to retain and enhance its effectiveness.

**The importance of labor market information.** In this context, two functions assume over-riding importance. First, the Employment Service should assume responsibility for the analysis, and dissemination of labor market information in the broadest sense, and the collection and use of such information at the local level. This information would, among other things, encompass the present and future demand and supply for specific occupations, the qualifications necessary for entry and career development in these occupations, and conditions in particular labor markets. In carrying out this task, the Employment Service must, of course, utilize the data available from other public and private agencies in order to avoid duplication of effort. The Employment Service should accept the ultimate responsibility for insuring the adequacy of existing labor market information and its dissemination in a usable form. The attainment of this objective is a precondition for intelligent planning and decision-making by all organizations or individuals with a stake in an efficient labor market.

**Toward a comprehensive manpower services center.** Second, the public Employment Service is in a strategic position to function as a manpower center at the community and labor market levels. Many of the technical services necessary for effective manpower development and utilization are already available. The efficient use of these services is thwarted, however, by the fact that they are too often provided on a piecemeal basis that overlooks the close interrelationships among the component parts of a manpower program. Under the circumstances, no single agency has been able to coordinate these services and bring them to bear in the interests of job seekers and employers. Such coordination is particularly important when dealing with persons who lack job experience or who must overcome special handicaps in the labor market.

A major step can be taken to rectify this administrative deficiency by strengthening the Employment Service as a comprehensive manpower services center rather than a passive adjunct of the "unemployment office." The 2,000 offices of the Employment Service constitute an established network connecting all the important labor market areas of the nation. Through these offices, job seekers who need help should be able to obtain the testing, in-depth counseling and current information that are essential parts of the job placement process. Moreover, the Employment Service should be the main governmental link between the diagnosis of deficiencies that impair an individual's employability and referral to the various government or private programs for training and rehabilitation.

In this framework, the placement function remains as the key objective in the operations of the Employment Service. But now it will be part of a systematic effort at manpower development rather than the primary concern of a labor exchange. The development of a comprehensive manpower services center can provide a powerful antidote to the casual, "one-shot" placement psychology that has frequently characterized the Employment Service in the past.

**The tasks of the employment service.** The potential contribution of the Employment Service to the operation of the labor market and national economic programs is revealed by an examination of its specific responsibilities. These responsibilities have been assigned by various statutes, Presidential Executive Orders, and inter-agency agreements. The major challenge at this time is to achieve statutory and administrative recognition of the close inter-relationships of the varied tasks of the Employment Service and to weave them together into a coordinated program of manpower services.

The tasks of the Employment Service may be classified as follows:

1. The maintenance of an active placement service for all workers and employers desiring assistance. This function involves developing better relations with employers, both large and small, to exchange information and to understand better their manpower requirements. Certain employers may need special help in recruiting, screening, and matching job applicants with their manpower requirements.

2. The collection and dissemination of information concerning present and future trends in the labor market and in the quality of the labor force. This information is derived from research initiated by other public or private agencies and by the Employment Service itself.

3. The improvement of employment counseling and testing services to help individual job seekers make intelligent decisions concerning occupational choices. The counselors of the Employment Service have not only an economic and social function but one that can be described as diplomatic. The psychological impression they create on their clients will determine in large measure the usefulness of the Service.

4. The provision of special counseling, job development, and placement services for young, inexperienced persons, members of racial and ethnic minority groups, including Indians, older workers, the physically handicapped, the mentally retarded, Selective Service rejectees, released prisoners, veterans and other job seekers whose capabilities may not be fully utilized in the labor market.

5. Active participation in support of the planning of various economic and educational programs involving important manpower questions such as vocational education, community and regional development, emergency mobilization, occupational retraining and rural development. In providing this planning support the Employment Service has a special responsibility for working closely with educational institutions so that school administrators and counselors themselves may do a more effective job of adjusting those parts of educational programs that bear upon labor market requirements.

6. The rendering of technical assistance and administrative support to other government agencies that are concerned with the employment process and manpower utilization, such as the

Office of Economic Opportunity, Council of Economic Advisers, the Bureau of Apprenticeship and Training, the Neighborhood Youth Corps, the Department of Defense, and public welfare agencies at state and local levels.

7. The certification of geographical areas for federal assistance under various statutes and Executive Orders, such as the Public Works and Economic Development Act of 1965.

8. The maintenance of standards and obligations involved in the administration of the Federal immigration laws, the Unemployment Compensation System, the Executive Orders banning racial and age discrimination by government contractors and related laws and directives.

**The Employment Service and pluralism in the job market.** This specification of the functions and needs of the Employment Service does not mean that it is, or should be, the dominant manpower agency in the economy. To the contrary, the importance of the Employment Service stems from the fact that in carrying out its responsibilities and functions it interlocks with a diversity of public and private institutions. We recognize that a majority of job seekers and employers are usually able to satisfy their needs through a reliance on usual labor market channels. Job seekers may be able to make an intelligent choice based on information provided by friends and other informal sources. Employers may be able to recruit a satisfactory labor force from the flow of applicants to the firm. In addition, both employees and employers will make a significant investment in the development of new skills for a variety of economic and non-economic reasons.

These informal processes are supplemented by a network of private labor market intermediaries. Unions organize the dissemination of information and the placement process in various occupational and industrial sectors. Private employment agencies are active in the placement of job seekers, particularly those in the more skilled or specialized occupational categories. In many cases, non-profit organizations render important services for job seekers who face special difficulties in the labor market.

Recognition of this pluralism in the employment process in the United States helps to define, rather than rigidly constrict, the role of the public Employment Service System. By supporting and supplementing existing arrangements, the Employment Service can and does make a vital contribution to the efficient operation of the labor market and national manpower development. Thus, the information provided by the Employment Service will benefit job seekers, employers and private agencies alike. In addition, by offering a wide range of services, the Employment Service can stimulate higher standards of performance on the part of other intermediaries that are active in the labor market. And most important, in a nation whose level of economic development permits it to contemplate an end to poverty, the Employment Service can render special aid to those individuals who have not been able to benefit from usual labor market processes.

**Equal opportunity and the Employment Service.** The Employment Service has an obvious and important role to play in the achievement of a society where all workers have equal opportunities to compete effectively in building and selling their skills.

The concept of "equal opportunity" must apply in the first instance to the operations and personnel administration of the Employment Service itself. It is not sufficient, however, merely to reaffirm existing laws and policies as they relate to this agency. Instead, Employment Service personnel at every level must make a positive effort to understand and cope with the special problems that confront members of racial minorities in the labor market. In addition, particular diligence should be exercised in helping these individuals to benefit from the various public and private programs that will enhance their employability. At the same time, the Employment Service can demonstrate its commitment to standards of equal opportunity by vigorously recruiting its own personnel from all groups of qualified persons.

**Toward a new mandate.** In the thirty-two years since the passage of the Wagner-Peyser Act, the Federal-State Employment Service has been asked to assume more and more of the responsibilities of a comprehensive manpower services center. This new role should now be affirmed and extended so that the Employment Service can respond to the changing economic environment with competence and imagination and so that the public will have a better understanding of this role. To achieve this objective, a variety of changes are recommended that will alter both existing concepts and administrative arrangements.

## III. A Separate Employment Service

The recent addition of many new responsibilities has greatly modified the nature of the public Employment Service system. An examination of these responsibilities clearly indicates that the Employment Service is now a center for the administration of various manpower services rather than an adjunct to the Unemployment Compensation system.

However, the agency's effectiveness in assuming this expanded role has been limited by its close identification with the Unemployment Compensation system. Since 1935, the Federal-State offices have been charged with administering the eligibility test for unemployment benefits. While this has been, and remains, an important activity, its dominant position in the operations of the Employment Service has had several unfortunate consequences for the efficiency of the overall system.

**Limitations created by integration with the unemployment compensation system.** Different personnel skills are required to operate a manpower services center as contrasted to the administration of the unemployment compensation laws. The latter essentially involves personnel well versed in the specific state Unemployment Compensation law, administrative rulings and other details relative to the effective administration of the program. On the other hand, the provision of manpower services requires personnel who are expert in labor market organization and trends and who have considerable skill in aiding job seekers to develop their full occupational capabilities. In addition, manpower personnel must be able to work closely with employers and become familiar with their problems as well as the needs of other agencies that are active in the labor market. To the extent that the Unemployment Compensation functions demand the attention of the Employment Service personnel they will tend to inhibit the development of satisfactory manpower services.

In addition, the emphasis on Unemployment Compensation has created a public image of the Employment Service that obscures other, more positive elements of its overall program. This "image" has influenced the attitudes of potential clients on both the supply and demand sides of the labor market. Thus, many job seekers who could benefit greatly from the services offered by the Employment Service office are reluctant to use these facilities because of the stigma attached to the "unemployment office." Similarly, many employers have not taken advantage of the Employment Service because they have felt that the placement and manpower functions have occupied a subordinate position in the offices' operations.

Considerations such as these have already led the Employment Service to separate its activities from Unemployment Compensation in cities of 250,000 and over. Furthermore several states, notably Arizona and Wisconsin, have completely separated the administration of the Employment Service from the operations of Unemployment Compensation.

We believe that this process should be extended to all states and to the national office.

We recognize that the Employment Service will continue to play an important role in the administration of the Unemployment Compensation system. This is especially true as it relates to the work test. Close working relationships between the two services are required for effective administration of the work test aspects of the claims certification process. However, it is important that the Employment Service should be a separate, identifiable organization whose over-riding interests lie in the area of manpower services. This means that, insofar as possible, administrative arrangements of the Employment Service should be separated from the administration of Unemployment Compensation, apart from the work test. To attain this objective, several steps should be taken.

**Recommendations for a separate Employment Service. 1.** Administrative arrangements. Separate administrative arrangements should be established for Unemployment Compensation and the manpower functions of the Employment Service at the federal, state and local levels. Some measures already have been adopted to achieve this end, but they should be strengthened and extended. There should be different executives for the two activities and each should have his own staff and line of authority, though reporting to an administrative head of an overall agency. This separation also means that the Employment Service should formulate its own policies to govern the selection of personnel, salary administration and training requirements, and, as discussed subsequently, be financed independently of the Federal Unemployment Tax Act. Although some individual differences may exist among the states, the federal agency should formulate basic requirements for the clear-cut administrative separation of Unemployment Compensation and the Employment Service.

2. Physical separation. A concerted effort should be made to provide physically separate facilities for the Employment Service and for the administration of Unemployment Compensation. Again, some steps have been taken in this direction, but they must be strongly augmented. The ultimate goal should be the physical separation of all Employment Service Offices from all facilities responsible for Unemployment Compensation with reasonable proximity maintained so as to minimize the inconvenience to claimants and job seekers. In the short run, these two activities may still be serviced from the same office in those cases where small offices in sparsely populated areas are involved. A long run program should be adopted, however, for consolidating these small offices, where feasible, as a preliminary to the establishment of separate facilities for Unemployment Compensation and the Employment Service. It may be that wider geographical areas could then be served by a single Employment Service office through the use of mobile teams who visit particular communities on a regularly scheduled basis. In this manner, the Employment Service will avoid the excessive duplication of facilities while also achieving the desired separation from the administration of Unemployment Compensation.

## IV. Scope of Service and Relations with Other Groups

The public employment agency shares its functions in the labor market with a diversity of individuals and organizations including school counselors, voluntary agencies, unions, employers and private labor market agencies and other governmental groups. In the past, however, relations between the Employment Service and other groups in the labor market have not been well defined or understood. As a result, opportunities have been lost for constructive cooperation among the interested parties, and relations between the Employment Service and other organizations have sometimes been strained, if not acrimonious. To clarify this situation, these guidelines are recommended:

1. No arbitrary limits on clientele served. No arbitrary limits should be placed upon the classes of clientele that may be served by the public Employment Service. If it is to function as an effective general-purpose manpower agency, it must be able to serve energetically all people who seek assistance in finding jobs. Because of the dynamic characteristics of the labor market today, any rigid definition of jurisdiction would impair the effectiveness of the Employment Service and also would deny aid to workers and employers who could not be adequately served by other private or public agencies.

2. Special services required. In some cases, special efforts may be called for to reach out to people in need of specialized services to improve their employability. These specialized services include:

(a) Identifying these persons and providing special counselling services in order to determine their rehabilitative needs;

(b) Developing plans commensurate with individual needs, such as referral to another agency for remedial education, institutional training or on-the-job training;

(c) Seeking employment opportunities of a special kind to accommodate the capabilities of persons in this group;

(d) Providing supportive follow-up services while they are on the job until they develop self-confidence in the employment relationship.

3. The need for flexibility and review. The absence of any fixed designation of the clientele of the Employment Service does not mean that it will serve all groups equally or at all times. Normally, the Employment Service should direct most of its resources to job seekers who are unemployed or who have special handicaps in the labor market. Also, in some cases, it will withdraw from certain areas where its objectives have been realized or where it is determined that another public or private agency can do a more effective job. The contraction or expansion of the operations of the Employment Service, therefore, should not arise from narrow bureaucratic considerations, but from an appreciation of its basic mission in a changing labor market and the economy. In this respect, useful recommenda-

tions can and should be made by the Advisory and Review Committee suggested elsewhere in this report.

4. Relationships with private groups. We urge the Employment Service to explore all possible ways to develop a more effective two-way flow of information and contacts with those private employment agencies which offer valuable services to workers and employers in particular labor markets and which adhere to professional standards in their own placement activities.

5. Relationships with other government groups. Recent Government programs for training, particularly of youth and low income groups, have involved the establishment of separate placement agencies, creating excessive demands upon employers and uneconomic duplication of counseling and placement activities. While we recognize that special problems often require special treatment, we feel also that the implementation of all these programs requires effective coordination in dealing with both employers and job seekers. The Employment Service has the potential, in view of its experience and facilities, to fulfill this coordinating role and it should equip itself to do so insofar as possible.

6. Special contracting arrangements. There may be occasional special situations where it is appropriate for the Employment Service to contract out to other qualified agencies in the community for the provision of manpower services such as special counseling, placement, or research activities. These agencies may possess specialized skills or special relations with certain clientele groups which make them better able to supply needed manpower services.

We therefore recommend that the Employment Service be given legislative authority to enter into contractual relations with non-government groups to supply specialized manpower services to certain clientele.

## V. Strengthening Personnel in the Federal-State Employment Service System

A critically important factor in strengthening the Employment Service is to improve the quality of personnel working in the system. While this has always been a problem, it has become more acute. The growing demands upon the Employment Service for comprehensive manpower services call for personnel with a more complex set of skills than previously required. To cite several examples, employment service counselors now select trainees for vocational training programs and work more intensively with the disadvantaged. Labor market analysts now have to provide more complete analyses of labor market conditions as a prerequisite for establishing training programs. Occupational analysts are more concerned with manpower requirements arising out of technological change. Local office managers are much more deeply involved in working with community groups to initiate and implement a variety of programs.

We believe that the needed improvement in the quality of personnel can be accomplished by (1) improving standards and raising salaries to attract and retain competent and qualified employees; (2) providing incentives for self-development through in-service and out-service training; and (3) enhancing employee job opportunity through facilitating movement among the states and between the states and the Federal Government. Changes in these areas should help make jobs in the Employment Service more attractive and provide the basis for more successful recruitment efforts.

**Existing procedures for salary administration.** To put the problem of improving salaries into perspective, it is necessary to review briefly the existing method of salary administration. Under the Wagner-Peyser Act and Title III of the Social Security Act, grants are made to the states for administration of public employment offices where the state's unemployment compensation law is in compliance with required administrative standards. Among these is the requirement that personnel standards on a merit basis be established and maintained. These requirements are promulgated by the Secretary of Labor and are identical with others issued by Federal agencies carrying out grants-in-aid programs.

Under the merit system, each state agency is required to establish and maintain a classification and compensation plan for all positions which are not exempt. The state has the final authority for levels and rates of pay but must comply with the comparability policy of the Federal Bureau of Employment Security.

This policy is primarily a fiscal control to assure that state Employment Service salaries are in line with comparable positions in other departments of state government.

**Problems of salary administration.** This policy has adversely affected the level of salaries for professional jobs in the Employment Service. One major problem is to determine what positions in state government are comparable. Aside from clerical and secretarial positions, the job duties of Employment Service personnel are not generally comparable with other state government jobs. More importantly, it has tied Employment Service salaries to low state salary levels in many states. Salary data from the Division of State Merit Systems in the Department of Health, Education, and Welfare, Reports of the Personnel Management Committee of the Interstate Conference of Employment Security Agencies and studies by the national office all attest eloquently that Employment Service salaries are generally low when compared to salaries presently being paid outside of state government for comparable jobs. For example, a sample survey in 31 states in 1963 showed that nearly a third of state Employment Service interviewers were paid less than $5000 a year. Furthermore, the low salaries are undoubtedly an important factor in the high turnover rates and the inability of the Employment Service to recruit and hold its share of the better college graduates and other qualified applicants. Nearly a third of the sample of interviewers had less than 3 years of service. Low starting salaries for employment interviewers in the states account for this. By January 1965 these starting salaries were still $4500 or below in half of the states.

**Recommendations for improvement of salary administration.** In light of these facts, it is strongly recommended that steps be taken to make salaries more attractive for qualified personnel and, hence, more competitive. Both the Secretary of Labor and the state agencies have responsibilities to work toward achieving better salaries for Employment Service personnel. The following steps are essential.

1. Salary administration and personnel qualifications. The general principle recommended is that higher salaries for Employment Service professional jobs such as counselors, interviewers, and labor market analysts, should be commensurate with the

qualifications and standards for these positions prescribed by the Secretary of Labor. Present incumbents in these positions should have an opportunity to receive higher salaries when, and if, they can satisfy the revised requirements. Federal funds for higher salaries would be made available to those states which meet the higher-qualifications, higher-salaries requirements. The general salary improvements which the states make periodically would continue to be recognized in determining the Federal grants to the states for personnel salaries.

The Secretary of Labor, according to a recent memorandum of the Office of the Solicitor, Department of Labor, has the authority to require the states to adopt minimum personnel qualifications for certain professional jobs in the Employment Service. On the basis of these new standards, the state agency would negotiate with either the Civil Service Commission or Merit System to revise salaries.

2. Salary levels and comparable jobs. To assist the state agencies in these negotiations, the United States Employment Service must modify the policy of salary comparability for professional jobs in include relevant factors, i.e., the salaries being paid for comparable jobs in the state, not only in the state government but in other public and private employment as well. To emphasize the importance of adequate salaries for effective administration, the Wagner-Peyser Act should be amended to provide that salaries in the state Employment Service agencies be commensurate with those prevailing in the area for comparable jobs, especially in view of pending legislation such as Senate Bill S.561. This bill specifically prohibits the use of federal grants-in-aid for the payment of salaries "in excess of the regular salary standards applicable to state employees generally."

3. Follow up on improvements. If, after a period of two years, there has not been substantial and general implementation of these standards in a particular state, the Secretary of Labor would appoint a public review panel from among the members of the proposed National Advisory and Review Committee to review the situation in the noncomplying state or states and [to] report its findings to him. The Secretary could make the report public if he deemed necessary.

4. Starting salaries for federal trainees. Starting salaries should

be raised since the recruitment problem is related to the inadequate salaries being paid to Employment Service personnel. State salaries at the entry level are too low in many instances to make them attractive to young college graduates. To facilitate the recruitment of college graduates, and other qualified employees, the Federal Civil Service Commission should set up a classification entitled *Employment Service Trainee,* relating the number of eligibles to the changing requirements of the Employment Service program. The salary of the trainee, who will be a Federal employee, would be at the entry professional level, which in many instances would be higher than the prevailing salary in the states.

A well defined training program at the national and regional level should be developed for these trainees. The Secretary of Labor should work out a cooperative relationship with the states to assign these trainees to state and local operations for a period of two years under the supervision and direction of the state Employment Service Director and paid by the national office. Afterwards, they will be reassigned in the national or regional office to a position commensurate with their ability and training, or, if preferred, they could transfer to the state if a mutually satisfactory arrangement could be worked out.

**Recommendations for the development of high quality personnel.** Related to the above recommendations on salary and higher qualifications is the provision of opportunities for self-development. The following are recommended:

1. Training programs. To improve the quality of the personnel at all levels, the Secretary of Labor should require that each state's annual plan of operation include a well-developed training program including provisions for orientation, in-service and out-service training, tuition refund, and educational leave. The curricula for these training programs should include, among other subjects, courses in race relations and community relations and should also provide the opportunity for first-hand experience in inter-racial situations.

The plan will thus include the various approaches to training activities which the particular state deems best suited to its needs. If the state does not include such a plan for its training activities, no funds would be made available for training of Employment Service personnel.

2. The financing of training. As a possible guideline for underwriting the cost of this training, the Secretary of Labor will allocate to each state a certain percentage of its grant for training purposes. The Secretary of Labor will also retain a certain percentage of the total amount appropriated by the Congress for Employment Service operations to underwrite the cost of training carried on by the national office on a national or regional basis.

3. Cooperation with colleges and universities. The Secretary of Labor should be authorized to make supporting grants to colleges and universities for development of appropriate curricula and training materials and for the establishment of regional centers for Employment Service personnel. Currently, he does not have such authority. Present programs for training personnel in colleges and universities could then be utilized where appropriate.

4. Budgets. The budget for Employment Service operations, which the Secretary of Labor submits to the Congress, should contain a line item with respect to training. This not only emphasizes the importance of training; it also underscores the Congressional intent as to how the money is to be spent.

**The mobility of personnel.** A third facet for improving the quality of personnel in the Employment Service is to facilitate their mobility within the Federal-State system. Freedom of movement enhances long-term career opportunities. This is important to college trained employees who tend to be more career-minded, and who want the opportunity to advance. Furthermore, facilitating mobility will enable the system to tap the reservoir of personnel qualified and experienced in the Federal-State program. The following are recommended:

1. The federal-state transfer of personnel. Provisions should be made for an employee in a state agency to be appointed to a Federal position if he has permanent status in the state agency which he acquired through competitive examination under a state Merit or Civil Service system approved by a Federal agency and if he passes such examination as the U.S. Civil Service Commission prescribes. A person so appointed may acquire a

competitive status upon completion of a probationary period of one year. This suggestion has been discussed within the Department of Labor for several years and has the support of the Secretary of Labor and the U.S. Civil Service Commission.

2. The movement of personnel among the states. The Secretary of Labor should be given legislative authority to develop a system permitting transfers or temporary leaves of absence for personnel to move among state agencies without loss in employment status, job protection rights, pension rights, and other accumulated benefits.

## VI. The Development and Dissemination of Labor Market Information

The intelligent formulation and implementation of national manpower policies requires current and comprehensive labor market and job information. The Employment Service has extremely important responsibilities in the collection, analysis and dissemination of such information. In carrying out these functions, the Employment Service must consider both its own requirements and the needs of other agencies and organizations.

**Research and data collection.** As a fundamental step, the Employment Service should be responsible for insuring the adequacy of existing labor market information. There is great need for a delineation of the responsibilities of the Employment Service, the Bureau of Labor Statistics, and other agencies of the Government with respect to the collection of labor market information. Considerable duplications of effort prevail and the public should not be burdened by requests from various agencies for similar information. The Secretary of Labor should take the lead in clarifying the assignment of responsibility for the collection of information about the labor market. Therefore, it is recommended that the following areas of authority be assigned to the Employment Service.

1. It should collect and analyze manpower information required for the efficient functioning of the public Employment Service and for the administration of other federal programs dealing with manpower development and utilization. In many cases, this will mean the gathering of data already available

from other government agencies. In other instances, the Employment Service may have to initiate the collection process itself.

2. It should be recognized as a major source for the development of information for occupational guidance, testing and employment counselling both for its own use in providing manpower services and for other users, public and private.

3. It should assist in efforts to strengthen community economic development activities.

4. It should be engaged in research which would facilitate manpower and labor force adjustments to automation and changing technology. To strengthen the research program, the Director of the national Employment Service should be given legislative authority to enter into contracts with universities and other institutions qualified to do research for the purposes of having them conduct specific studies related to the effective functioning of the Employment Service. Currently, he does not have such authority.

5. It should be given legislative authority to collect information from the Federal Government on job openings in governmental agencies and government corporations.

6. It should also work closely with employers, especially Government contractors, to obtain specific information on job openings and their characteristics and to obtain advance notice of mass layoffs in order to facilitate workers' job adjustments.

7. It should make better use of the considerable data concerning job openings now available as a result of the normal operations of the Employment Service network. In the course of its placement activities, each local office compiles a current list of unfilled openings with respect to specific occupations and industrial sectors. To utilize this potentially valuable source of labor market information, each local office should forward a monthly statement and analysis of its unfilled job openings to the USES. The USES could then compile and periodically publish an analysis of these data as another indicator of the composition of the demand for labor. We recognize that these data do not lend themselves to the estimation of a national aggregate figure on job vacancies and they should not be misused for this purpose.

**The dissemination of information.** When adequate labor market information is collected and analyzed, vigorous measures must be adopted to insure that it is widely and meaningfully disseminated to other public and private organizations with an interest in labor market trends. These organizations include schools, employers, unions, voluntary agencies, private employment agencies, and the Employment Service itself. Unfortunately, however, much of the information currently available has not been in a form that is usable by other organizations and only limited arrangements have been made to communicate this information on a regular basis.

1. Designation of labor market information officers. To remedy this deficiency, each metropolitan local office should have a staff member who will be designated as the Labor Market Information Officer (LMIO). Additional staff personnel should be provided as appropriate for local offices which serve large, metropolitan areas while the functions of the LMIO may be assigned as a collateral duty to the staff of an office in a smaller community or provided on an area basis.

2. Functions of the labor market information officer. The principal duty of the LMIO should be to communicate on a regular basis with schools, employers, unions, non-profit organizations, private employment agencies and other groups as appropriate, and to maintain the close contact with these organizations that will help develop quality manpower services. In the course of these communications, the LMIO can discuss with the organizations' representatives the relevant labor market information that is available through the Employment Service. At the same time, the LMIO should solicit suggestions concerning needed information that is not presently available and the best method for preparing the information so that it will have maximum utility for the user.

3. Benefits from the use of labor market information officers. This approach would have several constructive consequences. First, it will promote a comprehensive flow of information from the Employment Service to the users. Secondly, the quality of the information can be improved through the suggestions of other organizations that have special requirements in the labor market. And third, the use of a Labor Market Information Officer would build better relationships between the Employment

Service and other groups and help to create a positive "image" with the public at large.

4. Information at work: the need for effective counseling. Comprehensive and current job market information readily available is essential for an effective counseling program. Knowledge about the contents of, and trends in, occupations and industries in geographic areas is basic for reaching decisions for vocational choice, manpower training or other related actions. The counsellor has a key role in the translation of this information to effective actions. It is therefore imperative that Employment Service counselors develop a sound background and working knowledge of the various types of information necessary to provide guidance to job seekers.

## VII. The Interarea Recruitment Procedure

In order to retain its effectiveness the public Employment Service must adjust the distribution and use of labor market information in its internal operations to the changing structure of the national labor market. In this respect, the increased importance of professional and skilled workers, the improvement of means of transportation and the shift of industry have all served to expand the geographical scope of the labor market. Although the local labor market is still the primary unit for the matching of supply and demand, the market for many professional and technical occupations is now regional or national in scope.

In this manner, job openings in one area may only be filled by drawing on applicants with the necessary qualifications who currently reside in other sections of the country. The magnitude of the problem is indicated by a special survey carried out in July 1964 which revealed that the public Employment Service offices had 250,000 unfilled openings of which 45,000 were for professional and managerial jobs and 35,000 for other skilled classifications. A majority of these openings had remained unfilled for 15 days or more. To function effectively in these markets the Employment Service must develop modern techniques for the communication of this labor market information among its operating units.

**Existing interarea recruitment procedures.** To facilitate the matching of applicants and job openings between local labor markets the Employment Service has developed an interarea clearance procedure. However, this procedure is cumbersome and generally ineffective. As presently organized, it depends upon the initiative of the local office manager who lists unfilled jobs with a state clearance officer. The state clearance officer then compiles the vacancies on a periodic basis and distributes this information to other state offices. Many of the local office managers are slow or reluctant to incorporate job openings into the interarea procedures, and even when the positions are listed, they are often "stale" by the time the information reaches other local offices. In addition, there is no parallel procedure for the listing of applicants who might be willing to move to take a new job.

**Recommendations for an improved interarea recruitment procedure.** In order to improve the operation of the interarea clearance procedure and the flow of information across local labor markets, the following steps should be taken:

1. The establishment of multi-market recruitment centers. Multi-market clearance centers should be established throughout the public Employment Service system, and the centers themselves coordinated on a national basis. The exact number and location of these offices can be determined after an initial study and pilot project. In some cases, the boundaries of the regional interarea clearance office will include more than one administrative region of the Bureau of Employment Security, as presently constituted.

2. Listings with multi-market recruitment centers. Each local office shall be required to list with the multi-market recruitment office all job vacancies in shortage occupations, as currently illustrated in the professional, technical and managerial classification. This listing should be made after the opening has remained unfilled 15 days from the date it was listed with the local office. Initially, the new recruitment procedure should be limited to these classifications since the existence of regional and national labor markets is most evident in these occupations.

Also, the local office shall be required to list with the multi-market recruitment office the names of all applicants with professional, technical and managerial qualifications who have remained unemployed for 30 days or more. In addition, any other applicant with skills and experience in these occupational areas may, at their own initiative, avail themselves of this procedure.

3. Functions of the multi-market centers. The information on job openings and applicants supplied to the regional recruitment center can then be used to promote placement across local labor markets. In some cases, a local office may contact the regional center to determine if applicants are available for unfilled job openings in the local labor market. In other cases, the regional center on its own initiative, will notify the local office of the possible availability of qualified applicants in other areas or labor markets. At the same time, the regional center will inform the local office servicing the applicant of the availability of the job. The administrative responsibility for bringing the prospective employer and the applicant together within the framework of the multi-market recruitment procedure shall then be assumed by the local offices. The employer and the applicant can carry out the usual screening and interviewing procedures at their own discretion.

4. The use of information technology. In order to develop an effective interarea recruitment procedure it is necessary to have rapid and accurate methods for storing, analyzing and retrieving information concerning job vacancies and potential applicants on a current basis. Further advances in automatic data processing and computer technology in the organization and operation of the interarea recruitment procedure should be given high priority by the Employment Service. Some exploratory efforts have already been undertaken, but they should be expedited within the framework of the new interarea recruitment procedures.

We recommend that the Secretary of Labor appoint a committee to study and suggest the bast automatic data processing and computer approaches to handling this problem. The committee should consist of academic experts on electronic data processing and computer technology, Employment Service, business, and labor representatives. This committee should decide on a regional trial application, to be thoroughly tested and operated, before establishing an elaborate system. The existing

LINCS system of the Employment Service provides a basic unit from which to start.

## VIII. Administering and financing the Service

In addition to the changes in concept, personnel policies and the use of labor market information, several other administrative aspects of the Employment Service have been examined which are important to the maintenance of an effective Employment Service. These include the budget process and financing, emergency planning, the establishment of an Advisory and Review Committee and related matters.

**The budget process and financing.** 1. The importance of budgetary controls. The process of making and carrying through a plan of operation and a financial budget plays a central part in the administration of any well-run organization. This process involves thorough discussion among units at various levels in the organization so that general policies and local needs can be coordinated. It forces each administrative unit to develop objectives for the immediate future and to make these a part of plans for a longer time horizon. While putting emphasis on program objectives, it makes necessary the evaluation of these objectives in terms of the resources needed to achieve them and asks continually such questions as "How do the costs compare with the benefits of this undertaking?," "How central to other activities is the one under review?," "Are there ways to accomplish this aim in a more economical manner?," "What priorities should be established among objectives?"

The careful composition of budgets in the first instance is thus a constructive process. At the same time, it provides deeper and richer material for use by a reviewing group, such as the Congress, for purposes both of initial judgment about a proposed budget and of later examination on how well the estimates of various cost-benefit relationships have held up. In this manner, the budget process can be a continual source of planning and evaluation so essential to effective administration.

2. Inadequacies of the existing budget process. The Employment Service has been moving, though gradually, toward a more effective budget process. In many of the states, however, this process has been the prisoner of relatively routine rules of thumb

involving the counting of referrals and of estimating budget
needs on a cost-per-referral basis. This approach is obsolete, as
is recognized in policy at the national level. Placements, not
referrals, are the central objective. Effective placement activities in the short run result from effective programs that must
be worked out on a longer-term basis, and which are interrelated
to the central objective. The quality of the labor market and job
information, counseling, interarea recruitment and the relationship between employment opportunities and educational and
training activities in the community all affect placement activities.

3. A new approach required. The budget process should emphasize the programs to be undertaken, nationally, regionally, in the
states and at the local level. It should call for analysis of problems impeding full implementation of these programs and for
remedial steps to correct them. It should involve a thorough
reconciliation of local needs and general objectives. It should include careful and systematic methods of evaluation and review,
so that the organization may learn from experience and continually improve its effectiveness.

We recommend that the budget process and its improvement
be made a matter of first priority by the Employment Service
and that its organization and arrangements for planning, review,
and budgeting be made an important and well-staffed part of the
Director's Office at the national and state levels.

4. Financing the Service. The close relationship between the
Employment Service and Unemployment Compensation has created certain limitations on the supporting financial arrangements.
A basic deficiency is that the present reliance on financing
through the Federal Unemployment Tax does not reflect the
much broader functions and responsibilities that have been assigned to the Employment Service in recent years. This has
meant that the availability of funds has not been directly responsive to the changing requirements of the Employment Service. Serious questions are also raised by the fact that a tax levied
on employers' payrolls to finance the system of Unemployment
Compensation is used to support other and broader activities
as well.

Separate financial arrangements should be made for the administration of Unemployment Compensation and the manpower

functions of the Employment Service. Currently, the Federal Unemployment Tax on Employers' payrolls is the exclusive source of funds for the Employment Service, except for a few special appropriations made by Congress. An approximate estimate can be made of the cost of administering the work test aspects of the Unemployment Compensation through the Employment Service. This cost should then be defrayed from the Federal Unemployment Tax Fund. The appropriations for the other, manpower functions of the Employment Service, should be financed from general tax revenues, as determined by Congress. By adopting this approach, Congress would be in a better position to determine the needs of the Employment Service and to evaluate the efficiency of its operations in the manpower field on a regular basis.

**Emergency planning.** In addition to establishing effective procedures for carrying out normal, day-to-day operations, the Employment Service should take the necessary steps to develop plans and techniques for handling emergency situations in the labor market. Unemployment resulting from large-scale layoffs such as those arising from the cancellation of defense contracts or plant closings and unrest stemming from chronic unemployment may generate urgent problems for the community that cannot be dealt with by conventional programs. It would be preferable, of course, if the Employment Service had advance warning of impending emergencies in the labor market. Some measures have been taken to develop an "early warning system" for plant closings and related events and we have earlier recommended additional effort in this direction; but perfect foresight cannot be expected of any agency, especially when its relationships with outside groups are on a voluntary basis.

**Recommendations for effective emergency planning.** Consequently, the Employment Service should engage in systematic emergency planning as part of its on-going organization responsibilities. Such planning can be facilitated by the following steps:

1. The establishment of an emergency planning unit. A unit should be established within the United States Employment Service with the primary responsibility for emergency planning

within the Employment Service system. This unit would collect and evaluate information concerning the possible occurrence of emergency situations in the labor market, develop prototype plans for handling different kinds of emergency situations, maintain continuing communications with key operating officials in other Government agencies and throughout the Federal-State network.

2. Coordination with the regional offices. Each regional office of the Employment Service should appoint an official whose collateral duty is to keep informed of the plans and activities of the national emergency unit and to coordinate the emergency programs when they are undertaken in the region. This official would maintain effective communications with the administrators of the state Employment Service agencies and, from time to time, should convene regional conferences to inform the state agencies of the programs of the national emergency unit and to obtain the benefits of the experience and points of view of these state administrators.

3. Operating responsibility at the local level. Primary operating responsibility for the administration of emergency action programs should be retained by the local Employment Service office. It should be authorized to add professional personnel on a short-term, contract basis, if necessary. The local office will have the greatest familiarity with the grass roots situation and will continue to be on the scene long after the sense of urgency has diminished but before the problems that precipitated the emergency have been resolved. However, the national and regional officials should work closely with the local office to adapt the prototype plans to the special circumstances of the emergency and to insure that adequate resources are on hand to deal with each situation.

4. Budget requirements. Clearly, the Employment Service cannot respond effectively to emergency situations without adequate funds earmarked for this purpose. Accordingly, there should be a line item in the annual budget of the USES for emergency planning and for use in implementing extraordinary programs that are beyond the normal resources of the local office of the state agency. As a first approximation, the amounts necessary for this purpose can be estimated from past experiences.

The appropriation could then be adjusted in the light of subsequent experience and annual projections of labor market developments.

**Advisory and Review Committee.** The Wagner-Peyser Act provided for the establishment of a Federal Advisory Council for the Employment Service and for state advisory councils. The Federal Advisory Council, over the years, has concerned itself primarily with unemployment insurance matters. Where active, the state advisory councils likewise focused on similar matters. The role of the advisory committee, therefore, needs to be reexamined both as to its orientation and functions. We therefore recommend:

1. The need for an Advisory and Review Committee. A new Advisory and Review Committee can play an important role in helping the Employment Service assess the range and focus of its activities and in development of its role in the labor market, especially as related to the functions performed by others. Just as the administration of the Service should be separated from that of the Unemployment Compensation system because of their basic differences in outlook and functions, so separate groups at both national and state levels should be established to give counsel and to serve in a review capacity.

2. Composition of the Advisory and Review Committee. The Advisory and Review Committee should be small enough to gain coherence as a working group yet large enough so that a variety of special tasks could be undertaken on a panel-system basis. We recommend a Committee of 12–15 members, appointed by the Secretary of Labor for terms of four years, staggered in such a way as to provide continuity of membership as old members drop off and new ones are added.

Membership should be drawn from the ranks of private citizens and should include men and women with expertise in the labor market and employment process, and the members should be compensated for their services at the regular rate established for consultants to the Federal Government. Groups with an important stake in the operations of the labor market, such as employers, unions and racial minorities should be represented.

3. Functions of the national Advisory and Review Com-

mittee. The work of the Committee should be confined to issues of general policy, including areas of emphasis for the Employment Service, relationships with public and private groups, the adequacy of existing labor market information, emergency planning and budgeting, personnel and organizational matters. It should advise as requested with the Secretary of Labor and the Director of the Employment Service and report each year its assessment of the overall operation of the Service.

In addition, it should be empowered to undertake, on its own initiative or at the request of the Secretary, an investigation and analysis of particular problem areas or of issues about which it has received critical comments. The results of these analyses and any related recommendations should always be available to the Secretary and the Director and should be presented at a time of maximum usefulness for planning purposes. If the Committee so chooses, its studies and reports should be a matter of public record and be included in full as Appendices to the Annual Report of the Service.

The Committee should have a full-time staff director of high competence, with adequate secretarial assistance and a separate budget. His work should be considered a part of the Office of the Secretary of Labor.

The Committee should meet in plenary session at least twice each year.

4. Establishment of state Advisory and Review Committees. The governor of the state should appoint an Advisory and Review Committee whose functions would parallel those of the national committee. The members would serve for a 4-year term, staggered in such a way as to provide continuity of membership. One member would be designated to serve as chairman. The committee would file an annual report which would take the form of an overall assessment of the state Employment Service. Their report would be an appendix to the annual report of the state Employment Service Director.

**Annual report.** As part of the process of evaluation and review the public should have access to a comprehensive report of the Employment Service on a regular basis. Therefore, the following recommendations are made for the filing and publication of annual reports:

1. Annual reports by the USES. The Director of the USES should be required to file an annual report at the end of the fiscal year to the Secretary of Labor which is an analysis of both the manpower services provided and its internal operations, i.e., resources made available and how these resources were used. The report should include an analysis of developments and trends in the job market.

There should also be included in the President's Manpower Report an analysis of the manpower services provided by the Federal-State Employment Service system for the calendar year.

2. Annual reports by state agencies. The state Employment Service Director should be required to file an annual report at the end of the fiscal year to the national Employment Service Director which includes an analysis of both manpower services provided and its internal operations, i.e. resources made available and how these resources were used. This report should take the form of an annual state manpower report.

# Discussion

## BY GEORGE P. SHULTZ

If the Employment Service is to be a cornerstone in the building of a manpower policy, as so many here have indicated in their papers and as I would agree it should, then the Service must have more and more direct financial support, a shifted organizational form, a strengthened personnel system, and more deftly articulated relationships in three crucial dimensions: with respect to federal, state, and local sharing of responsibilities for its own performance, with other units of the federal government, and with employers and the broad range of private groups now active in the labor market.

The report of the Employment Service Task Force suggests a variety of means designed to achieve those ends and to get started promptly at both the legislative and administrative levels. In these respects, S.2974 and the companion House bill, sponsored by Senators Clark and Kennedy and Representative Holland, together with various internal developments are heartening. But political and administrative prognostication are not our business, so let us turn to a few questions about the recommendations in the Report.

1. *Why not federalize the Service?* This is recommended by such groups as the AFL-CIO, the President's Commission on Manpower, Automation, and Technological Change, and the White House Conference on Civil Rights. Why not join the parade?

The Task Force, addressing itself to questions of what might be useful in the immediate future, chose to concentrate on key problems and possible solutions within the framework of a federal-state system. It was our belief that a great deal could be done within that system to work out central issues. In general, if our recommendations are followed, there will be more active

174

national and regional offices having more responsibility for budget planning and review and for the operation of interarea clearance systems. There will also be far more opportunity to get things done at the local level and more resources to do them with.

To put the matter another way, we identified what we felt were the key problems of organization, personnel administration, finance and budgets, and interarea clearance. We then went on to see whether, within the framework of the federal-state system, reasonable solutions could be found for the problems. It seemed to us that the answer is "yes," given good fortune on the legislative and administrative fronts mentioned earlier. The reader will judge for himself whether the Task Force recommendations do deal effectively with key issues.

Of course it is true that certain goals would be much easier to achieve under a unified federal system, for example, mobility of personnel. Nevertheless, it is far from true that all the arguments fall on that side of the ledger. After all, the vast majority of placements are within local labor markets, and the work of an individual office and its relationships with other public and private groups and programs take place there. The present system gives recognition to that fact and to the great diversity in American labor markets. Overcentralization in the administration of manpower programs can be as great a problem as the reverse.

2. *Is there any chance that the financial implications of the Task Force recommendations will be accepted, especially by the Congress?* These financial implications are of two sorts: (1) the higher cost per placement of programs that serve disadvantaged workers, and (2) the shift to general revenues as the primary means for supporting the Service.

Obviously, the members of the Task Force were not selected for, nor did they try to exercise, political expertise. We would not have made our recommendations, however, if they had seemed to be so clearly out of bounds as to have no chance of acceptance. I would only say that on the whole Congress has shown itself over the past few years and on both sides of the aisle to be genuinely concerned with manpower problems, including those involving disadvantaged groups. This seems a good time, there-

fore, to put forward in programmatic terms the contributions
that can be made by the Employment Service and the associated costs. It is our further hope that the Employment Service
will be able to avoid the kind of "cost-benefit analysis" that in
effect forces the management of the Service to emphasize work
with easy-to-place groups in order to achieve a good-looking
ratio of costs to placements.

The Task Force members felt strongly about the importance
of distinguishing the Employment Service from the administration of unemployment compensation, and they fully accepted
the concomitant implication of separate financing. It seems unlikely that such a move would be made in one fell swoop; but
the establishment of the principle is important, and a gradual
shift in budget composition seems entirely practical. In a small
way, this is already happening, and, as the Service becomes
more and more involved in the variety of manpower programs
not associated with unemployment compensation, this development seems a natural one.

There is no more reason for the system of unemployment
compensation to bear the costs of administering these programs
than there is to expect the administrative considerations of the
University of Chicago not to be dominant when the University of
Chicago pays the bill. Let us allocate costs to the appropriate
programs and seek direct support for their administration.

3. *Is there any chance of a working rather than a fighting
pluralism involving public and private employment services?*
Here I can only say that we hope so and that we have suggested
a number of ways in which better relationships may be developed.
Feelings in this area run high, and the taste is bitter. Nevertheless, better understanding and working relationships are already
emerging in some areas, and positive and helpful actions by the
Employment Service should create an environment of at least
mutual toleration. In the long run, it is obvious that both public
and private agencies have an important role to play in the economy and important contributions to make to each other. As in
labor-management relationships, improvement will come only
when the people involved in offices throughout the country work
in a day-to-day sense at that task. Nevertheless, an improved

tone and leadership at the national level will help to set an encouraging framework for those day-to-day efforts.

In the past few years, this country has become acutely conscious of its manpower problems and has developed some feel for the kinds of programs through which to deal with these problems, and it has demonstrated a willingness to supply resources to that effort. At the same time, it has become more and more obvious that programs and resources mean little if not accompanied by good administration. The Employment Service is in a key position to contribute heavily to that administration, given the chance to do so. The Task Force recommendations were designed to help provide that opportunity.

# Discussion

## BY LEONARD P. ADAMS

The Task Force Report on the Employment Service sets forth an ambitious set of responsibilities for the Service, identifies several significant weaknesses in the Service, and makes some useful suggestions about how these shortcomings might be overcome. If the Congress approves either of the bills which translate the major recommendations into law, the Service will be considerably strengthened.

As I see it, there are two important questions about an effective Employment Service program which the Report does not discuss or does not cover adequately. Perhaps these problems were not given the attention they deserve because of the desire for consensus and a unanimous report. These questions are:

1. What represents a "model" or optimum functioning Employment service policy and program? This question has two corollaries: (a) What are acceptable standards of performance for a public employment service? (b) What constitutes an optimum staff in numbers and in quality?

2. What should be the relationship of the public service to fee-charging employment agencies?

### A Model Is Needed

There is a good deal of truth in the contention that the recommendations in the Report do not very much modify the scope of present activities of the Service, or at least its authority, under present legislation. The Employment Service has a number of tools for dealing with manpower problems on both the demand and supply side of the labor market. Its authority, as shown by the programs developed, is much greater for helping to adjust workers to jobs rather than the other way round. The Service

178

has become the operating arm in local areas for translating virtually all of the recent manpower legislation into programs of service to workers and employers. It is engaged in helping workers who have trouble in finding jobs at both ends of the working-age spectrum, as well as many who are "hard to place" in between. These duties have often been added piecemeal and without much indication of what should have priority in case, as has usually been the situation, there was not staff enough to carry on all the old, as well as the new, programs.

It is useful to have an operating agency in touch with employers and workers to carry out new manpower policies and programs whenever the time is politically propitious. But what, in addition to flexibility, are the other desirable qualities in a model public service? Its authority to influence the jobs available at present is limited to what it can do by way of helping to prepare people to meet a need for which there is a potential demand. The Swedish Service, in contrast, spends about 25 per cent of its budget on measures to change the job opportunities for workers.[1] Our service has no power to influence the number of jobs in private industry or on public construction work. Perhaps we do not wish to go as far as the Swedes have done in giving the Employment Service leverage on the demand side, but it would have been helpful if the pros and cons of this issue had been discussed in the Report.

It is also clear that the performance of the Service in a federal-state organization will vary considerably from one state and area to another depending on the quality of the staff. Under the circumstances, a more definite understanding of the dimensions of a "model" service becomes very important. It is also necessary to establish definite standards of performance by which one may judge the effectiveness of the Service both as a whole and in its component parts.

**Standards of Performance**

How much of an influence on labor markets should we expect a public employment service to have? How can the effectiveness of a public service be measured? These questions are not discussed in the Report. Yet the answers will help to determine the concept of a "model" service as well as its day-by-day administration and the amount of influence over manpower problems it can be expected to have.

There is, for example, the question as to what level of penetration of job markets a public service should have if it is to be fully effective. Professor Reynolds has suggested that it should fill at least half of the job openings for which workers are recruited in the open market.[2] Mr. Olsson suggests in his paper that the ratio should be one-third to one-half, but he, like Professor Reynolds, offers no specific reasons for setting such goals. It is inferred that such a high level of penetration is considered necessary to give the Service prestige, to make it known as *the* place to go for a variety of services, and to provide the Service itself with sufficient information on a wide variety of markets and conditions so that it becomes the recognized authority on such matters. Presumably, however, penetration *per se* is not the important consideration but rather what it implies in terms of speed in getting jobs filled and hence higher production, and also what more manhours of work mean to the employees who otherwise might be idle.

There seem to be substantial differences in penetration rates of public-employment services in industrialized nations. Rates in European countries such as Sweden, West Germany, and Great Britain range from 25 to 30 per cent according to published reports.[3] In the United States they are probably about half as much.[4] Data on relative penetration rates are not very reliable because of differences in definition of vacancies and the lack of comprehensive coverage. But the figures, such as they are, suggest that the national rate in the United States is substantially lower than in the countries mentioned above.

What is an optimum penetration rate? It seems probable that there is no single answer that makes sense for every area at all times. The answer given will also depend on how important we think the public service should be, relative to other methods of bringing workers and jobs together, in order to do its work effectively. But it is obvious that, if one decides that an overall rate of about one-third to one-half is necessary, the placement operation in the United States needs to have considerably more staff time and imagination put into it.

Some possible criteria for reaching an answer to this question which might be considered are:

1. Cost-benefit analysis of the results of adding additional staff. A recent experiment in Indiana, in which the staff of a local office was increased by 25 per cent, produced an increase in placements of about 65 per cent.[5] The increase in costs to government in this case may well have been more than offset by the gains in wages earned, by increased production, and by additional taxes collected.

2. The best past performance of local offices in the nation. Some offices are said to have rates as high as those in the foreign countries mentioned.[6] These might serve as models for the others.

Similar problems of setting standards exist with respect to other aspects of Employment Service operations. Time does not permit further discussion. In determining what these standards should be, the advice of local advisory committees representing the users of the services could be helpful.

## Optimum Staff

It is obvious that the "model" one adopts for the Service and the standards of performance established will (or should) determine the numbers and qualities of the staff required to do a satisfactory job. The Task Force Report recognizes that the quality of the staff needs improvement and that something must be done to raise standards and salaries and to attract and hold able young people. But there is no indication in the Report that the question of an optimum staff was discussed. It seems to me there is a real danger that the present opportunity to take a fresh look at the personnel required to operate an effective Employment Service will pass, leaving the question of budgets and staff in an unsatisfactory state. The result is likely to be more of the same kind of experience that characterized the Service's history during the period of the Second World War, i.e., a constantly changing and growing set of responsibilities with a staff that in numbers and quality does not keep pace with the work load.

The old numerical measures for budgeting based on estimated

volume of operations such as placements, registrations, counseling interviews, and tests administered have been abandoned. What has taken the place of this system is much less definite. Presumably the offices are being budgeted on the basis of need for services. The information available suggests that not much change in staffing patterns has taken place since additional funds were obtained in fiscal 1961 and 1962 to provide more personnel for local offices and at the federal level, except for assistance with special programs such as those for youth.

Statistics on work done in 1961, as compared with activities in 1965, suggest that special programs such as those under the Manpower Development and Training Act (MDTA) and for youths under the Office of Economic Opportunity (OEO) have diverted the staff of the Service from some of their regular responsibilities.[7] For example, counseling and testing activities increased over 40 per cent between 1961 and 1965, but field visits to employers declined.

One measure of adequacy of staff in a local office is the ratio of staff to the labor force of the area being served. If this measure is used, wide variations appear among the states and labor-market areas of the nation. In general, the small states and areas are more adequately staffed than the large ones. There is some evidence, too, that performance varies with the adequacy of staff.

The whole problem deserves more study and analysis than it has had. In Sweden the ratio is about 1 staff person to 2500 workers in the labor force. This is about the same as the ratio in the smallest one-third of our states. Perhaps this is a goal that should be aimed at by the others. At any rate, it would seem more desirable from the standpoint of the national welfare, as the country becomes more and more an urban society, to have the most favorable staffing patterns in the largest, not the smallest, areas.

### Relationships with Fee-Charging Employment Agencies

The Report advocates closer cooperation between the public service and "private employment agencies which adhere to professional standards in their placement activities." It is not clear to me what this means. Does it mean that only information on labor market conditions should be exchanged, or should the public service refer applicants whom it cannot place and orders that it cannot fill to private agencies? There has been a long-standing policy directive against such a procedure which in my opinion still has merit. For one thing it would make it too easy for the staff to avoid hard work. Secondly, it is likely to result in requiring the applicant to pay a large fee for a job which, as a taxpayer and citizen, he has the right to expect the public service to get for him.

It is hard to visualize a cooperative arrangement whereby the public service could develop an exchange of information about individual claimants and specific openings with private agencies. But it may be possible to arrange for a better exchange of general labor-market information. The private agencies, which deal mainly with professional, technical, and white-collar jobs, could provide interesting and useful data on their placement activities if they cared to do so. At present we have no meaningful information at all on their activities except in a few states. It would appear from the scanty data available that they have larger staffs than the public service, more full-time offices, and deal mainly with white-collar occupations.[8]

## Concluding Suggestions

In view of the many unresolved questions about the public service, it seems important that the recommendation in the Report for a separate Advisory Council with a staff of its own selection be included in the proposed new legislation. Neither the Administration's nor the Clark-Kennedy bill does this. Such a body could undertake some of the kinds of reviews of performance and studies that are needed.

It would also be helpful to reestablish the idea of experimental offices such as the one in Rochester, New York, in the early 1930's. Such experiments would provide laboratories for testing ideas about "model" offices, "standards," and "optimum staffing," and the resulting experience could be used to great advantage to improve the Service throughout the nation.

## NOTES

1. See Bertil Olsson's paper in this volume.
2. Lloyd G. Reynolds, *The Structure of Labor Markets* (New York: Harper and Brothers, 1951), p. 68.
3. *Employment Service Review*, III March, 1966), p. 11.
4. Robert C. Goodwin in *Hearings on The Nation's Manpower Revolution*, U.S. Senate, Subcommittee on Employment and Manpower, Part 3, 88th Cong., 1st sess. (Washington D.C.: June, 1963), p. 836.
5. *The Labor Market Role of the State Employment Services*, U.S. Senate, Subcommittee on Employment and Manpower, 88th Cong., 2d sess. (Washington, D.C.: January 24, 1964), p. 725.
6. *Key Facts: Employment Security Operations*, U.S. Department of Labor, Manpower Administration (Washington, D.C.: April, 1966), p. 3.
7. See Leonard P. Adams, "The Public Employment Service," in J. M. Becker, editor, *In Aid of the Unemployed* (Baltimore: Johns Hopkins Press, 1965), p. 209.
8. "Selected Services. Summary of Statistics," *U.S. Census of Business*, V (1958), 1–6. See also the statement by C. Kleath Kembel, General Counsel, National Employment Association in *Hearings on S. 3259*, U.S. Senate, Subcommittee on Public Health, Education, Welfare and Safety, Committee on the District of Columbia, 87th Cong., 2d sess. (Washington, D.C.: June 26 and 29, 1962).

# Discussion

## BY DANIEL H. KRUGER

In recent years the Employment Service has been given a range of new assignments. Greater responsibilities have been imposed piecemeal. Since the beginning of this decade, 13 major legislative enactments and executive orders have specifically assigned the Employment Service to perform some new function. Among these are the Area Redevelopment Act, Manpower Development and Training Act, Economic Opportunity Act, Public Works and Development Act, Trade Expansion Act, Vocational Education Act, Immigration and Nationality Act, and a Presidential Order on selective service rejectees.

The Employment Service has become intimately involved in implementing national manpower policies. Senator Joseph Clark has called the public Employment Service "The first line of defense in any manpower program." The recent legislative enactments not only assigned additional responsibilities to the Employment Service; they concomitantly focused attention on the role of the Employment Service and its effectiveness. In the hearings conducted both by the House of Representatives Select Subcommittee on Labor (the Holland Committee) and by the Senate Subcommittee on Employment and Manpower (the Clark Committee), questions were raised as to the role and mission of the Employment Service.

### The Changing Environment

To put the Task Force Report into some kind of perspective, it is necessary to review briefly the environment in which the Employment Service seeks to carry out its missions. Prior to the recent federal manpower legislation, labor market institutions—such as the Employment Service, private employers, and civil service arrangements—followed what was, in effect, a policy of exclusion. Only those job seekers who could overcome the obstacles were admitted as active participants in the world of work. Tests of all kinds, educational and medical requirements, color of skin, age, and a perfect social record (for example, no police record) were among these obstacles. In the postwar period the selection procedures became more refined. With each refinement the policy of exclusion became more institutionalized. The exclusions were introduced on the basis of "objectively determined job requirements" so as to obtain the best qualified worker for the available job.

Under the policy of exclusion, job qualifications as prescribed by employers were raised. The placement agencies, both private and public, responded. If the job applicant did not measure up to the specifications, he was excluded from consideration. Of course, the state of the labor market affected and altered the requirements for the available jobs. With high levels of unemployment, the requirements tended to become more stringent. As the levels of unemployment fell and the labor market became tight, the requirements were relaxed. Despite the current high levels of employment, there are still large numbers of unemployed workers who are not able to compete realistically in the labor market. These are the excluded.

The policy of exclusion falls most heavily on the unskilled, the uneducated, and the unwanted. The excluded group embraces more than the young worker, the older worker, and Negroes. It includes all of those persons who by reason of personal characteristics, background, emotional deficiencies, lack of skills, deprivation, or economic denial are excluded from active participation in the job market.

As a result of recent legislation, especially MDTA, Civil Rights Act, and the Economic Opportunity Act, the policy of exclusion has changed. The intent of these public declarations is that everybody is to be included in the world of work if he so chooses. Thus, from a policy of exclusion we have moved to a policy of inclusion. This is indeed a significant change which has affected the operation of the public employment service.

The policy of inclusion has altered the composition of the clientele of the Employment Service. Much of the current criticism directed towards the Employment Service has its roots in this changing composition. More specifically, it is contended that the Employment Service has not moved fast enough in changing its *modus operandi* to accommodate the excluded. At the same time, another criticism with a similar ring is that the Employment Service is not effectively serving the white-collar worker.

While this is no defense of the Employment Service, it does take time to develop new techniques and new approaches and to change attitudes and work habits. This is especially true when the emphasis for many years has been on serving employer manpower needs. Furthermore the Employment Service seems to have played a passive role in the sense that it served only those who came into the local office. Those job seekers needing manpower services, especially many of the excluded, did not utilize the Employment Service. Their reasons for not doing so varied.

The Employment Service did not until recently have what has been called an "outreach" approach—going out into the community to establish personal contact with those needing work. The organization was not equipped to serve this group. The local offices were not located in the areas in which the excluded live. In some instances, perhaps many, the local office staff were not able to relate well to this group of job applicants. Their value system may have indeed served as an obstacle. Further, past experiences of the local offices hampered their efforts to reach out. The excluded had not been served well in the past, and they were not convinced that local office personnel really wanted to help them. The excluded, in many instances, were not only reluctant to use the services of the Employment Service; they were also suspicious. They may also have been unaware of the very existence of the local office.

### Recommendations of the Task Force

The Task Force called attention to the need for improving manpower services to the excluded or disadvantaged. It also recognized that the public Employment Service does not in every instance possess the kinds of resources needed to reach out to the excluded. There are two ways for the Employment Service to reach out. It can do so itself, or it can establish relationships with organizations and agencies in the community which have a special relation with the excluded groups. The Task Force urged the Employment Service to utilize both methods. In addition, it recommended that the Employment Service be given legislative authority to contract out for specialized manpower services with certain kinds of organizations in the community. The underlying rationale is that those organizations which have special relations with certain clientele groups can, in all probability, do a more effective job in providing manpower services to the excluded. The Employment Service would prescribe standards which the organization would be required to meet if it desired to have such a contractual arrangement.

The excluded are not the only group needing manpower services. Workers at the other end of the occupational spectrum, namely, the skilled, technical, and professional workers, may also require assistance. The emerging shortages of skilled workers in certain occupations and in certain geographical areas have highlighted the need for more effective manpower services directed toward these groups. The problem of serving these groups of workers has three dimensions. Such workers have to register at the local Employment Service office; the office must have job openings for these kinds of jobs; and the job seekers and the job openings must be linked together effectively. The first two conditions are highly interrelated. These workers will not seek assistance at the local office if they feel that the local office does not have the kinds of job openings which they desire. There is reason to believe that if the local office did, in fact, have such job openings, these workers would use it much more extensively. The Task Force, therefore, recommended that the Employment Service be given legislative authority to collect information on job openings in governmental agencies and government corporations; that it should work closely with employers, especially government contractors, to obtain information on job openings and their characteristics; and that it should make better use of the existing data now available as a result of its normal operations.

Linking together the job seeker and the job may mean that the Employment Service must look beyond the local labor market. Although the local labor market is still the primary unit for the matching of supply and demand, the market for many skilled technical and professional occupations is now regional or national in scope. The Employment Service has developed a procedure, called interarea recruitment, to facilitate the matching of job seekers and job openings among local labor markets. The procedure, however, is cumbersome and generally ineffective. Accordingly, the Task Force recommended that steps be taken to improve both the operation of the interarea recruitment procedure and the flow of information across local labor markets. Specifically, it urged the establishment of regional multi-market clearance centers throughout the federal-state system of public employment offices.

These centers would operate as follows. Each local office would be required to list with the Regional Center all job vacancies in shortage occupations which had remained unfilled 15 days from the date they were listed with the local office. In addition the local office would be required to list with the Center the names of applicants in the professional, technical, and skilled-job classifications who had remained unemployed for 30 days or more. With such information the Regional Center could promote interarea recruitment, making use of the appropriate automatic data-processing and computer equipment.

The quality of manpower services provided by the Employment Service is directly related to the quality of personnel working in the system. Therefore, a critically important need is to improve the quality of personnel. The Task Force believes that needed improvement could be accomplished by (1) improving standards and raising salaries to attract and retain competent and qualified employees, (2) providing incentives for self-development through in-service and out-service training programs, and (3) enhancing employee advancement opportunities through facilitating movement by personnel among the states and between the states and the federal government.

Improving salaries in the federal-state system is not easy. Each state has final authority for levels and rates of pay for its personnel, but must comply with the comparability policy of the federal Bureau of Employment Security, of which the United States Employment Service is a part. This means that state Employment Service salaries must be in line with comparable positions in other departments of state government. One major problem is to determine what positions in state government are comparable. In the past, this policy tied Employment Service salaries to low state salary levels in many states. The Task

Force strongly recommended that steps be taken to make salaries more attractive for qualified personnel. Higher salaries for professional jobs should be commensurate with qualifications for these positions as prescribed by the Secretary of Labor. The Task Force also recommended that the Employment Service modify the policy of salary comparability for professional jobs to include other relevant factors such as the salaries being paid for comparable jobs in both public and private employment.

The Task Force linked improved salaries with higher qualifications, and the latter are obtained through self-development. Therefore, there must be opportunities for such development. Accordingly the Task Force recommended that the Secretary of Labor require each state to include in its annual plan of operation a well-developed training program covering provisions for orientation, in-service and out-service training, tuition subsidies, and educational leave. Each state would develop the program best suited to its needs. If, however, the state does not include such a plan for its training activities, the Task Force recommended that no funds be made available for training of Employment Service personnel in that state.

The last method of improving the quality of personnel recommended by the Task Force is to facilitate the movement of personnel within the system. Freedom of movement enhances long-term career opportunities. This is especially important to career-minded employees who want the opportunity to advance. In the view of the Task Force, facilitating mobility would enable the system to make better use of the reservoir of qualified and experienced personnel in the Employment Service. Specifically, the Task Force recommended that provisions be made for an employee in a state agency to be appointed to a federal position if certain conditions with respect to examinations are met. It also recommended that the Secretary of Labor be given legislative authority to develop a procedure permitting personnel to move among state agencies without loss in employment status, job rights, pensions, and other accumulated benefits.

Another important area of Employment Service operations on which the Task Force focused attention was the development and dissemination of labor-market information. Since there are several government agencies involved in the collection of such information, the Task Force recommended that the Secretary of Labor should take the lead in clarifying the assignment of responsibility for the collection of this information among these agencies. The Employment Service should (1) collect and analyze manpower information required for the efficient functioning of the Employment Service and for the administration of other federal programs dealing with manpower development and utilization; (2) develop information for occupational guidance, testing, and employment counseling, both for its own use and for other users, public and private; (3) assist in efforts to strengthen community development activities; and (4) engage in research that might facilitate adjustments to automation and changing technology.

Collecting and analyzing adequate labor-market information is but the first step. Such information must be widely disseminated in meaningful form to those organizations, both public and private, with an interest in labor-market trends. The Task Force recommended that vigorous measures be adopted by the Employment Service to insure this kind of dissemination. It urged that each metropolitan local office have a staff member designated as the labor-market information officer, whose principal duty would be to communicate on a regular basis with various organizations in the community, both public and private. In the Task Force view, the effective use of a labor-market information officer would build a better relationship between the Employment Service and other groups in the community, which, in turn, would help to create a more positive image of the Service.

As the Task Force put it, labor-market information to be effective must be put to work. Comprehensive and current information, readily available, is essential for the counseling program. Equally important, the Employment Service counselors must have the background to use this information to provide maximum assistance to job seekers.

These are some of the highlights of the Report of the Employment Service Task Force. Its recommendations dealt with the need for both administrative improvements and legislative changes in order to strengthen the Employment Service. Some of its recommendations dealing with the former have already been acted upon by appropriate officials in the Department of

Labor. Many of the recommendations dealing with legislative changes have been incorporated into several bills currently being considered by the Congress. One such bill in the Manpower Services Act of 1966, which the Senate recently passed. It is now before the House of Representatives.

In view of the interest in improving the Employment Service, it seems highly likely that a new legislative mandate will be given to the federal-state system of public employment offices. The Task Force strongly recommended that such a mandate be given. The basic legislation—the Wagner-Peyser Act of 1933— did not envision the role the Employment Service would be called upon to play in the implementation of national manpower policies.

CHAPTER **7**

# The Value of Vocational Education

## BY DAVID S. BUSHNELL*

These are exciting times in education. The forces of innovation have swept before them many of the highly valued practices of the past. Graded classes are giving way to the nongraded. The one-room schoolhouse has recently emerged as the educational park. With increased federal resources becoming available, educators for the first time are in a position to support with adequate funds major changes which give promise of meeting the needs of all segments of our society. Our efforts in the past to strengthen the hand of the teacher and to introduce more effective instructional techniques and materials have been small in scale and fragmented. Even recent innovations, such as Opera-

*Director, Division of Adult and Vocational Research, Bureau of Research, U.S. Office of Education. This paper represents the views of the author and draws upon current research being sponsored by the Division of Adult and Vocational Research.

tion Headstart and the Neighborhood Youth Corps (NYC), have created in many communities a patchwork quilt which fails to provide the necessary articulation and continuing support needed by most students throughout their formal (and informal) years of education. Dramatic improvements in dropout rates and in the number of really literate graduates from our high schools are not yet in evidence. Much has been learned about learning, but much has yet to be accomplished in fully implementing these promising developments. We are now capable of building the kind of curriculum and the institutional framework which will enable a youngster to realize his full developmental capability during his formal years of education. Such an articulated program should nurture the intellectual, manipulative, creative, and social skills potentially present in each pupil. The major hurdle before us is the narrowing of the gap between this potential development of latent human resources and the implementation of such a program in our schools.

## Investment in Education

To achieve this educational goal will require an investment well beyond the approximately $40 billion spent last year on education. The National Education Association has stated that to achieve the quality of elementary and secondary education which will fully develop the individual student's productive potential would involve an increase in annual current expenditures per pupil from $341 in 1960 to $720 by 1970.[1] Leonard Lecht estimates that to achieve a national goal of full educational opportunity, as laid down by President Johnson in his Message to Congress on Education in January 1965, will require an expenditure of $82 billion by 1975.[2] Increasing the length of enrollment and the numbers enrolled, adding more and better paid teachers, and building an up-to-date instructional system for the 66 million students anticipated at all levels of education by 1975 will raise expenditures on education to about 8 per cent of the near trillion dollar Gross National Product anticipated at that time.[3]

Viewed from the perspective of potential cost, the question needs to be asked: Is education worth it? The resounding answer of most American families is "yes." The pressure for education from employers and parents alike in this country has brought us well along the path toward universal education. At earlier grade levels, universal education has been achieved in the United States for virtually all children between the ages of 6 and 13. At the high school level, we are well ahead of other nations. The demand for higher education continues unabated. In the past, high school graduation was an acceptable goal for most students. Today, employers and parents alike emphasize the need for more schooling so that young people can enter and succeed in occupations and professions that offer better incomes and high status.

I was interested to note in a recent *Wall Street Journal* article that Common Market nations are working diligently to overcome serious shortages of educated manpower by opening up educational opportunities for youngsters from working-class backgrounds.[4] Only 4 per cent of college-age youths in these European countries receive university degrees in contrast with 20 per cent of their American counterparts. The article goes on to state that the increased pressure for higher enrollment stems partly from the growing awareness on the part of working-class parents that college degrees will help to raise the social and economic status of their children. Additional evidence of this country's heavy investment in education can be found in a recently completed UNESCO survey which compared the percentage of 17-year-olds enrolled in full-time schooling in various countries, with the following results: United States, 81 per cent; England, 56 per cent; Belgium, 30 per cent; and Germany 13 per cent.

In spite of the "flattery by imitation" conferred upon us by our European associates, many economists were arguing as late as 1950 that the United States was overtraining its potential job seekers. In 1949, for example, Professor Seymour Harris of Harvard estimated that "a large proportion of the potential college students within the next twenty years are doomed to disappointment after graduation as the number of coveted openings will be substantially less than the number seeking them."[6] Investments in physical capital (plant and equipment, housing, inventories, etc.) were viewed as having contributed the major gains in productivity in this and other countries. This belief led to a shortsighted view of the role of education in the economic growth of underdeveloped countries. It was assumed that a fixed relationship between the amount of physical capital invested and the increase in output could be expected. Development economists found that the actual increase in output fell short of the expected additional output because the labor force was not adequately trained to utilize efficiently the additional physical capital.

More recently, economists have come to recognize that investments in human capital not only provide handsome dividends for the individual but many account for a large share of the economic growth achieved in this country in recent years. Edward F. Denison,[7] Theodore Schultz,[8] and others have demonstrated that education and training have played a much bigger role in our economic growth than was previously realized. Denison estimated that the rising educational level of the labor force was responsible for 23 per cent of the growth in real national income between 1929 and 1957. Using a different method but with similar results, Professor Schultz has estimated that the yield on our investment in "educational capital" over roughly the same period accounted for about one-fifth of the rise in national output.

Two recently completed follow-up studies of vocational and comprehensive high school graduates argue successfully for the wisdom of investing in vocational education at the secondary school level. Max Eninger's study of vocational and comprehensive high school graduates suggests that vocationally trained high school graduates found jobs more quickly, were subject to less unemployment, and enjoyed greater employment security than did graduates of academic programs from the same schools.[9] By means of a selected sample of male graduates of the classes of 1953, 1958, and 1962 from 100 high schools surveyed, the post high school occupational and educational experiences of 5500 graduates of trade and industry vocational courses and 1800 academic course graduates were studied. Parallel results were obtained in a Pennsylvania State University comparative study of approximately 8000 graduates of vocational, academic, and general education programs in 9 Eastern cities.[10] Vocational graduates were found to have higher pay levels than their academic counterparts. Nonwhite vocational graduates surpassed their white counterparts; just the opposite relationship held among white and nonwhite academic graduates.

It is becoming increasingly apparent that a healthy modern economy depends to a large extent upon our ability to adapt to changes in productive capacity resulting from the adoption of better and more efficient machinery. Not only are skilled engineers needed to design and install the improved equipment but more technically trained personnel are required to plan and manage production, to maintain and supervise expensive automated equipment, to sell and service the product, and to conduct research for newer and better products. A growing modern economy also requires more and more teachers, scientists, professional managers, advertising and sales people, computer programmers and technicians, and mechanics and maintenance workers of all kinds.

Gardner Ackley in an address in Washington recognized that "recent economic research has given us a new understanding of the role of education in producing a highly skilled and adaptable labor force, and in providing the basic research and the technological support for rapid and continuing economic growth." [11] It was out of the studies of patterns of economic growth of underdeveloped countries, Ackley argues, that economists began to be aware of the significance of investments in human capital. Compared with most school systems abroad, our public educational programs do pay heed to the need for optimizing the success of all students and do not stress the desirability of screening out students along the way. This commitment, while costly, helped put the United States first in the ranks of countries graduating students at higher educational levels. It has been our policy, not always successful, to provide our students at the high school level with a rich resource of instructional material that would be useful for both the college and the noncollege bound. The comprehensive high schools are uniquely qualified in this way. The community colleges and the new area vocational schools offer to those who wish to have some specialized training at a post-secondary level the chance to complete a terminal-degree program without having to qualify for a four-year college program. Counseling at each stage of the way helps to insure the continued adjustment and realistic goal-setting for students of varying abilities. Sometimes in our rush to improve a system grown sluggish with age, we fail to recognize its strengths and contribution to a vital economy.

### New Needs and Opportunities

It is not my purpose, however, simply to applaud our achievements to date. Too many sobering facts impinge upon what might otherwise be a happy view of the future. Many of these have been well documented by the other papers presented at this meeting. Recent shifts in the structure of the labor market have imposed increased demands upon public education to prepare young adults and experienced workers alike for changing work careers. The shift from production-oriented occupations to service occupations has accelerated the need for communicative and social skills in addition to the more familiar manipulative skills. Many of the more traditional entry-level occupations are now unavailable to the high school or junior college graduate. With 26 million young workers entering the labor force this decade, new jobs must be created. Unskilled or low-skilled jobs frequently offer only interim employment opportunities. Qualifying for entry-level occupations is a necessity but should be viewed as only the first step in a series of job changes leading, hopefully, to a more stable and remunerative working career.

Unfortunately, much of what is now taught in our public schools fails to recognize that technology is generating profound changes in the nature of work. As muscle power gives way to brain power, each of us needs to understand and master, to some extent, the man-made environment about us. The heavy emphasis in the past upon verbal reasoning skills, "book learning," has unfortunately penalized those most in need of adapting to these demands, the socio-economically disadvantaged.

Through research and the support of new and innovative programs, a number of techniques and instructional methods have recently been identified which, if implemented on a sufficiently large scale, give promise of major breakthroughs. It is foolhardy to think that such techniques should only be applied at certain time periods in the formal education of the child or the adult. Deutsch,[12] Hunt,[13] and others have all readily demonstrated that improvements can be dramatically achieved but that continued

reinforcement is needed to prevent fall-back. When children return to the traditional school programs, they respond in the
traditional way. Dropouts and "pushouts" are the result.

New efforts must be consistently applied to an articulated program at the various grade levels with built-in review and reinforcement techniques at each step of the way. It is not sufficient
any longer to graduate students who meet only the minimum
requirements for functioning as a mature adult. Entry-level job
skills alone are not sufficient to insure a profitable and satisfying
work career. Nor should we simply strive to produce assembly-
line graduates, each of whom looks like a carbon copy of the
middle-class child. The objective should be to tap each child's
unique strengths and background by creating a link between
their vocational and avocational interests and the broad array
of information to be learned. Dr. Melvin Herman, Director of
the Center for the Study of Unemployed Youth at New York
University's Graduate School of Social Work, commented in the
press recently that a long-term program is needed for identifying
potential dropouts and devising a suitable educational program
geared to their particular needs as well as providing the placement service and follow-up help required. He points out that under the Manpower Development and Training Act (MDTA) most
of the effort is limited to less than one year of training. "Long
range planning is still a dirty word," he states, "but it is the
kids that suffer when programs are haphazard." [14] Frank Riessman argues that tapping the strengths of the disadvantaged child
may offer advantages beyond that of simply bringing the child
back into the mainstream of American life.[15] Through attention
to the special needs of these students, the teacher may develop
a rich repertory of instructional skills with less emphasis on
verbal-reasoning abilities and more attention to alternative styles
of learning.

A number of recently pioneered techniques for responding to
individual student-learning needs within and outside the classroom setting have been tested through federally supported research programs. Special motivational techniques which link
learning achievements with desired rewards have proved to be
very effective. One group of delinquent boys who had dropped
out of high school proved very receptive to earning credits to-

wards the opportunity to play chess once or twice a week by successful participation in classroom activities. Other researchers have used money as an incentive in an attempt to exploit the more acceptable employer-employee relationship with students who dislike any learning situation which smacks of formal education. Computer games have been successfully employed as a method of teaching teenagers to think through appropriate career choices. Much of this type of effort grows out of the stimulus-response studies conducted by learning theorists during the last three or four decades.

Attempts to individualize the instructional process through the use of computers and other instructional technology have succeeded in permitting the student to involve himself at his own rate in the learning process. How far this can be carried in our schools with current and future restraint on the cost of education has yet to be determined, but a number of optimists see computer-assisted instruction in most of our classrooms in the next four or five years. New textbooks are appearing which gear the information to the background and reading level of the student. "Hiptionaries" have been used to introduce "hip" words which translate into other linguistic concepts. Students who might not understand the word "tranquil" can learn it through use of the "hip" word "cool it." [16] Tutorial programs with sixth graders helping fourth graders to read have again demonstrated the often observed phenomenon that those who help frequently benefit more than those being helped. Even the expanded use of subprofessionals offers some modicum of hope in giving more intensive attention to those children needing it, while at the same time helping to offset the spiraling cost of education. Each of these examples illustrates that we are in the take-off stage and can, with appropriate planning and funding, begin to make major inroads into those educational problems which still face us.

Under the recent stimulation of new federal legislation, research into the problems of vocational and technical education has taken on new dimensions. Fortunately, this resurgence of interest and activity is occurring at a time when teachers and school administrators are under pressure by local employers and parents to provide today's youngsters with the kind of education which will qualify them to find and hold jobs. It would be a mistake, however, to let employers with their specialized entry-job skill requirements or parents with their frequently provincial view of the existing employment market to dictate the type of training which should be made available in our schools. The educator has much to offer in assessing the appropriate skills and attitudes that will carry today's students successfully through the role of working adult and citizen.

The tendency in the past to separate general and vocational education has penalized both those who are college bound and those who plan to terminate their formal education at the end of high school or junior college. The academically oriented students are directed to those college preparatory courses which will enhance their performance on the college entrance examinations. Some teachers have argued that these students do not require a knowledge of the functioning of the business and industrial community. At the same time, vocational students must be competent in the basic learning skills if they are adequately to cope with present day society. "There can be no adequate technical education which is not liberal and no liberal education which is not technical"; states Whitehead, "education should turn out pupils with something they know well and can do well."

The tendency to separate those in the college preparatory programs and those who have been tagged as vocationally oriented handicaps both groups. Those who plan to go on to college are not at all prepared to cope with the question, "What happens if I have to drop out?" On the other hand, those exposed to current vocational programs find themselves being trained for a narrow range of job skills. Even if such a student should qualify for his first job, he is still faced with the frequent demand to adapt to a changing labor market. Another segment of our public school population is not enrolled in either vocational or academically oriented programs and receives very little in the way of occupational preparation. From the perspective of providing for the optimum development of all students, the present allocation of resources and the type of curriculum available for occupationally oriented students is inadequate.

This recital of the problems and shortcomings associated with what passes today for vocational education establishes the need for major revisions in this field. Research and development efforts supported by the enactment of the Vocational Education Act of 1963 are helping to accomplish several broad objectives in bringing about a change in the junior-high, senior-high, and junior-college curriculums.[17] Better information systems funneling industry's job needs to vocational curriculum planners in our schools are a necessity. Computers are serving as intermediaries between employers and school counselors. Students are being permitted to pursue special vocational interests in depth, often in ways tailored to their individual needs and abilities.

## Improving Vocational Education

As new instructional techniques are developed and pilot curriculum efforts completed, several areas of emphasis have begun to emerge which support the need for fostering a major effort aimed at curriculum revision. It is this specification of the criteria for structuring a "new" vocational education for all students which will characterize the major thrust of the remainder of this paper. While content and structure are difficult to state without a great deal more specificity, I should like to outline several objectives for consideration. A new vocational curriculum should:

1. Emphasize the articulation between academic and vocational learning for the purpose of fusing the two programs. With vocational preparation used as the principle vehicle, the inculcation of basic learning skills could be made more relevant to many students who would otherwise have difficulty seeing the value of a general education.
2. Expose the student to an understanding of the "real world" through a series of experiences which capitalize on the universal desire of youth to investigate for himself. Abstract, verbal principles could be acquired through nonverbal stimuli, such as seeing, feeling, manipulating, and even smelling.
3. Train students in manipulative, cognitive, and interpersonal skills. Stress not just one specialized occupation, but a common core of skills related to a cluser of occupations.
4. Help students cultivate the attitudes and habits which go with undertaking adult responsibilities, particularly those appropriate to the work setting.

5. Provide a background for the prospective worker by helping him to understand how he can play an active part in the economic and social institutions of our country. Civil liberties represent one arena in which many workers are or could be involved.

6. Maximize opportunity by providing a range of positive learning experiences for students at all levels of ability and with different backgrounds. Utilize the full range of new instructional technology.

7. Help students cope with a changing labor market through developing their problem-solving ability and a series of career strategies leading to an adequate level of income and responsibility. Help them to cope with the problems of changing status.

8. Create within the students a sense of self-reliance and awareness which leads them to seek out appropriate careers and aspiration levels.

While we must educate our youth by making them adaptable to changing job demands, it is nevertheless important to recognize that most employers still require competence in some skill before accepting a new job applicant. This is particularly true of minority group members who must evidence excellent credentials to compete with the more advantaged. In an attempt to provide vocational programs in growing occupational fields, the Office of Education is pushing hard for curriculum-development efforts in such fields as health services, landscape gardening, public and social welfare, and engineering-technician occupations. A number of these call for work-study arrangements under which the student can gain on-the-job experience while attending school. At the present time, some 96 research and development efforts sponsored by the Office of Education are focused on these new and emerging occupational clusters.

In general, the proposals being supported seek to tap the total capacity of the individual, including the intellectual, the manipulative, the creative, and the social. They emphasize the discovery of abstract concepts through the examination of "real world" events. Experientially based learning provides an underpinning for the more traditional academically oriented subjects such as mathematics, science, and English. Shop and laboratory experiences are being emphasized to provide a counterbalance to the present heavy emphasis on verbal reasoning in most curriculum offerings at the high school and post secondary school level. Communication skills, social skills, and work attitudes are being stressed, together with the more familiar manipulative and cognitive skills. As you can see, this focus concerns itself with all education and treats vocational education as an integral part.

## NOTES

1. *Financing the Public Schools, 1960–1970* (Washington: National Education Association, 1962), p. 16.
2. Leonard Lecht, *Goals, Priorities, and Dollars—The Next Decade* (New York: The Free Press, 1966).
3. *Ibid.*, p. 160.
4. *Wall Street Journal,* July 14, 1966, p. 1.
5. UNESCO, *World Survey of Education, III* (New York International Documents Service, 1961). See also U.S. Department of Commerce, "Population Characteristics," *Current Population Reports,* Series P-20, No. 148 (February 8, 1966), p. 2.
6. Seymour Harris, *The Market for College Graduates* (Cambridge: Harvard University Press, 1949), p. 62.
7. Edward F. Denison, *The Sources of Economic Growth in the United States* (New York: Committee for Economic Development, Occasional Paper No. 13, 1962).
8. Theodore W. Schultz, "Education and Economic Growth," in Nelson B. Henry, editor, *Social Forces Influencing American Education, The Sixtieth Yearbook of the National Society for the Study of Education,* Part II (Chicago: The National Society for the Study of Education, 1961), p. 81; and Schultz, "Investment in Human Capital," *American Economic Review,* LI (March, 1961), 13.
9. Max U. Eninger, *The Process and Product of T and I High School Level Vocational Education in the United States* (Pittsburgh: The American Institutes for Research, 1965).
10. Jacob J. Kaufman, "Job Placement and Employment Experiences of High School Graduates: A Preliminary Report," presented at the Conference on Research in Vocational and Technical Education, The Center for Studies in Vocational and Technical Education, The University of Wisconsin, June 10–11, 1966.
11. Gardner Ackley, "Policies for the Promotion of Economic Growth," *Seminar on Manpower Policy* (Washington: U.S. Department of Labor, 1966), p. 12.
12. Martin Deutsch, "Facilitating Development in the Pre-School Child: Social and Psychological Perspectives," *Merrill-Palmer Quarterly,* X (July, 1964), 249–263.

13. J. McVicker Hunt, "The Psychological Basis for Using Pre-School Enrichment as an Antidote for Cultural Deprivation," *Merrill-Palmer Quarterly*, X (July, 1964), 209–248.

14. *New York Times,* May 29, 1966, p. 38.

15. Frank Riessman, *The Culturally Deprived Child* (New York: Harper and Row, 1962).

16. For further information on the use of "hiptionaries," see Frank Riessman, *Hiptionary Word Games* (Chicago: Follett, 1966) and Gerald Weinstein, "Do You Dig All Jive?" *Scholastic Teacher,* LXXXV (January 14, 1965), 13-T–14-T.

17. For a description of the Vocational Education Act of 1963 and its implications, see Walter M. Arnold, "New Directions in Vocational Education," *American Vocational Journal*, XXXIX October, 1964), 8–12.

# Discussion

## BY LOUIS J. KISHKUNAS

Modern American society, according to John Gardner, Secretary of Health, Education, and Welfare, needs both good plumbers and good philosophers. Education, he warns, must see to it that both our pipes and our ideas hold water. There was never a time in history when such universal concern and abundant support was focused on education, especially job-centered education, as we see today.

Mr. Bushnell's call for the merging of our efforts in vocational education and general education is most timely and welcome. In the very recent past the mere acquisition of a high school diploma insured employability. This is no longer true in today's more complex and technological society. In addition to his high school diploma, today's job seeker must be able to tell the potential employer that he possesses a specific skill. More than that, his previous educational experiences, optimally, must be such that he can return to classes within the formal educational establishment or partake of the in-service opportunities offered by industries and technical societies so that advancement can be insured. The opportunity for upward mobility is essential to the mental health of our working force today.

Our experiences with the G. I. Bill following the Second World War and more recently with MDTA give us ample experience to demonstrate the thesis that moneys expended for education (especially job-centered education) are indeed a fruitful investment. The economic growth that we have enjoyed since the Second World War can be attributed, at least in part, to the training acquired by the masses of returning veterans. The costs of this training have been reimbursed several times over through the increased personal income taxes paid by these veterans due to their increased earning capabilities and through the dramatic increase of the Gross National Product. Another illustration is provided by MDTA, under which unemployed or underemployed people have been literally taken from the relief rolls, trained, and employed, thus becoming tax-paying members of society rather than recipients of government welfare payments.

Those states which made the largest investment in educational facilities and programs during the depression years and after the Second World War are today reaping the harvest in the form of very rapid economic growth—particularly in those industries which have the most promise for further growth in the emerging technologies.

Too often in the past we have been guilty of overtraining, that is, using professionally trained people in positions which could be handled just as effectively by people with narrow skills. We are familiar with the example of the engineer who, to operate most effectively, must have from four to twelve technicians working with him performing those operations they can do as well as he, thus freeing him for the more important tasks that only he is qualified to do.

Mr. Bushnell's endorsement of the comprehensive high school is most welcome because too often in the past young people have had to make commitments at much too tender an age—commitments which were virtually irrevocable.

Our industrial labor market is changing so rapidly that we must face up to the task of preparing our students for frequent job changes. It has been estimated that a young person entering the labor market today will be retrained and change his job at least six times during his working life. This is a new problem facing our workers—a problem that they must be prepared to cope with.

One of the characters out of Greek mythology was the Macedonian bandit, Procrustes. You will remember that Procrustes' specialty was capturing caravans and holding his captives for ransom. Procrustes had a warped sense of hospitality; he wanted his "guests" to be comfortable. He would measure them to his bed. If they were too short, he would put them on a rack and stretch them so that they would fit the bed. If they were too long, he would chop off their legs. Too often in the past, our schools have played the role of Procrustes; that is, they expect the students to fit their programs. If they were too long, they were to be cut down to size; if they were found inadequate, they were stretched or forced out. Our schools must seek to offer a tailor-made program for each student, recognizing individual needs and the different backgrounds from which the students come.

These same concerns have been expressed by the Research Council of the Great Cities, which since at least 1960 has been examining vocational and technical education as it relates to the total high school program. Several cities have conducted surveys to determine whether their high school programs are preparing students for the lives they will be leading upon graduation. Almost universally, the cities have concluded that the vocational programs, as conducted under the Smith Hughes Act of 1917, and the academic programs in the same systems do not realistically prepare young people for the careers they will pursue. Vocational education as it has been offered has not been able to attract the numbers of students that it should. Too many students and parents (and guidance counselors) have interpreted this type of education as being suitable only for the "academically unfit" and as preparing young people for "dead-end" occupations.

There is a definite trend in the large cities of America today toward high schools which are truly comprehensive. These institutions offer the full array of academic programs but give each student the opportunity to learn a skill by means of which he can get his first job.

Ideally, the vocational and academic programs are not mutually exclusive—that is, for students who are aggressive enough and have the necessary prerequisites and ability, it is possible to pursue both an academic diploma and the acquisition of a salable skill. Carried to fruition, this movement towards establishing truly comprehensive high schools, large enough to offer a complete spectrum of programs, will help to realize the oft-cited goal of equal educational opportunities for all.

# Discussion

## BY BURTON A. WEISBROD

David Bushnell's paper deals principally with two matters: (1) evidence that expenditures on education constitute a good investment in increasing real output of the economy, and (2) criteria for, or goals of, curriculum development, with particular reference to preparing youngsters for their working careers. By presenting his views, Bushnell raises some important issues concerning public policy toward education—issues that deserve careful consideration.

Before I present my specific comment on his paper, I should like to note, in a sympathetic vein, a natural and yet rather fundamental difference in viewpoint between a government official, such as Bushnell, who is charged with responsibility for action programs, and an academician, such as myself. With respect to decision-makers' errors of types 1 and 2—errors of omission and commission—the government official is, no doubt, more prone to act and thereby to risk committing errors of commission, while the academician, confronted by the same incomplete information, is more prone to delay action in order to study matters further and thereby to court errors of omission. Thus, I sympathize with Bushnell, given the pressure on him to make proposals and urge changes, but at the same time I must point up the fact that such proposals may rely upon information that we simply do not have and on reasoning that is by no means beyond question.

### Education As an Investment

Let us turn now to education as an investment. Are we on strong ground in defending expenditures on education as a profitable investment in labor productivity and economic growth, as Bushnell has done? This is not the place for a full-scale evaluation of the economic literature on rates of return to investment in education, and yet a few comments are in order concerning what that literature does and does not show. First, little is known about how much of the observed earnings differentials among persons with different levels of educational attainment are attributable to their education and how much are attributable to difference in "ability" or other variables that are probably correlated positively with educational-attainment levels. Second, the existing data that appear to show relatively high rates of return to schooling apply to males; returns to females—who average less time in the labor force—are probably lower than returns to males. This is especially noteworthy since the rate of increase of school-going has been greater for females than for males. Can increased amounts of schooling for females also be regarded as a sound investment in economic growth? The answer is by no means clear.

Third, whatever the "profitability" may be of education expenditures in general, the profitability of such "investments" in "disadvantaged" youngsters—with whom Bushnell is particularly concerned, as am I—is another matter. The moral, equity case for helping such children is powerful, but the evidence is yet to be produced that additional expenditures for their education will produce payoffs in increased productivity that justify the expenditures on this ground alone. Of course, there may be returns from education in forms other than increased output, e.g., reduced crime and social discontent (although little is known about these matters), and, in addition, society may wish to provide added education for the disadvantaged even if there is little or no identifiable return. But in the latter case it could not be said that such expenditures are "efficient" investments in the (Pareto) sense in which the term is used conventionally in economics.

## Improving Vocational Education

Bushnell's brief attempt to show the financial payoff from education appears to be a sort of introduction, albeit a nonessential one, to his main point—that instructional techniques in public schools need to be altered so as to better equip all students for work careers that change unpredictably. The remainder of my comments deal with this main thrust of the paper—the need for and the criteria for developing such a "new vocational education."

If this employment-oriented goal were the only one that Bushnell proposed for the junior high school, senior high school, and junior college, the implementation of a program for achieving it would be difficult enough. But he actually provides a list of *eight* "objectives" of a vocational curriculum—including helping the student to understand the "real world," fusing academic and vocational learning, creating a sense of self-reliance, in addition to training students to have both *specific* work skills and *flexibility* with respect to changing job demands.

These objectives are laudable, but even if all were defined operationally—and in Bushnell's paper they are not—is there *any* known curriculum that could achieve all of them? Are these objectives consistent with each other, or are some attainable only at the expense of others? If some of the objectives conflict—and they do—what trade-offs should society be willing to make? Unfortunately, Bushnell's paper does not even recognize the existence of these issues. The assertion of eight goals, without consideration of their compatability, their *relative* importance, the cost or even the technical possibility of their achievement with present knowledge and technology, is a weak foundation upon which to build a "major curriculum revision effort." Of course, Bushnell surely agrees with the need for developing measures of educational output, that is, measures of the degree of attainment of educational objectives, and with the need for learning more about the education production function, that is, the combinations of imputs by the use of which any of the objectives can be reached. There is no doubt that a great deal more research is needed. There *is* doubt, however, as to whether Bushnell's policy measures ought to be pursued, given the present state of knowledge.

The education production function framework is useful for organizing much of Bushnell's paper. Consider the general relationship, $P_a = F(E, S_a)$, which says that the outputs of education for student $a$, $P_a$, depend on the quantities and qualities of educational inputs through the schools, $E$, the nature and ability of the student, $S_a$, and the state of knowledge, $F$. This relationship tells us how to combine $E$ and $S$ so as to produce the outputs. As already noted, Bushnell suggests that $P$ is in at least eight forms. He also appears to suggest that the same eight forms of output should be sought for all students. If this view is held, the usefulness of the traditional separation of "vocational" from "general" or "academic" schooling is, as Bushnell observes, called into question. These different types of educational programs should then be viewed as alternative *means* (techniques of production) for producing a *given* set of outputs. Depending upon the type of student, $S_a$, one combination of educational inputs, $E$, or another is most efficient. Although the question of whether, and in what respects, the goals of vocational and general or academic education are the same deserves further exploration, it does seem reasonably clear even now that the stated objectives of vocational education are not entirely job-oriented, and neither is most acadamic education devoid of concern about subsequent employment and income opportunities for students.

Moreover, the available empirical evidence—limited as it is— suggests that schooling not termed vocational nevertheless does have vocational value (that is, produces an output in this form). In saying this, I am observing that additional schooling appears to bring additional income, even though the great majority of schooling is not avowedly vocational. It remains to be seen whether further study will show that vocational education pays a greater or smaller rate of return in the form of added earnings than does academic education, which is less costly per student-year. Nevertheless, Bushnell has performed a real service by questioning whether the *objectives* of different types of schooling should be thought of as differing.

Although Bushnell's list of eight educational goals is wide-ranging, he places primary emphasis on the importance of providing occupational *flexibility* along with *specific* job skills. Behind this prescription is an implicit judgment that production techniques in the economy are changing more rapidly than they have in the past, and so workers must be increasingly adapatble if they are to obtain employment and satisfactory incomes. The empirical basis for this judgment is not given in the paper, and its validity is open to doubt. Is it really true that the importance of labor flexibility is *growing*? Flexibility has always been an advantage, *ceteris paribus*, but is the extent of that advantage increasing?

It seems fair to describe Bushnell's view of an "ideal" education—ideal from a vocational viewpoint at least—as one that produces students who are trained *broadly* (to make them flexible) and *narrowly* (to make them able to fit easily and quickly into the world of work). There is a question, though, as to how far flexibility ought to be carried. How many of life's uncertainties ought schooling attempt to cope with? Bushnell would not only have schooling provide for easy job-switching *after* the person has completed schooling; he would also have it deal with the possibility at every stage in the educational process that the student might decide, unexpectedly, to drop out. The implications of such attempts to plan for a wide variety of contingencies are not well specified by Bushnell. For example, we might agree that one type of high school education is optimal for a student who will not go on to college; another type may be optimal for the student who will go on to college. But what about the student who does not plan to go to college but then changes his mind? Since such cases are not unheard of, should those high school students who have any chance whatsoever of going to college receive a college preparatory education in addition to their vocationally-oriented schooling? And what about the student who intends to go on to college but subsequently drops out of high school before graduation? Should all students who are even slightly in danger of dropping out be given a "vocational" course of study, in addition to their broader college-preparatory schooling? In short, should all students be prepared at all times either to continue in school or to enter the job market?

It is possible, one might guess, to develop an educational curriculum that combines breadth with specialization. It is possible but at a price in terms of either the resource costs of education or the duration of schooling or both. How high is the price? Are the outputs—the benefits—worth the price? For any given total cost or total duration of schooling, what is the optimal balance between breadth and depth? These critical questions remain unanswered. Unfortunately, they are not even raised in the Bushnell paper.

Since Bushnell emphasizes so strenuously the importance of educating for employment flexibility, it may be worthwile to consider the case for the defense—for narrow, job-specific education. In so doing I shall abstract from nonemployment-oriented goals of education, as Bushnell has done.

Rather than incur the costs of educating youngsters to be highly flexible—ready to adapt to contingencies many of which will never confront them—might it not be better to train for relatively narrow skills and then, later, to provide retraining if and when it seems worthwhile? After all, retraining will probably not be desirable for every person over his lifetime. It is, thus, somewhat wasteful to train everyone to be flexible. Moreover, training, however broad and general, inevitably depreciates and obsolesces through time and disuse; hence, it would seem inefficient to provide people with flexible skills well in advance of the need for them. Perhaps the most useful curriculum revision would be in the *time* dimension: to provide opportunities for *adult* workers to attend classes at night, on weekends, and so on, rather than to encourage, from a vocational viewpoint, larger investments of time and other resources in the broader vocationally oriented education of *youngsters*.

These issues and choices should receive more attention. Even at this stage, though, I am happy to support Bushnell's urging to take advantage of the preferences of some students for "practicability" to teach them a variety of things that do facilitate adaptability, that are sometimes learned most easily when one is young, and that can be done at little or no cost. To say this is to note that student preference patterns ($S_a$ in the production function above) are an input to the education production-function. Thus the economically optimal way to provide education would appear, in principle, to vary with the type of student. If it is further agreed that the broad objectives of "vocational" and "academic" education are the same, then Bushnell is probably right in calling for "a major curriculum revision effort." It is by no means apparent, however, that this revision should emphasize labor-market flexibility, bearing in mind the attendant costs.

CHAPTER **8**

# Our Experience with Retraining and Relocation

## BY GERALD G. SOMERS

While some may deplore the continued lack of a comprehensive, coordinated manpower policy in the United States, others rejoice in the multitude of piecemeal programs that have been initiated in the past few years. The retraining and relocation programs provide grist for the mills of those who deplore and of those who rejoice. They represent significant recent departures in American manpower legislation; but our initial experience indicates the crucial need for their coordination with each other and with other educational and labor-market policies.

It is the principal premise of this paper that the establishment of the appropriate relationship between these manpower policies requires a detailed research evaluation of each; and this discussion is focused primarily on the present status and future prospects of such evaluations.

215

### Evaluation of Retraining Programs

The experience with federal retraining should be evaluated in the context of the goals of the legislative programs which call for retraining. These include the Area Redevelopment Act of 1961 (now replaced by the Economic Development Act), the Manpower Development and Training Act (MDTA) of 1962 (as amended in 1963 and 1965), the Trade Expansion Act of 1962, the Vocational Education Act of 1963, and the anti-poverty programs of the Economic Opportunity Act. At the risk of doing some violence to the language of these enactments, the goals they set for retraining can briefly be summarized as follows:

1. For the trainee
   (a) Reduction of unemployment and underemployment
   (b) Increased income through higher skill and productivity
2. For society
   (a) Reduction of national unemployment and welfare payments
   (b) Reduction of poverty and related social ills
   (c) Increased skills and productivity to fill shortages, expand output, and combat inflationary pressures

**The individual trainee.** The agencies entrusted with responsibility for operating the training programs have placed evaluation where it undoubtedly belongs on their priority list: in second place to the carrying out of the actual operations. Although this lower level of priority can be justified, it has meant that the evaluations published by government agencies have gone little beyond 1 (a) and 1 (b) in assessing achievements of the goals listed above. And, even here, government reports thus far published do not permit a conclusive judgment on the role of retraining programs in bringing about gains in employment and income.

It is indicated that, among those who have completed institutional MDTA courses, somewhat over 70 per cent of the trainees are employed, and of those who have completed on-the-job training programs over 85 per cent.[1] A sample interview survey of 1000 trainees shows that an even larger percentage work at some point after their training, 70 per cent in training-related jobs, while 70 per cent stated that "training helped them to get their jobs." [2]

Government data are also available on the costs of the programs (now averaging $1900 per institutional trainee and $520 per on-the-job trainee), and earnings of those who have completed training (a median of $74 per week, a gain of $5 over median earnings in their last period of employment before training).[3] Unfortunately, no analysis is presented of the relationship between costs and income gains for particular trainees or training programs.

Although we are promised more sophisticated government evaluations soon, the missing link in the government reports to date is the absence of studies including control groups of nontrainees. Even though we are told that most of the trainees are placed in "training-related" jobs and most feel that their training "helped them" in getting their jobs, these terms are sufficiently vague to leave questions concerning the impact of training when isolated from other influences on employment and income. For example, national unemployment rates were falling in this period, and earnings were rising. We could expect improvements in employment and earnings regardless of training. One would feel more confident of the beneficial effects of retraining if the experience of the trainees were compared with that of "similarly-situated" nontrainees and if benefits were related to costs.

This approach has been adopted in a few nongovernmental evaluations of the retraining programs. The gain in methodological techniques is partially offset by the limited size of samples; and, moreover, it cannot be said that the control groups were similar to the trainees in *all* respects except their training. However, efforts were made to control for such basic variables as age, education, and race; and the differences in earnings between trainees and nontrainees were related to the costs of the training programs, including the opportunity costs of the trainees —their foregone earnings during training.

These limited private studies indicate the substantial benefits derived by the *individual trainees* from their retraining. Whether one uses such simple measures as a "pay-back period" (the period of time before accumulated gains in earnings offset the costs of training) or calculates a rate of return on the training investment or the increase in capital values, the favorable impact of retraining is underscored. A multiple regression analysis has also emphasized the crucial role of the retraining programs in explaining the post-training benefits derived by the trainees.[4]

**Social gains.** As heartening as these results may be for the individual trainees, they say little about achievement of the objectives for society as a whole. It is possible that the trainee's improved employment status was achieved at the expense of a decline in status of other unemployed workers competing for available jobs. The retraining programs could be said to reduce total unemployment in the economy only if training resulted in an increased number of jobs for the unemployed or in the more rapid filling of previously "unfillable" job openings by newly qualified unemployed men.

The retraining programs can be said to create jobs in three possible ways: (1) The government expenditures on training facilities, instruction, and allowances augment aggregate and regional demand and do not merely replace other expenditures which would have been made in the absence of training. (2) Employers are induced to establish plants in depressed areas—which would not have been established elsewhere—because of the availability of newly retrained workers. (3) Employers are willing to hire trainees because their new skills are found to be attractive, even though these employers had no "job vacancies" before the trainees presented themselves on the scene. Whereas these effects might assume some importance if expenditures on retraining programs were increased manifold, there is little evidence that they are currently of sufficient magnitude to have a significant impact on the number of jobs in the nation as a whole. Similarly there is little evidence at the present time of unemployed workers moving into "unfillable" job vacancies.

Considerations of this type also apply to the reduction of poverty. Although individual trainees have clearly gained in increased income through retraining, others in the poverty ranks—who have not had retraining—may be doomed to an even longer period of poverty because they have suffered a further decline in *relative* employment qualifications. Needless to say, there have been no studies to appraise this possible effect on the employment and earnings position of nontrainees.

The social welfare has been most clearly advanced through the national increase in productivity brought about by retraining. Here, too, however, the effect on productivity has not been measured. We do know that large numbers of MDTA trainees complete courses in occupations well above their previous skill level. Since most trainees obtain jobs in "training-related" occupations, it can be assumed that their productive contribution is greater than it was on jobs held prior to retraining.

These higher skills will be especially in the social interest if they result in the elimination of occupational shortages created by the general expansion of the economy. Indeed, there are some who would say that government-subsidized retraining programs can be fully justified only in such a period of tight labor markets and inflationary pressures. The reasoning is that government retraining programs in a period of general labor surplus will merely change the composition of the unemployed, but in time of labor shortages public retraining can become an important anti-inflationary force.

Although this position has some merit, there are caveats that must be observed. First, in a period of tight labor markets, the remaining unemployed are likely to be heavily concentrated among the hard-core disadvantaged. Increasing emphasis can be given to retraining programs for these workers in such a period, but they are the very workers who are least likely to be trained for the critically short occupations. These occupations usually require a higher level of general education than is customarily found among the most disadvantaged.

Second, private employers can be expected to increase their own training efforts in a period of labor shortage. Since the evaluation of federal retraining should be based on a determination of what would have happened in the absence of this public activity, a period of full employment may be one in which the social net "benefits" of subsidized retraining are less than one would suppose. The relationship of public and private retraining is one that requires considerably more study. It is discussed further below.

Finally, as my colleague, Burton Weisbrod, has noted, even if the benefits of retraining (in employment, earnings, and productivity) increase in a period of full employment, the costs of retraining may also be expected to increase in such a period. The costs of good instructors and facilities will be higher, and the opportunity costs of the training will rise. Although one might anticipate an improvement in the motivation toward retraining in a period when trainees are more likely to find post-training employment, it must be noted that such a period also offers more ample pretraining employment opportunities, and workers may prefer an immediate lower-skilled job to a "distasteful" return to the classroom.

At any rate there is little evidence, as yet, that the government retraining programs have made a sizeable dent on the "hard core" occupational shortages that have almost become a tradition in the labor market. In spite of the many MDTA courses in these occupations, draftsmen, welders, auto mechanics, secretaries, nurses aides, and others continue to be in great demand. In the absence of more detailed national and regional occupational vacancy data the reasons for these persistent shortages cannot be conclusively determined. To what extent are the vacancies in these occupations increasing at an even faster rate than the increasing supply of trained manpower; and to what extent are the trainees found to be inadequate by employers, or the wages found to be inadequate by the trainee, so that the "shortage" persists in spite of retraining?

## Retraining the Disadvantaged

If careful evaluations of the regular MDTA programs are rare, controlled evaluations of the newer programs for welfare recipients and other disadvantaged groups are almost nonexistent. And yet increasing emphasis is being accorded these training projects under the anti-poverty programs and in the experimental and demonstration projects of MDTA. The Manpower Administrator has announced that a substantially larger proportion of the total MDTA training budget—perhaps as much as 65 per cent—will be concentrated on the disadvantaged in coming years. At the same time an ever-growing number of state and local welfare departments are determined to reduce their relief roles through retraining. But in spite of the Administration's hopes for the future it is clear that in the past year the proportion of disadvantaged in institutional MDTA programs did *not* increase significantly. This is seen in the following summary tabulation culled from MDTA reports:

TABLE 1.

| | Percentage of MDTA Enrollees | |
| --- | --- | --- |
| | 1965 | 1964 |
| Less than 8th grade education | | |
| Total | 7.1 | 7.6 |
| Male | 9.7 | 10.4 |
| Female | 3.2 | 3.4 |
| Nonwhite | | |
| Total | 33.6 | 30.4 |
| Male | 28.9 | 27.0 |
| Female | 40.7 | 35.6 |
| 45 years and over | | |
| Total | 10.0 | 10.6 |
| Male | 9.0 | 9.9 |
| Female | 11.5 | 11.7 |
| Pretraining unemployment over 52 weeks | | |
| Total | 12.0 | 14.3 |
| Male | 6.9 | 7.2 |
| Female | 28.8 | 31.4 |

Source: *1966 Report of the Secretary of Labor on Manpower Research and Training Under the Manpower Development and Training Act of 1962.*

The percentages of enrollees with less than an 8th grade education, of those 45 years of age and over, and of those with 52 weeks or more of unemployment before training actually decreased slightly between 1964 and 1965. There was an increase in the percentage of nonwhites. Whereas the percentages of older workers and of those with low levels of education among the trainees were considerably below the percentage of these groups among the total unemployed, the long-term unemployed and nonwhites had a greater than proportional representation among trainees as compared with their representation among the total unemployed.

It should be noted, however, that nonwhites selected for retraining were usually more favorably situated with regard to other characteristics than their counterparts among the general unemployed. Thus the very young, older, and less-educated nonwhites were underrepresented in the selection of trainees.[5]

The obstacles in the path of expanded institutional retraining for the disadvantaged stem primarily from their problems in obtaining employment upon completion of training. As is shown in Table 2, those in the least advantageous categories of age, education, previous unemployment, and race had lower post-training employment ratios than trainees with more favorable labor-market characteristics. This was true in both 1964 and 1965. The most disheartening finding in this comparison, however, is that in spite of the improvement in national employment between 1964 and 1965, the employment ratio of the disadvantaged trainees actually suffered a slight decline. Whereas the employment of disadvantaged workers can usually be expected to increase more than the average in a national employment expansion, this was not true among the disadvantaged MDTA trainees relative to other trainees. The sharp decline in the employment ratios of nonwhite trainees is especially discouraging. It seems clear that at the 1965 stage of the employment expansion, employers were still able to bypass many of the disadvantaged trainees.

The picture is much less discouraging, however, if one compares the post-training and pretraining experience of the disadvantaged; or if one compares the labor-market experience of disadvantaged trainees with that of disadvantaged nontrainees. Government agencies have now conducted the former type of analysis, but it is necessary to fall back on our own studies (with their limitations of sample size and data acquisition) for controlled comparison of the second type.

A special study of a sample of trainees reported by MDTA finds, as indicated above, that employment rates, job retention,

TABLE 2. EMPLOYMENT EXPERIENCE OF PERSONS COMPLETING MDTA INSTITUTIONAL TRAINING, BY AGE, EDUCATION, RACE, AND DURATION OF UNEMPLOYMENT, 1964, 1965

| Characteristic | Per Cent Employed | |
|---|---|---|
| | 1965 | 1964 |
| Total | 71.3 | 71.7 |
| Age | | |
| Under 22 years | 69.8 | 71.0 |
| 22 to 44 years | 73.5 | 72.2 |
| 45 years and over | 66.8 | 66.9 |
| Education | | |
| Under 8th grade | 67.9 | 68.2 |
| 8th grade | 67.8 | 69.6 |
| 9th to 11th grade | 69.2 | 71.0 |
| 12th grade and over | 73.6 | 72.5 |
| Duration of unemployment prior to training | | |
| Under 5 weeks | 82.5 | 76.0 |
| 5 to 14 weeks | 78.0 | 73.7 |
| 15 to 26 weeks | 75.4 | 69.5 |
| 27 to 52 weeks | 67.8 | 66.0 |
| Over 52 weeks | 57.1 | 64.2 |
| Nonwhites | 63.2 | 70.1 |

Sources: *Manpower Research and Training, Report of the Secretary of Labor, March 1965; 1966 Report of the Secretary of Labor on Manpower Research and Training Under the Manpower Development and Training Act of 1962.*

and earnings are all lower for Negro trainees. At the time of the follow-up interviews, only 61 per cent of the Negroes had jobs compared with 77 per cent of the other trainees. Negro trainees earned $11 per week less than others, largely in low-paying service occupations. However, there is also evidence of *greater benefits* to Negro trainees compared with whites. The post-training weekly earnings of Negroes were on the average, $13 higher than earnings on pretraining jobs, whereas for whites the differential was only \$4.[6]

Among the 116 Negroes in our West Virginia evaluation, 92 per cent of the trainees were employed after the training period compared with only 40 per cent of the nontrainees.[7] On the other hand, the employment ratio of white trainees was only 8 percentage points above that of white nontrainees. However, these results are far from conclusive because the Negroes selected for training were more advantaged, with respect to such characteristics as age and education, than the average Negro nontrainee. Thus the nontrainees cannot be construed as as a "pure" control group. Unfortunately the size of the initial sample precluded analysis within common age and education cells.

In a study of training programs for Milwaukee welfare recipients, it was found that the average gain in weekly earnings per trainee ranged from \$7 over pretraining earnings after "Operation Alphabet" to \$36 as a result of a course for custodial work. Most of the workers enrolled in these programs were Negroes. The trainees' increase in earnings stemmed primarily from a longer tenure in employment for trainees as compared with nontrainees during the post-training period.[8]

When the welfare trainees were compared with a control group of nontrainee welfare recipients, an effort was made to match trainees and nontrainees with common age, education, race, previous welfare experience, and other characteristics. It was found that in 30 of the 57 matched pairs, trainees were "off welfare" more than nontrainees in a comparable post-training period. In 25 of the pairs, the matched workers had a similar welfare experience, and in only 2 matched pairs were the nontrainees "off welfare" more than the trainees.[9] Thus here, too, training proved to be a significant force for advancing the welfare of a disadvantaged group relative to similar disadvantaged workers who had no training.

The results for other trainees are mixed. In one of our studies it was found that older workers gained after their training, but that they were not able to gain as much from their training as were younger workers. It is seen in Table 3 that in all age categories those who completed their training enjoyed a more favorable employment experience after training than the comparable

TABLE 3. PERCENTAGE OF TIME EMPLOYED DURING EIGHTEEN MONTHS AFTER RETRAINING, BY AGE AND TRAINING STATUS

| Age (Years) | Training Status | 0–25 | 26–50 | 51–75 | 76–100 | Total Number | Total Per cent |
|---|---|---|---|---|---|---|---|
| | | Percentage of Trainees | | | | | |
| 0–21 | Completes | 11.4 | 20.0 | 12.8 | 55.7 | 70 | 100 |
| | Drop-outs | 20.7 | 20.7 | 13.8 | 44.8 | 29 | 100 |
| | Rejects | 33.3 | 33.3 | 16.7 | 16.7 | 18 | 100 |
| | Did not report | 58.3 | 8.3 | 8.3 | 25.0 | 12 | 100 |
| | Nonapplicants | 33.3 | 14.6 | 18.8 | 33.3 | 48 | 100 |
| 22–34 | Completes | 13.7 | 10.9 | 13.7 | 61.6 | 211 | 100 |
| | Drop-outs | 22.5 | 11.2 | 13.8 | 52.5 | 80 | 100 |
| | Rejects | 33.3 | 22.2 | 25.9 | 18.5 | 27 | 100 |
| | Did not report | 26.1 | 21.7 | 26.1 | 26.1 | 23 | 100 |
| | Nonapplicants | 35.1 | 22.5 | 11.7 | 30.6 | 111 | 100 |
| 35–44 | Completes | 22.3 | 9.8 | 10.7 | 57.1 | 112 | 100 |
| | Drop-outs | 20.8 | 18.9 | 11.3 | 49.0 | 53 | 100 |
| | Rejects | 51.6 | 12.9 | 16.1 | 19.4 | 31 | 100 |
| | Did not report | 33.3 | 6.7 | 6.7 | 53.3 | 15 | 100 |
| | Nonapplicants | 46.2 | 12.5 | 12.5 | 28.8 | 104 | 100 |
| 45+ | Completes | 28.3 | 13.3 | 16.7 | 41.7 | 60 | 100 |
| | Drop-outs | 44.4 | 11.1 | 3.7 | 40.7 | 27 | 100 |
| | Rejects | 53.8 | 10.2 | 12.8 | 23.1 | 39 | 100 |
| | Did not report | 50.0 | 33.3 | — | 16.7 | 6 | 100 |
| | Nonapplicants | 52.0 | 11.8 | 10.2 | 26.0 | 127 | 100 |

*Percentage of Time Employed* is the overall heading spanning columns 0–25, 26–50, 51–75, 76–100, and Total.

Source: Ford Foundation Retraining Project in West Virginia, 1962–1964.

groups of nontrainees. Among workers 45 years of age and over, 41.7 per cent of the "Completes" were employed more than three-fourths of the time during the eighteen-month post-training period, as compared with only 23 per cent of the "Rejects" and 26 per cent of the "NonApplicants." But the differences in the corresponding percentages for trainees and nontrainees were considerably greater in the younger age categories.

The data also indicate that older trainees were not so continuously employed as younger trainees. For example, over 60 per cent of the trainees in the 22–34 age category were employed more than three-fourths of the time after their training. And even those who were under 21, the problem children of the labor market, had a better post-training record than the older trainees.

If training cannot fully remove the disadvantages of older trainees in the job market relative to younger trainees, the data *do* reveal that retraining can provide older workers with an advantage over younger nontrainees. The young workers in all age categories who failed to apply for training experienced shorter periods of employment than the 45-year-olds who completed a training course.

In summing up the position of the disadvantaged, it can be said that their employment and earnings after retraining are not as favorable as the employment and earnings of other trainees; but the labor-market position of the disadvantaged is considerably enhanced by their retraining, as compared with their own pretraining experience and as compared with disadvantaged workers who have not been retrained.

This divergent result gives special emphasis to the need for careful benefit-cost analyses of retraining programs for the disadvantaged worker. Since the labor-market rehabilitation of the disadvantaged often requires basic and remedial education as well as occupational training, the costs incurred may be unusually high; and given their less-favorable post-training experience compared with nondisadvantaged trainees, one might conclude that our retraining dollars would best be invested elsewhere. However, if it is true that retraining can do more to *improve* the position of the disadvantaged worker relative to his own pretraining status than it can do for other workers, retraining for disadvantaged workers may be the soundest economic investment of all.

Finally, it should be noted that noneconomic considerations are especially important in the evaluation of retraining programs for the disadvantaged. Regardless of the level of economic returns, one might wish to give the highest social priority to programs which aid in the reduction of squalor and all of its attendant social ills.

## On-the-Job Training

The effectiveness of the new retraining programs for unemployed and low-income workers must be appraised in relationship to the total educational system and to on-the-job training (OJT). In spite of recent legislation it will continue to be true that most general knowledge will have been absorbed by the worker in the traditional system of public education; and most specific occupational skills will be acquired on the job. This procedure has much to commend it in view of the constantly changing skill requirements of a dynamic economy. The greater the emphasis on skill acquisition on the job, the more general can be the education and training provided through public institutions.

On-the-job training has many advantages; and these have undoubtedly stimulated the expansion of OJT programs under MDTA in the past year, as well as the plans for expansion in the future. After a very slow start, the number of workers in OJT programs more than doubled between 1964 and 1965. Although the guidelines are still in process of formation. it is apparently planned that on-the-job training will become relatively more important, in terms of numbers of trainees, than institutional training in the total MDTA effort. The proposed expansion is undoubtedly influenced by the following considerations.

1. The overall goals set for the training and retraining of unemployed and underemployed workers can be met much more readily if training on the job is widely used as a supplement to institutional training in the vocational schools.

2. Training on the job is traditionally the most common means by which specific occupational skills have been acquired in American industry. One would expect employers to welcome so familiar a procedure.

3. The government's expenditures per trainee in OJT projects are substantially below costs in comparable MDTA institutional training programs.

4. The equipment used in OJT training is usually more expensive, more up-to-date, and better adapted to changing tech-

nology than the equipment found in most vocational education facilities.

5. The job placement ratio of OJT graduates is substantially higher than that of MDTA institutional trainees because most employers hire their own OJT trainees before, during, or after their training.

6. These placement results enhance the motivation of workers in entering the training course and in completing their training, relative to institutional trainees.

It has been noted that in spite of these advantages the MDTA's on-the-job training projects have lagged because, unlike the situation in institutional training, a whole new system of procedures and standards had to be developed for OJT. Staff limitations hindered not only the establishment of these procedures, but also the necessary promotional technical assistance. Moreover, unions have been concerned about the possible wage effects of such training and the possible reduction of employment and advancement opportunities for their own members.[10]

The reasons for the delay in establishing OJT programs in the early stages of MDTA are relevant for the prospects of future expansion. Aside from the general and administrative factors influencing the rate of introduction of OJT projects, the decisions of private employers must be accorded the central and most crucial role. To a much greater extent than in institutional training, the successful growth of MDTA's on-the-job projects will depend upon employers' evaluations of the potential costs and benefits of such projects.

Light can be cast on the past problems as well as the future potentialities of federal OJT programs through surveys of employer attitudes toward governmental activity in this field. In addition to impressions gained from the public statements of managerial officials, useful insights are provided by three surveys of employer opinion, conducted as part of the University of Wisconsin's overall evaluation of retraining and vocational education. The first interview survey of 132 employers was carried out in 1962–1963 primarily among employers in West Virginia who had hired trainees of programs established under the Area Redevelopment Act and state retraining legislation.[11] The second, a nationwide mail questionnaire survey, was conducted in 1964 with the cooperation of the American Society of Training Directors (ASTD). Responses were received from 1048 members of the ASTD.[12] In the third survey, a mail questionnaire was sent to over 1000 employers in apprenticeable trades in Wisconsin in order to determine their attitudes toward the apprenticeship form of OJT. Useable responses were returned by 457 employers.[13] Some of the major conclusions derived from these surveys are summarized briefly below:

1. The attitudes of employers toward government-subsidized OJT are influenced by their views on government intervention in general on behalf of the unemployed.

2. A somewhat larger group of employers prefer government-aided institutional training as compared to those who prefer subsidized OJT. However, the ratio of OJT:institutional preferences greatly exceeds the ratio of OJT:institutional projects currently included in the total MDTA program.

3. Employers who have had experience in hiring retrained workers and who are aware of government-sponsored programs in their areas are more favorably disposed toward government-sponsored training in general, and toward OJT projects in particular, than are those who have not hired trainees and who are unaware of training programs.

4. The preference for government-subsidized OJT increases with the size of the responding firm.

5. Within industry classifications, the greatest relative employer interest in subsidized OJT is found in hospitals and other service establishments. Many trade establishments and local government units also prefer OJT, but even more of the respondents in these latter two categories give first preference to government-sponsored courses in the vocational schools.

6. The advantages of OJT indicated by employers include (in order of importance): (a) greater company control over the training course; (b) training for specific company jobs; (c) use of up-to-date equipment; and (d) immediate placement of trainees.

The surveys encourage the view that employers will be willing —under appropriate economic circumstances—to expand government subsidized OJT programs on their premises. But problems arise in the relationship of the planned expansion of OJT to the Manpower Administrator's other goal of expanding retraining for the disadvantaged. If MDTA selection has generally tended to favor the cream of the unemployed in the past, the OJT component of MDTA has taken the cream of the cream. Because the employer plays a greater role in the selection process of OJT programs, relatively small proportions of disadvantaged workers (relative to MDTA institutional courses) have been included. In addition to their reluctance to depart from their customary hiring standards, employers are especially loath to absorb workers in whom a very substantial training investment will be required. Given the mobility of American labor, a sizeable private investment in the retraining of disadvantaged workers may be lost through turnover.

Three possible approaches may be adopted to ease these problems. First, the government subsidies, through wage payments during training or through tax credits or some combination of the two, could be increased to cover the employer's risk of later loss of the trainee. Second, the subsidies could be arranged on a sliding scale based on the characteristics and qualifications of the trainee. That is, employers would be especially compensated for absorbing the disadvantaged. Third, financial procedures could be established so that large companies (with extensive training staff and facilities) would have incentive to train workers for small companies, and regional or industrywide subsidies could be established in order to safeguard individual companies against loss of the trainee through turnover. Variants of these procedures have been adopted in other countries, and precedents are beginning to emerge here.

Although detailed benefit-cost analyses of the MDTA OJT programs—none of which now exist to my knowledge—would probably show an initially favorable result, a lengthy period of follow-up would be required for a full assessment of their value relative to institutional training.

### Retraining and Relocation

A number of significant questions arise in the relationship between retraining programs and schemes to relocate workers through travel allowances and other forms of assistance. Does the retraining of a worker encourage his geographic mobility or discourage it? Is relocation a substitute for retraining or a complement to it? What are the benefits and costs of retraining and relocation assistance for different groups of workers, occupations, and areas?

These questions have recently become more critical for the United States. As a result of the 1963 Amendments to the MDTA, the Department of Labor conducted 16 pilot projects in 1965 providing relocation assistance to unemployed workers who had limited labor-market prospects in their own areas. In all, only 1200 workers and their families were helped to move, but the number of projects is being expanded this year, and there are proposals to incorporate a regular program of relocation allowances in manpower measures currently before Congress. Schemes of relocation assistance have existed in a number of European countries for some time.

There is some evidence that retraining and relocation are substitutes for each other in the preference scale of many workers; and yet it is found that retraining and relocation often complement each other, resulting in increased earnings for those who engage in both. Our West Virginia surveys of retraining and geographic mobility were conducted prior to the inception of the relocation demonstration projects, and, as usual, the comparative analysis is hampered by limitations of sample size. Analysis of the training-mobility nexus is still under way but some rough, tentative patterns seem to be emerging.[14]

For many workers in a depressed area outmigration is often seen as a substitute for retraining. Frequently, retraining is taken only as a last desperate resort by workers who are determined to find employment in their home area, and mobility is a last desperate resort for trainees who cannot find local work. Since training is frequently viewed by the worker as a means to local employment, it is found that training does not necessarily encourage mobility.

In all age and education categories of the trainees, continued difficulties in the labor market after their training were associated with their eventual outmigration. On the average, those who later moved had lower earnings *prior* to their move than those who stayed. In fact, contrary to the general advantage in the earnings of trainees over nontrainees in the West Virginia surveys, those trainees who eventually migrated had lower earnings before they moved than the nontrainees. This was especially true for the older and less-educated trainees, but the finding occurs in all age-education categories.

The fact that the move was a rational one (in gross financial terms) is seen in the improvement in earnings of the mobile trainees *after* their move relative to the earnings of nonmobile West Virginia trainees. Between the time of their geographic move and the summer of 1964 (our final follow-up survey), the mobile trainees gained substantially in earnings relative to the nonmobile nontrainees, even though the latter group had higher earnings before the mobility occurred. Thus, mobility may be an act of desperation, stemming from unemployment and low income; but once forced to move, workers find that their retraining serves them well in the new area.

In appraising the experience under the relocation assistance scheme, it should be noted that a very substantial movement out of depressed areas occurs in any case, and most of this movement is "rational" from the standpoints of employment security and earnings. But our West Virginia surveys indicate that there is still much "irrational" mobility among unemployed trainees and nontrainees. By directing workers to areas and firms with more bouyant employment opportunities, the relocation scheme might make a major contribution. Inducing improvements in the *direction* of migration may be more important than inducing an increase in the *amount* of migration.

The demonstration relocation projects have not yet spawned sufficient data to permit a thorough follow-up evaluation. Qualitative appraisals[15] confirm some of the accepted doctrine on geographic mobility and offer a few surprises. Although financial aid for travel and moving has induced some movement that would not have occurred otherwise, it was often not the most important factor. It was found that an opportunity for the worker to appraise the job environment and for his wife to appraise the community environment might be more crucial to successful transfer. Counseling and other assistance provided in the new locale for adjustment of the worker to his new job and for adjustment of his family to the new community were also found to be important.

Most important of all, however, is the attractiveness and the security of the new job relative to prospects in the worker's home area. Similar conclusions have been reached in appraisals of relocation provisions under private industrial or union-management auspices, especially those studies conducted in connection with the Armour Automation Committee.

The labor-market influences on relocation raise the most serious questions concerning the allowance system and render benefit-cost analyses desirable in periods of changing regional and national employment conditions. Most of the initial 1200 relocatees in the demonstration projects were young (40 per cent under 25), and many, if not most of them, probably could be expected to move from a depressed area to an expanding area in any case—with or without assistance. Even many older workers may feel forced to move under such circumstances. In South Bend at a time of very high unemployment following the Studebaker shutdown approximately 150 workers, out of almost 3000 over 50 years of age who had been laid off, migrated to other areas. This was prior to the inception of the scheme of government assistance. By the time the relocation demonstration project started in 1965, employment conditions in South Bend had greatly improved and of the remaining older workers, clearly less mobile, only 2 of the over 700 considered to be eligible were relocated under the project.

Similar problems of inducing relocation have occurred in other areas as a result of the pick-up in national and local employment in 1965. In two of the projects, over 50 per cent of the relocatees returned home, partly because of improvements in employment conditions. This compares with an average of 20 per cent who returned in other projects, the same percentage as in European experience.[16] Under these circumstances, when other relevant variables are changing at the same time that retraining and relocation allowances are being provided, it is difficult to evaluate the impact of the relocation investment on the quantity of movement, its rationality, or its economic return.

Two additional questions remain in relating relocation policies to retraining and other labor-market policies. From the standpoint of the receiving area, at what point should the induced immigration of distant workers be initiated or discontinued while thousands of hard-core, disadvantaged workers may remain unemployed amid the city's affluence? The project designed to move workers, some trained and some untrained, from northern Wisconsin and northern Michigan into Milwaukee is a case in point. When the migrants are almost all white and the local unemployed are almost all Negro, how should this fact affect the decision?

From the standpoint of the supply area, when is fully fledged vocational training necessary or desirable for potential migrants to areas of tight labor demand? Persons connected with one southern retraining-relocation project were convinced that literacy training and some counseling alone would have sufficed for job placement after relocation to cities of low unemployment.

Clearly, detailed data on the characteristics of the workers involved and the labor supply and demand situations in both supply and receiving areas would be required for a truly judicial answer to these questions. Such data, if sought, are seldom forthcoming.

## Conclusions

The new government retraining programs for the unemployed have now been accepted, largely on faith, as an integral part of our economic way of life. Fortunately, the few detailed evaluations made of these programs indicate that they are effective in improving the economic status of the trainees and have a high rate of return. But much more extensive and sophisticated benefit-cost analyses will be required to determine whether the new programs are significant as a factor in reducing national unemployment and poverty and to determine whether they are making a significant contribution to the easing of skill shortages or to the reduction of inflationary pressures.

We can say even less about the economic benefits and costs of relocation allowances. Presumably they aid the individual, but the extent of their usefulness as a social investment still remains to be established.

An even more critical need of sophisticated economic analysis arises when we are forced to make choices with regard to these and related policies. For example, we may wish to expand training for the disadvantaged and also increase the number of OJT projects. Are these objectives now compatible, and, if not, can they be made compatible? Hopefully, economic analyses can also help us to determine when, where, and with whom to start and stop government aid to general education, vocational education, literacy training, remedial education, vocational retraining, counseling, and relocation. They might also tell us when the whole package or some combination of its components is appropriate to meet some specifically defined social goals.

## NOTES

1. *1966 Report of the Secretary of Labor on Manpower Research and Training Under the Manpower Development and Training Act of 1962,* U.S. Department of Labor, March, 1966, pp. 18–19.

2. *Ibid.,* p. 54.

3. *Idem.*

4. A number of these studies have been supported by a grant from the Ford Foundation to the University of Wisconsin. The methodology of the major studies, those in West Virginia, was described in the author's earlier paper in this series, "Retraining: An Evaluation of Gains and Costs," in Arthur M. Ross, editor, *Employment Policy and the Labor Market* (Berkeley: University of California Press, 1965). See also, Gerald G. Somers and Ernst Stromsdorfer, "A Benefit-Cost Analysis of Manpower Retraining," *Proceedings of the Industrial Relations Research Association,* December 1964; Glen C. Cain and Ernst Stromsdorfer, "An Economic Evaluation of the Government Retraining of the Unemployed in West Virginia," in Gerald G. Somers, editor, *Retraining the Unemployed,* to be published by the University of Wisconsin Press; Michael E. Borus, "The Economic Effectiveness of Retraining the Unemployed," *Yale Economic Essays,* 1964; and David A. Page, "Retraining Under the Manpower Development Act: A Cost-Benefit Analysis," Studies of Government Finance, Reprint 86 (Washington, D.C.: Brookings Institution, 1964).

5. *1966 Report of the Secretary of Labor . . . ,* p. 181.

6. *Ibid.,* p. 55–56.

7. Glen Cain and Gerald Somers, "Retraining the Disadvantaged Worker," Conference on Research in Vocational and Technical Education, University of Wisconsin, June 10, 1966, p. 8.

8. *Ibid.,* p. 15.

9. *Ibid.,* p. 17.

10. *Manpower Report of the President,* March, 1965, p. 129.

11. Reported in detail in Harold A. Gibbard and Gerald G. Somers, "Government Retraining of the Unemployed in West Virginia," in Somers,

editor, *op. cit.* A few employers who had hired trainees in depressed areas of Tennessee and Michigan were also included in this survey. The results of this survey and the two surveys listed below are summarized in *Hearings before the Subcommittee on Employment and Manpower of the Committee on Labor and Public Welfare,* U.S. Senate, September, 13, 1965.

12. Reported in detail in Edward C. Koziara, *Employer Views and Evaluations of Government Retraining Programs* (unpublished Ph.D. dissertation, University of Wisconsin, 1965).

13. Reported in detail in G. Soundara Rajan, *A Study of the Registered Apprenticeship Program in Wisconsin* (unpublished Ph.D. dissertation, University of Wisconsin, 1965).

14. The analyses are currently being conducted at the University of Wisconsin with the assistance of Graeme McKechnie. See his forthcoming Ph.D. dissertation, *Retraining and Geographic Mobility: An Evaluation.*

15. *1966 Report of the Secretary of Labor* . . . , pp. 45–50.

16. *Ibid.,* p. 48.

# Discussion

## BY MELVIN ROTHBAUM

The main thesis of Professor Somers' paper—"that the establishment of the appropriate relationship between these [retraining and relocation] manpower policies requires a detailed research evaluation of each"—can be readily accepted. And much of our limited stock of knowledge in this area we owe to Professor Somers and his colleagues at the University of Wisconsin. As to the paper itself, there are striking differences in both the scope and concreteness of his review and analysis between programs that have been subject to such research evaluation and those that have not. The extensive and multi-faceted commentary on institutional training and the richness and insights of the preliminary research on relocation contrast sharply with the generality of the OJT section. Thus the content of the paper impressively supports its own main thesis.

### Evaluation of Retraining Programs

Although the number of cost-benefit studies is limited, they consistently show large returns to individuals in institutional training programs. (Somers hazards a guess that at least the initial results would be favorable also for OJT, presumably in part because of the lower costs and higher placement rates in these programs.) While the information on disadvantaged groups appears to be mainly on the benefit rather than on the cost side, it also suggests large gains to individuals from retraining as compared to their own previous experience and to the experience of nontrainees with similar characteristics.

The analysis of the disadvantaged provides emphatic support for Somers' point about the need for control groups in the research evaluations. Without this, no meaningful standard exists by which to measure benefits, and the simple application of placement rates and post-training earnings among different groups may be seriously misleading. The rapid introduction of studies which utilize control groups in the analysis of retraining benefits appears to be the minimum requirement for intelligent policy-making. The conclusive demonstration of substantial benefits is a prerequisite even for equity (or what Somers has called non-economic) decisions—those cases in which the relation of costs to benefits is not controlling because of overriding social priorities. But the more comprehensive study of both costs and benefits clearly would be desirable. Sound information on relative costs and benefits can permit a more efficient choice among alternative programs, whether or not there is an equity constraint in the decision. And perhaps as important as the economic result, the attempt to identify economically efficient programs yields the kind of detailed information that can give us a better understanding of the needs and prospects of various trainee groups as well as of the strengths and weaknesses of alternative institutional arrangements to meet these training needs.

While there have already been exciting results in the study of individual gains from retraining, the problem of social gains remains murky. The rise in productivity levels associated with retraining and any contribution that may be made to the solution of occupational shortages appear to be the most clearcut social advantages. On the other hand, some of the gains associated with retraining as a job-creating device are open to question. Even in the unlikely case in which training expenditures were to rise to the point where they were no longer a minor budgetary item, the fact that they (like any other budget expenditure) augment demand may not be a very sound reason for calling them job-creating. The fiscal policy decisions on expansion or contraction of demand involve changes in budget deficits or surpluses and the overall tax and expenditure policies that will achieve the desired results. The allocation to specific tax and expenditure items reflects current Congressional and Presidential views about program priorities. For example, a decision to maintain the budget at approximately the same level may involve an increase in training expenditures that is offset by an appropriations cut elsewhere or vice versa. It is difficult to see why the training expenditures should be singled out as job-creating or job-destroying under these circumstances.

Creating jobs by filling a previously "unfillable" job opening by a newly qualified unemployed man appears to have more merit. The assumption here is that current output is limited by the scarcity of particular types of labor not available in the pool of unemployed. The final result is subject to the same caveat that Somers later applies to shortage occupations. Since private employers are probably increasing their expenditures in such a period, the government may simply be replacing training that would have been generated privately or redirecting the flow of trainees occupationally or geographically from that which would have taken place.

The impact of training on the reduction of poverty may depend on which of several views of the labor market are correct. If the unemployed are viewed as a single queue, then all those who are leapfrogged by a newly trained worker do suffer a relative decline in employment qualifications and, presumably, in potential employment opportunities. However, if the unemployed actually make up many queues, then training may shift an individual from an unskilled to a skilled queue (e.g., training him to be an auto mechanic). Under these circumstances, employment opportunities for those in the unskilled (poverty) queue may rise. Perhaps the most realistic view is to recognize both the substitution possibilities inherent in the single queue and the obstacles to cross-occupational mobility inherent in the multiple queues. In such a model, one might consider each individual as having a position on several queues. The indirect effect of training given to others would involve both gains and losses. The impact would be more immediate for the queue in which the individual was currently qualified and more potential for queues in which he had some expectations of becoming qualified through admission to training programs.

## On-the-Job Training and the Disadvantaged

Current emphasis in government training programs is on expanding the relative importance of OJT programs as compared to institutional training. Somers has summarized the arguments in favor of such a change, including tradition, lower costs, better equipment, and easier placement. The survey results cited in the paper begin to give us a better idea of employer reactions to such an expansion and the degree of support that might be expected. Employers evidently fear government intervention in the training process, and even employers in those industries with the greatest relative interest in subsidized OJT programs show a preference for institutional training. On the other hand, a substantial pool of employers express interest in OJT, the interest rising with size of firm and familiarity with government programs.

In general, Somers concurs with the increasing emphasis on OJT as part of a rational division of labor: the public education system providing general education while the private sector provides the specific training needed to adapt the labor force to continually changing skill requirements. The line between the two is fuzzy, however, and specific circumstances will undoubtedly dictate breaching the general rule in many cases. Thurow's view of the training situation as a continuum between completely general and completely specific training investments is perhaps the most useful to employ here. His dynamic model indicates the likelihood of more general training by private employers than one would at first expect, because various institutional factors tend to reduce mobility and thus reduce training investment losses through turnover. Moreover, the development of internal labor markets through patterns of promotion from within the plant increases the need for private training expenditures. While these larger training expenditures appear desirable, from a broader viewpoint the economy might be better off if mobility were greater, private training expenditures lower, and the general training shifted to the public sector. In addition, the growth of internal labor markets may have adverse effects on disadvantaged workers as employers apply more rigorous hiring standards to low-skilled jobs because they view them as the first step in a career pattern.

If one accepts the proposition that more OJT is desirable, then there appear to be several possible alternatives. Additional private training could be encouraged in general through changes in the tax system, or specific subsidies could be used to encourage specific training efforts (e.g., in shortage occupations), or these incentives could be linked to the training of specific groups of people (e.g., the disadvantaged).

General tax incentives to encourage training may create a serious windfall problem. Much of the tax revenue loss may involve training already being done or that would have been done in the absence of the incentives. While safeguards might be built into the program to limit tax benefits to additional training efforts, the ingenuity of private parties to reap the benefits of tax incentives at minimum cost to themselves is impressive. Stieber's comments on British experience indicate the distinct possibility that much of the gain might be an accounting rather than a real phenomenon. In addition, European experience warns against the possibilities of abuse, particularly the establishment of so-called training programs that actually are geared more to production than learning.

These problems may be somewhat more manageable when subsidies are related to specific training programs. As noted earlier, however, these are precisely the shortage situations in which one would expect the market mechanism to generate increased private training expenditures. As Thurow suggests, an increase in the amount of training might perhaps best be achieved by a guarantee of continuing high employment. On the other hand, it might well be profitable for the government to invest in subsidies to help private companies reorganize the pattern of training more effectively and to spread risks. Somers' suggestions on the use of large employers, or multi-employer arrangements, would move in this direction.

By far the most difficult problem arises when one adds the requirement that the training should be directed mainly toward disadvantaged individuals. European experience indicates some tendency for employers to avoid government efforts to direct training programs toward the unemployed, particularly those recruited through the public employment service. Directing a training program toward the disadvantaged unemployed would enhance this problem. The survey results cited in the paper and Somers' own conclusions support this view.

The question, then, is whether OJT, with its extensive area of employer control over the program, is compatible with the emphasis on training the disadvantaged. To overcome the reluctance of employers, both Somers and Thurow suggest the possibility of using sliding-scale subsidies, the amount varying inversely with the qualifications of the trainees. Presumably there is some level of subsidy that will induce employers to train people from the back of the queue, i.e., to apply hiring standards substantially below those required by current market conditions. Whether this will involve very high costs in the form of subsidies not justified by differential training costs in order to overcome existing employer preferences, it is impossible to say. In part this may depend on whether noneconomic factors can be brought to bear on employer decisions in the form of convincing them to make a contribution to the solution of an important social problem. In any case, it should be possible to experiment with various ways to test the employer's demand curve for disadvantaged workers.

On the other hand, rather than treating training costs as a whole and applying subsidies that are related inversely to trainee qualifications, it might be useful to specify the special needs of disadvantaged workers and the training costs associated with those needs. Such an approach might have several advantages: (1) It would require a fairly precise definition of and agreement on the deficiencies involved. Thus, it might more easily permit a shift from a very general negative attitude toward the disadvantaged to a more realistic and specific problem-solving approach. (2) It might allow more intelligent choices between public and private programs for removing deficiencies. In some cases, institutional work prior to OJT might be desirable, or there might be institutional classes simultaneously with OJT; or the employer might provide the classes as part of his obligation under the OJT contract, the cost of the classes and of released time from the regular training program being picked up as a specific item under the subsidy.

While there are various possibilities for making the OJT program compatible with a major orientation toward the disadvantaged, the difficulties involved in framing such alternatives suggest that one should not be dogmatic about de-emphasizing institutional training in favor of OJT. Enrollment figures for 1965 indicate that institutional programs have enrolled a higher percentage of disadvantaged trainees than OJT programs, whether one measures disadvantage in terms of race, previous unemployment, duration of unemployment, educational levels, or age. These differences may perhaps narrow in the coming year with the expansion and redirection of OJT programs. But there is no doubt that the government's ability to influence the choice of trainees is greater under institutional programs, and foreign experience shows a similar tendency for institutional programs to succeed more easily in directing training toward disadvantaged groups.

In summary, there appears to be no neat way of dividing the functions of public educational systems and private training on the basis of general education and specific skill training, though the distinction between the two is a reasonable first approximation. The division will be determined partly by the economics of training in the private sector, and partly by the public goals of the training programs in terms of the amount of training desired, the occupations involved, and the particular groups to which it is directed. The public programs, in turn, will be affected by a complex set of variables including employer receptivity, trainee preferences, training costs, the quality of training in terms of the experience and teaching skills of the instructors, and the types of equipment available. A variety of experimental approaches, accompanied by careful evaluation, will be required in order to determine the training approaches that best fit the diverse circumstances and goals in the current labor market.

## Relocation and Retraining

The preliminary findings on retraining and relocation are particularly illuminating, especially the various complementary and substitution relationships between the two programs. From the evidence presented so far, the substitution effect appears to be the most significant, i.e., individuals tend to look at the programs as alternatives. This issue is central to the question raised in the paper as to whether substantial training is necessary for potential migrants to labor-scarce areas. Unfortunately, the ability to place nontrainee migrants is not sufficient to answer the question. If training resulted in better and more secure jobs for the migrants, then relocation and retraining would be complementary. Whether the benefits of the training exceed the costs, including effects on the number of migrants returning to the point of origin, would appear to be a crucial point for future evaluation.

On the relocation program itself, Somers has quite properly emphasized the importance of spontaneous migration and the gains to be achieved from more rational migration as against simply increasing the amount of movement. It is clearly in the public interest to help individuals make the "best" move. But the fact that much migration is spontaneous and that many migrants do not rate financial aid high in their decision to move should not obscure the important relationship between such aid and the choice of "best" moves. Feasible alternatives are determined by individual preferences and ability to finance the move. And the extent to which public policy should seek to expand the feasible alternatives may be a difficult policy issue.

For example, should public policy be limited to helping an individual move to the nearest place where any job is available? To the nearest place where a job is not only available but the long-run outlook for employment is good? To the nearest place where superior wages, working conditions, and advancement possibilities are available for someone of his qualifications? To the place he most prefers provided that jobs are available? Obviously there is a range of public policy positions. At one end, public policy centers on moving the individual from the category of the unemployed to the employed; at the other end, the major public interest is in maximizing the employment prospects and satisfying the preferences of the individual.

Although it is trite to say that manpower programs should be flexible, it does appear that this advice applies especially strongly to relocation programs. While the furnishing of labor-market information to increase the rationality of migration should be a continuing activity throughout the nation, the use of loans and grants might well shift rapidly with changing labor-market conditions. Not the least difficult problem in deciding when to halt positive inducements to mobility is Somers' point about encouraging in-migration when there is a reservoir of unemployed in the receiving market. This only emphasizes that relocation and retraining may be substitutes not only from the point of view of the single individual but from a broader policy viewpoint. It also reinforces the view that the labor market should be viewed as consisting of many queues and that relocation raises many of the same problems in regard to poverty as retraining.

## Conclusion

Professor Somers has not only demonstrated the importance of careful evaluation of retraining and relocation programs and the insights that can be gleaned from the small number of studies currently available, but he has also raised enough pertinent questions for a decade of future research. His ultimate goals are wide-ranging and difficult to achieve, varying from the impact of retraining on unemployment and poverty to providing a mechanism for choosing among a large number of interrelated programs touching upon education and training. Fortunately, the more limited studies have considerable value in their own right, for our knowledge in this area is more likely to accumulate in small steps rather than burgeon forth in the form of any spectacular breakthrough. Perhaps the most important requirement at this point is methodological: that the growing number of independent studies be cumulative in their design and results. Current trends in research in education and training, systems analysis, and government planning and budgeting procedures give some indication that this may indeed happen.

# Discussion

## BY CURTIS ALLER

I have only a relatively few comments to make. First, I agree with Professor Somers' paper. He covers the literature, the analysis is unexceptional, and some important issues are highlighted. But let me add some more as grist for the mill.

Several commentators have already noted, and rightly so, that present training efforts are so small in scale relative to the need that they can only be described as experimental or demonstration efforts. We have very little analytical basis for determining the appropriate size or composition of the program. Instead, five-year planning, which is now in vogue for government agencies, tends to take place within the twin constraints of estimates of budgetary possibilities and capacity for growth of the training agencies. We need substitute for this primitive approach some sophisticated models of the economy that would give us guidelines to follow in terms of key variables, such as general unemployment, changes in the composition of output, demographic changes, geographic location of economic activity, migration of people, and so forth. Much of our present effort along these lines is fragmented and largely intuitive. Moreover, such models would have to allow for the unique variability of local needs, as Mr. Mangum has noted. I take it that something of this kind lay behind Somers' concluding remarks.

Questions as to the appropriate mix, i.e., institutional vs. OJT, are not sufficiently understood to enable us to arrive at any accurate decisions. Research in this area needs to be carried much further. We now have a variety of manpower tools, but we know very little about how to combine them most efficiently. Nor do we have much to go on if we try to decide whether a marginal shift in resources from training to labor-market information systems, or vice versa, would be desirable.

On these questions and others, I should note that we have

several things under way that should be helpful over the long run. We have recently added to our planning division a small cost-benefit unit. This has been supplemented by a contract with an outside firm possessing skills in this area. Our research division is also contemplating more contract-research support of model-building efforts, including the development of outside capacity to begin applying techniques such as systems analysis to manpower planning and policy formulation.

In the area of cost-benefit analysis, more narrowly conceived, I would agree with Professor Somers that one of our missing pieces is the absence of suitable control groups. Some progress can be noted. The Office of Economic Opportunity is presently contemplating a national study focusing on the youth segment. An effort will be made to study simultaneously the Neighborhood Youth Corps, Job Corps, and Special Youth Projects (MDTA) with a suitable control group.

But as a single indication of the difficulties faced in a situation in which we cannot control all the variables, let me remind you of one of our earlier studies which found that rejectees did better than the trainees. The answer to this puzzle became clear as we looked at the data further. An expanding economy pulled the rejectees into sweeper positions in auto plants at about $2.70 an hour, while trainees went into service jobs with a wage roughly half of this.

Now let me strike out into new directions and go beyond Somers' paper. We have found that, given the effort, virtually everyone can be made employable. Certainly it is important to discover more efficient means of doing this, but it remains true that concentrating on the best qualified of the unemployed yields a "better" return. Even so, we may still decide, as I hope we shall, that we should focus on the "underservicing unemployed" i.e., on those who have the least, simply because we believe this is the way to honor our commitment to the American dream.

But in pursuing this American dream, we should not think solely of isolated individuals in an amorphous mass we call Society or the Economy. There are a host of intermediaries to be considered if we are to maximize desirable changes in the operation of the relevant institutions. If this is the larger goal, then evaluation of training efforts that focuses only on the indi-

viduals flowing through a particular training program may be far
too narrow and, hence, incomplete. I suggest, therefore, that
Somers' outline at the beginning of his paper be extended further
by adding to his "For Society" section a new item (d) that would
specifically embrace this goal of institutional change.

To avoid misinterpretation, I should emphasize that, both as
an economist and a program administrator, I welcome and look
forward to the contributions of cost-benefit analysis. We do have
limited resources and face problems of choice. Hence, we need
measures of relative efficiency if we are to utilize these resources
wisely. But at the same time I want to emphasize that I am
also a revolutionist, albeit a modest and disciplined one, and
these objectives should somehow also enter into our calculus.

Perhaps I can make this plea more tangible by taking as a
recent example some contracts my office has recently developed
with Mexican-American groups in the Southwest and California.
Here we have a community largely outside the mainstream of
American life, presently restive and with an emerging leadership
largely untried and inexperienced. We can and do reach many
individuals with our present training programs, but these represent a small part of the total need. Moreover, we know that these
efforts, as well as the effect of other American institutions, may
produce for this group in another generation or two full participation in American life in every sense of the phrase. Given this,
we ask the question: Can we cut this time in half or more by
supporting a set of activities that will develop a leadership
group able to penetrate the whole community so that we are
working with the entire social fabric instead of autonomous individuals? If we can, it is well worth the costs and the risks.
Yet the effort may not fit either the formal statement of goals
now enshrined in legislation or the usual boundaries of cost-
benefit analysis. Should this kind of effort be of concern to those
now embarking on rigorous, formal evaluation studies? I think
they must, or we may end up with our hands tied and the larger
opportunities missed.

# CHAPTER 9

# Labor-Market Policy
# in Modern Society:
# With Particular Reference to
# Marginal Manpower Groups

## BY BERTIL OLSSON

The employment service has a tradition of more than fifty years
in most industrialized countries. It can also be said to be the
product of industrialism, with its more differentiated labor market, which created the need for employers as well as for employees to have an institution collecting information on vacancies as
well as on labor supply. In the same way industrialism created
the banking and credit market as a natural agent of the other
production factor, capital.

In the early stages, it was not taken for granted that the employment service should be a public institution, free of charge.
Private employment agencies, self-financing as well as profitable,
could very well have been imagined. In fact, such employment

services arose here and there in different countries. Many of them degenerated, however, and were especially criticized by the job seekers, who felt that these private employment services were interested only in the returns. They appeared to take little interest in giving "the right service" to the applicants. Growing demands were made for governmental control of the exchange of manpower, and it was not by mere chance that some of the first international agreements on labor legislation concerned the employment service. In this connection, the conventions and recommendations of the International Labor Organization should particularly be mentioned. The agreements took two forms: (1) exhortation to governments to start public employment services, and (2) recommendations to supervise and/or prohibit private employment services. In almost all countries developments since then have proceeded along these same lines, i.e., in setting up stronger public employment services and in reducing the importance of the private exchange field. In the United States, however, the private employment service retains a strong position, beside the public employment service.

If we consider the development of the employment service in industrialized countries from the historical point of view, much has happened during the last fifty years. Nowadays all industrialized countries have public employment services, more or less popular of course, but they are there, and it would be unthinkable for any industrialized countries to do without them. After some weakening during the Great Depression of the 1930's, when the employment service in many countries was left alone to solve the unemployment problem—a hopeless task—the public employment service has gradually become stronger and acquired increasing influence, especially during the last decade of full employment in the industrialized countries. And it is in a society of full employment that the employment service has best managed to justify its existence, not in the old unemployment society of the twenties and thirties.

Though the organization of the public employment service varies from country to country, some of the most important principles are similar. It is most important, for example, that the public employment services should be free of charge to both applicants and employers. They also have to be neutral. The so-called "golden rule" is also valid in most countries, i.e., "to the employer the best manpower available, and to the applicant the work best suited to him." Today we are, however, more inclined to replace "the work for which the applicant is best suited" with "the work he himself wants to have." But generally the type of work he desires and the type for which he is best suited fit quite well together.

The main activity of the employment service has been and still is the exchange itself, i.e., the establishing of contacts between the applicant and the employer. Today this is generally done with the help of modern methods of communication, it is true, but often without any means of influencing either the applicant or the employment opportunity. This can be called "mechanical exchange." It is important enough, and there is nothing disparaging or robot-like in the expression "mechanical." But it is an indication of the fact that the means and measures of the employment service up to now have been limited.

The question may be asked whether "mechanical exchange" is enough in today's society. It is very easy to give an answer. Mechanical exchange is not enough. Something more is required.

Today we have to have an *active labor-market policy*. It is quite natural to give the public employment service a more active part in carrying out the new labor-market policy. But we have to preserve what is good in the "mechanical" exchange— the traditions, the inherited contacts—we cannot do without them. However, the important thing is to supply the employment services with the many new and different instruments of labor-market policy. In short, the employment service should be made the *channel* through which the instruments of labor-market policy are made available to all those who are going to take advantage of them. That is why we say that we have to have *"an active employment service"* in the society of today. But it should be built upon the traditional basis of the public employment exchange.

## The Need for an Active Labor-Market Policy

Why do we need an active labor-market policy today? Up to now we have mainly explained the need for such a policy from the economic point of view. We also want to consider labor-market policy in a broader context as one of the tools of national economic policy. It contributes to creating full employment without jeopardizing the balance of the economy and the labor market. There is a risk in using only the general economic-political means—credit, money, and fiscal policy. This may cause a high demand for goods and services and consequently an excess demand for manpower, and this in its turn can result in continuous inflation. On the other hand, a more restrictive general economic policy with lower employment goals may cause unemployment. This cannot be accepted in a society which aims at full employment. If, however, selective labor-market policy means are used, we can avoid unemployment, while preserving economic balance.

Significant for a modern labor-market policy is that it can use *many different means*. These have to be selected in such a way as to influence the individual or groups of individuals without influencing the rest of the labor market (which the general means have a tendency to do). The means, or methods, have to be administered through an *organization*, which is widely spread all over the country, so that they reach all employees and employers. Furthermore, this organization has to act very fast, because imbalance on the labor market appears quickly, and the aim of labor-market policy is continuously to restore the balance. To summarize, the three characteristic features for an active and selective labor-market policy are as follows. The many different means have to be used selectively and not for the whole labor market. The organization has to *cover the whole country*—unemployment areas as well as inflation centers. *A fast way of acting* is necessary (within days or a few weeks), because the effect of the general economic-political means operate too slowly (sometimes requiring months or years).

Accordingly we want to consider labor-market policy as one of the components of economic policy. It can influence the margin of the total labor force, perhaps 2 to 3 per cent. Together with the other economic means it acts to achieve full employment and rapid growth under conditions of overall economic balance. From this point of view, it would seem natural for labor-market policy to be administered by the Ministry of Finance. But this is not the case in any country; generally it belongs to the

Ministry of Social Security or to the Ministry of Labor and Social Security.

This is a remnant from the time when labor-market policy mainly had socio-political aims. Much of this still remains today. But it seems completely unnecessary that there should be any conflict between labor-market policy and other areas of economic policy, as there is in many countries today, merely because the different activities are dealt with in difference ministries. In this case, there is a need for a change in organization.

The ideas discussed above are also the main characteristics of the international agreements on labor-market policy which have been adopted in recent years; namely, the recommendation on employment policy by the International Labor Organization and the convention on an active labor-market policy by the Organization for Economic Cooperation and Development (OECD), both adopted in 1964.

However, it is not only economic-political motives which justify an active labor-market policy and an active employment service. We also want to make the employment service an outstanding service organ. The individual in the labor market today asks for better and different services than he sought before. Although this makes the labor market more complex and more difficult to survey, it also provides more and better possibilities for the individual than ever. The increased opportunities for the individual to choose between different jobs means that he now requires a better labor-market service. Both employers and employees call for better service. Educational and vocational-guidance questions become more and more related to the labor market. The problems of vocational training of adults and their adaptability on the labor market become more important.

There are different ways to obtain more effective service. A great deal of service can of course be provided by private institutions. This takes place partly through consultative activity on the labor market, which is gaining ground. It is also conceivable that the different kinds of labor-market services could be administered by some other public institution, leaving the employment service responsible only for the "mechanical exchange service." But the most natural development seems to be for the public employment service to become responsible for the new labor-market policy. One of the main reasons for this is that the "mechanical exchange service" is after all the most important and decisive factor—the service organ which brings the applicant into contact with the opportunity to work. And in his field scarcely anybody can compete with the public employment service, which is often the last link in the whole chain of service functions. Moreover, if the same institution which administers labor-market policy also provides the service, it is the most convenient solution and the one which is most likely to prevent conflicting and ineffective administration. In addition, this solution offers the best guarantees that the social-political interests of labor-market policy (the interests of the individual) can be combined with the more general economic-political interests. In other words, macroeconomic and microeconomic considerations can be reconciled more effectively if they are handled by the same agency.

Consequently, the conclusion is that nowadays we need an active labor-market policy and an active employment service as a means of serving general economic-political objectives as well as giving better labor-market service. This policy also aims at using manpower resources in the best possible way in order to increase productivity and the rate of progress.

The keynotes here are first and foremost *adaptability* and *mobility*, and these are the things that the labor-market policy and the employment service have to promote.

Why then is adaptability on the labor market so necessary today, more necessary than before? There are many reasons.

In Sweden—and in many other industrialized countries in Western Europe—manpower resources are no longer growing rapidly. In the next two decades there will be very little increase in manpower resources, perhaps none at all. Indeed, if we take the shortening of working time into consideration and estimate manpower resources in terms of manhours, we can expect an actual decline in the future. There is perhaps no reason to worry about this. We can maintain full employment and a rapid rate of progress independent of the amount of manpower. We cannot, however, count upon achieving increased production and a better standard of living through an increase of manpower. If we want to have increased production, output per man has to be increased.

This can be done, e.g., by improved mobility and adaptability of the labor force. In fact, the adaptability questions become more important in a society of stagnant manpower resources, and there are good prospects for solving these problems with the help of an active labor-market policy.

In such a situation it is also of importance to increase the utilization of manpower resources that are now dormant—married women, who still do not participate in the labor force, the handicapped, and elderly people. These resources can be counted in hundreds of thousands (although the numbers will, of course, vary from country to country). Several different labor-market policy means have to be used if we are going to utilize these resources. Foreign workers also belong to these manpower resources. Through an active immigration policy, they can make a considerable contribution, and the employment service is of considerable importance to a well-ordered immigration policy.

The labor market changes faster under full employment conditions and with an expanding economy. Moreover, the changes are accelerated by technical development and foreign competition. We have to take the *rapid advance* of technology into consideration. We live in the age of automation. Technical progress nearly always leads to a saving in manpower resources at some point in the production or distribution process. But technical progress also creates new needs, increased possibilities for a better life, demands for new articles and services, and hence new demands for workers. The problem caused by technical evolution and automation is therefore not an unemployment problem. It is a problem of adaptability on the labor market, which has to be solved by all the methods of labor-market policy. If this is done in a proper way people can benefit from rapid technical progress.

Nowadays not only trade but also competition among countries is increasing. Small countries, like Sweden and some other European countries, are very dependent on foreign trade in order to maintain a high standard of living and full employment. They have a so-called high foreign trade ratio—in Sweden it is 25 per cent of the national income. In the future we have to expect more intense competition on the international market. This will be reflected on the national labor market. Some products and some companies will perhaps not survive this competition. But we may also expect that some other products and companies will fare better, that they will be able to compete effectively on the international market and produce more. Consequently they will need *more* manpower. And so, for this reason, also, the same adaptability problems will arise. We must meet the increasing foreign competition not with duties and restrictions but with an active labor-market policy. This will counteract the disadvantages which can result from more liberal world trade. In fact, if we succeed in doing this the advantages of a more liberal exchange of goods between countries will be even greater.

The progress of technology and foreign competition frequently causes variations in labor productivity in the short as well as the long run. These variations are unavoidable if we want to have full employment and rapid progress. But these structural changes in commercial and industrial life can be facilitated and accelerated by an active employment policy, which provides the practical means for helping workers who are hit by structural changes to shift to other jobs and other fields. These jobs are as a rule more profitable and offer better pay. Thus, in this way an active employment policy also contributes to speeding up progress. Indeed, it has been calculated that the gains from mobility are responsible for nearly half of the rate of economic growth.

## Measures of Labor Market Policy

The means and measures for the implementation of labor-market policy are many and various. They have to suit the different individuals on the labor market, and they have to be used selectively.

The following means and measures are at the disposal of labor market policy in Sweden:

I. Measures to stimulate geographical mobility
II. Measures to stimulate vocational mobility
III. Measures to influence the location of industries
IV. Measures to encourage the employment of the handicapped: rehabilitation activity

V. Measures to create new opportunities to work, during seasonal and economic fluctuations and within special regions

VI. Measures to suppress a too high demand for manpower

VII. Measures to give information, including vocational guidance and advice.

**Geographical mobility.** To stimulate geographical mobility of manpower is one of the best and most frequently used means of bringing about a balance between demand and supply. The best instrument in this case is *the employment service*, which gives information about vacancies and applicants within the whole country. In other words, the employment service acts not only as a leveling factor on the local labor market but also must coordinate the activities of the different employment service offices, in order to bring about a clearing of applicants and vacancies all over the country. It is also necessary for the employment offices of different countries to maintain contact with one another in order to organize the international clearing of vacancies and applicants. This already takes place within the so-called Nordic labor market in Scandinavia and within the European Economic Community. The labor force is, however, slow in adapting itself to the ever-changing needs of the market, and we still know too little about the causes underlying this slowness. Consequently research in this field must continue even more intensively than before.

In many European countries *economic stimulants* are being used in order to facilitate geographical mobility. In Sweden we have gone very far in this respect. A worker who moves from an area of manpower surplus and is a breadwinner can receive as much as 6000 Sw. kr. ($1200) in cash, if he moves to a permanent job outside the unemployment area. In connection with this the housing question is of importance, since the housing shortage is the major obstacle to mobility. In order to solve these housing problems, special arrangements have been made, e.g., houses are being built especially for workers moving to new jobs, and sometimes such workers are given priority on the waiting lists for new housing. The most important measure needed to stimulate mobility is, however, a better coordination of housing policy with employment policy. A housing problem of another kind arises in the depopulated areas, because of the difficulty faced by people who are moving out in selling their houses without any loss. In Sweden the labor-market authorities can intervene in such cases, helping the moving workers to sell their houses and subsidizing any financial loss.

All these means of stimulating geographical mobility are as a rule in the hands of the employment service offices. In some countries, including Sweden, support is given not only to un-employed persons but also to those who have jobs but could be more effective if they changed work and working place. In order to influence geographical mobility, the employment service has to know thoroughly the trends and details regarding va-cancies and applicants. There is, however, no reason for the public employment service to aim at a monopoly of job-place-ment activities. In some cases other methods, which are cheaper as well as more practical, can be used. But if the employment service is to accomplish its task as a labor-market institution, influencing mobility, it has to administer one-third or one-half of total placements. Probably only a small number of countries have reached such a high ratio today.

There are measures belonging to mobility policy that require a fast solution. For example, workers moving to a new area need a better reception and more assistance to get quickly adapted. This adaptability has to do not only with work and housing but also with many other things, like schooling possi-bilities for children, leisure-time activities, social conditions, and family activities. In Sweden, we have conferences and discus-sions with the employers, trade unions, local governments, and the employment services in order to facilitate this adaptation. In these cases the responsibility for carrying out different tasks is divided among the participants mentioned above, the em-ployment service serving as the uniting power. Adaptability can also be promoted by better and more reliable information about vacancies, which can best be distributed by the modern mass media, e.g., TV and radio.

**Vocational mobility.** As the labor market is continuously changing it becomes more and more important to support vocational mobility. In the future it will certainly be the rule that people have to change occupations twice or more during a lifetime. A *good general basic education* is of the greatest value for productivity and also for the possibility of changing jobs. Thus, much stress is put upon basic education in all industrialized countries. During the next generation it might become quite common for people to go to school up to the age of 20. Of course, the ideal is to educate them for the needs of the future. But few, if any, dare to anticipate the needs of the labor market forty to fifty years into the future or during a lifetime. This may be an impossible task even with the assistance of the most ingenious computers. What we are able to do today is to forecast the development of a few industries and attempt to find out whether they are likely to expand or decline with regard to manpower. In connection with education we naturally have to consider these forecasts in order to plan educational facilities as realistically as possible.

But it is equally important to have educational capacity enough for the training, retraining, and further training of adults, so that the labor force can continuously be occupationally adapted to the needs of the labor market. The most important aspect of the system is its flexibility. In many countries such retraining has started only recently. It has developed faster in Sweden than in any other country, and about 1 per cent of the labor force can now be enrolled during a year. The activity will be extended to provide for occupational retraining of 2 per cent of the labor force each year.

Thus the labor market requires two systems of training. One system has to provide basic education and is administered by the general school authorities. The other system is required for retraining purposes according to the various requirements of the labor market. It should preferably be administered by the labor-market authorities. The system has to be very flexible and provide opportunity for fast action. The element of time is often of decisive importance. For this reason there has to be a continuous receiving of trainees, age limits should not be established, and the system must always fit the individual. In order to make it possible for the trainee to concentrate on his courses, he should get benefits enough to avoid economic worries for himself and his family. As a rule, the benefits should not be much less than the wages paid on the open market in different occupations.

The labor-market authorities should administer the retraining or at least have a considerable influence on it, because vocational mobility very often has to be combined with efforts regarding the geographical mobility of the labor force or with location policies. The goal is to reach the best coordination of the tools of labor-market policy—and this coordination is most efficiently carried out by the labor-market authorities.

**Location policies.** Lately, policies have been developed in many countries to increase employment opportunities in areas with very high unemployment rates. There has been an active program to support the starting of industries in such areas. This support has been of different kinds. Thus there exist direct subsidies or loans on favorable conditions. Sometimes the local authorities supply the industries with buildings on a leasing basis. There are also efforts to facilitate vocational training for work in the new industries. In other cases the government adopts the policy of increasing the number of orders to industries in development areas. The most common approach is to carry out a large general action program for a whole area—regional development policy—with the purpose of improving the infrastructure of the area.

The different types of actions mentioned above can also be used in combination with each other. Their common goal is to create new opportunities for work in unemployment areas. This policy, however, is to some extent contrary to the policy of geographical mobility which aims at stimulating people to move out of the region.

Location policy is mainly aimed at solving the labor-market problems in a certain region and should be seen as one of the means of labor-market policy. However, location policy is not enough. As a rule, the other means of labor-market policy also have to be used, namely, geographical and vocational mobility and adaptation of the labor force.

**Rehabilitation.** In spite of vigorous efforts to create full employment by utilizing all the means of economic policy, there still remain a lot of individuals who are difficult to place on the labor market. These individuals, who have handicaps of different kinds, may not get jobs in the absence of special measures to assist them. We can estimate that their number is somewhat more than 5 per cent of the total labor force. However, they are an important marginal manpower resource. Many of them contribute more or less permanetly to the rate of unemployment in a country. Attacking this unemployment through instruments of general economic policy may lead to such a high level of aggregate demand that it will create a danger of permanent inflation. Thus, the labor-market policy of a country should include means that are especially adapted for this kind of manpower without having a marked influence on the rest of the economy. These measures are aimed at *rehabilitation.*

Among the different groups of handicapped who require rehabilitation, we may first consider *elderly manpower.* In many industrialized countries elderly workers, in spite of general full employment, have difficulties in getting suitable work because of a certain amount of age discrimination. In Sweden a special program covering elderly manpower has been adopted for the employment service. It includes the following points:

1. It is important that everyone who is working with personnel questions be familiar with population trends. Information about this should be widely distributed. The Labor Market Board should continuously observe "the elderly manpower on the labor market," make the necessary investigations, and disseminate the conclusions.

2. The Labor Market Board should give information about problems connected with elderly manpower in its own personnel education.

3. The County Labor Boards are requested to make an inventory of suitable employment for elderly people based on their own experience and also on that of employers. This is coordinated with a request from the Confederation of Swedish Employers to its members that they also make an inventory of suitable jobs and—as far as possible—give the jobs to elderly people. Moreover, emphasis is placed on the importance of the companies having their own internal employment service to take care of the placement of elderly personnel.

4. There should be the possibility of trial employment in cases where the staff manager has some doubt about the applicant because of his age. The possibility of part-time work should also be given special attention.

5. Examinations have shown that middle-aged or elderly people with little education are finding it more and more difficult to keep pace with rapid technical progress. Steps to increase vocational education can be expected to reduce future problems with elderly workers. A

further build-up of adult education for retraining and further training is also required.

6. Special courses for elderly people should be arranged. In connection with these courses one should especially examine the capacity of elderly people to absorb education.

7. The Labor Market Board must make every effort to abolish age limits in recruiting and education. Special attention should be paid to age requirements given in radio advertising or in vacancy lists supplied by employers to the Labor Market Board. The employment service officies should request explanation of the motives for age limits before the vacancies are included in official lists.

8. The entire employment service organization should be engaged in assisting elderly workers instead of having special employment service offices for their assistance.

9. A description of successful examples of placement is being made in a new edition and will be distributed to elderly workers.

10. Local employment boards with representatives of trade unions, employers, and municipal authorities should be attached to the employment service offices. Their task should be to discuss general problems connected with elderly workers and also to take the initiative in the placement of individual cases.

11. The employment service offices should continuously make an inventory of elderly applications. Cases with long unemployment periods —more than two months—should be the object of special attention. An obligation to report such cases will also be introduced.

12. Research is very important regarding the adaptation to work of elderly manpower. The Labor Market Board should initiate and stimulate such research in close cooperation with experts on labor physiology and medicine.

13. The Labor Market Board should make a request to the employer organizations that they urge their members not to stress the age of the applicants when hiring them. The Labor Market Board should also request the employee organizations to encourage their members to accept elderly people as fellow workers and to avoid age discrimination. The requests should be directed especially to staff managers and to people active in the trade unions.

14. The Labor Market Board and the national employer and employee organizations should appoint a central delegation with the aim of overseeing the elderly manpower situation and of making arrangements to facilitate placement of elderly people. The delegation should be the central authority for the carrying out of this program.

15. The Labor Market Board requests that the problem of elderly manpower be taken into consideration by the Labor Market Committee—an organ for cooperation between the central organizations of employers and employees.

16. A central conference with participation from the County Labor Boards should be arranged.

17. Each one of the larger employment service offices should consider appointing a special officer with the task of coordinating actions regarding elderly workers.

18. Within the Labor Market Board actions regarding elderly people are dealt with in the appropriate divisions. A special officer has to coordinate the actions. He is also responsible for coordination with the program which has been developed to increase the effectiveness of vocational rehabilitation.

Another large group of handicapped people who need special services consists of those with *physical handicaps.* Through better methods of rehabilitation, not least by use of improved mechanical equipment, it is nowadays to a large extent possible to rehabilitate people with physical handicaps. The success in this field has also led to attempts to take care of persons with psychological handicaps. We probably are only at the beginning of a development in which we can expect to succeed in using labor-market policy measures for the psychologically handicapped. Further, there is a large group of people who have difficulties in participating in modern social life. Among these are the emotionally disturbed, alcoholics, and those who have violated the laws of their country. Persons in the latter group may have paid their penalties, but afterwards it is usually very difficult for them to find suitable work.

All these groups require individual measures of different kinds to become adapted to the labor market. In Sweden a special program has been adopted for them, and special rehabilitation sections, connected to the regional labor-market boards, are now working with all these different problems.

The contents of the program are as follows:

1. An important prerequisite for efficient rehabilitation is that the needs are detected at an early stage. The rehabilitation program thus should include more systematic methods than hitherto to find the cases. This can be done through (a) organized cooperation with hospitals, social institutions, organizations of persons with impaired working capacity, etc.; (b) organized cooperation with the sickness funds according to the guidelines proposed by the Investigation on Social Assistance (Security) and Adaptability; (c) rehabilitation examination at the employment service of those applicants who are difficult to place.

2. Rehabilitation should begin as early as possible with an examination of the personal, vocational, and medical qualifications of the applicant. This requires among other things (a) more efficient vocational guidance for people with impaired working capacity; (b) increased possibilities for the use of aptitude tests; (c) increased activities concerning job analysis and industrial physiology research regarding vocational requirements; (d) a strengthening of the medical authorities of the County Labor Boards.

3. Among the activities required to cover more completely the needs for vocational testing (a) certain institutions for work training and the vocational schools for the handicapped should be equipped with special facilities for vocational testing; (b) for medically complicated cases there should be possibilities for work training at the future rehabilitation clinics; and (c) the National Work Training Clinic should be provided with increased resources and in the future should concentrate exclusively on the most complicated cases, functioning also as an Institute for Education and Research in the field of vocational testing and work-training techniques.

4. Work-training activities should be made more efficient (a) by preparing systematic working methods, by increased participation of physicians, and by organized supervisory activities; (b) by increasing governmental subsidies, e.g., for installing machines and tools, for medical fees, and for supervisory activities; (c) by introducing governmental grants to the clients, mainly according to the norms for vocational schools; (d) by trying to organize a training center for civil servants and others in connection with archive work activities.

5. The educational possibilities for certain handicapped groups should be more differentiated than before through (a) expanding the adaptation courses for people who are crippled or have visual or hearing defects, and starting special vocational courses for people with low I.Q.'s, as well as regional vocational courses for difficult orthopaedic cases, epileptics, and alcoholics; (b) continuously adapting the vocational departments of the special schools to the needs of the market; (c) providing benefits (students' allowances, etc.) for a theoretical education which is a prerequisite for a planned vocational education; and (d) utilizing the educational possibilities offered by industry and trade to a greater extent than before for individual education as well as for courses.

6. The placement service should continue on a voluntary basis. For the time being there is no need for quota legislation or other means of coercion. However, the following steps are necessary in order to increase efficiency: (a) there should be intensified information activity regarding the possibility of using handicapped people; (b) the representatives of the employers' and employees' organizations should be more closely connected with the Rehabilitation Delegation of the Labor Market Board, and an advisory committee for cooperation should be created at the county level, including members from the rehabilitation

organs, the employers' and employees' organizations, and the organizations of persons with impaired working capacity: (c) the employer service should take special care of the placement of rehabilitation clients—this should be done through a systematic review of vacancies and through acquisition of suitable jobs (in both cases having in mind the special needs of people with impaired working capacity); and (d) the rehabilitation organization should have adequate personnel resources to assist its clients with social rehabilitation when required (in cooperation with the social-security authorities).

7. A change should be made in the regulations concerning governmental help towards self-employment, purchasing of vehicles, technical facilities, etc., in order to extend the scope of subsidies. The following changes are proposed: (a) the help should be given to individuals as well as to economic societies or foundations connected with the organizations of handicapped (provided that one of their purposes is to provide work and means of subsistence to the handicapped), with subsidies available for acquiring tools, etc., needed for getting and keeping a job, or for special motor cars or other devices required for rehabilitation; (b) the present maximum subsidy amount of 5000 Sw. kr. ($1000) should be increased; (c) this help should be administered only by one central authority; and (d) the County Labor Boards should receive grants to cover the cost of assistance by industrial and technical experts.

8. There should be an intensified program of building sheltered workshops, and opportunities for work for the handicapped should be expanded in the following ways: (a) an intensified information program; (b) planning that takes into account the regional organization within the Labor Market Board and probable future changes in municipal organizations; (c) greater differentiation in types of jobs; (d) special institutions for those who need work as well as care; (e) an increase in investment and management subsidies in relation to what has been proposed for the work-training clinics; (f) better resources for the Labor Market Board to assist in the securing of orders and technical advice; (g) courses for educating new personnel and retraining existing personnel; (h) a coordinated purchasing and sales activity; (i) a program to increase employment in industry for people with subnormal ability to work by compensating companies for the higher cost; (j) an increase in governmental subsidies for archive work to 50 per cent in order to achieve the desired expansion in this activity; and (k) a systematic inventory of all types of uncomplicated work (including indoor work) in the municipal sector, which might be suitable for people who are difficult to place.

9. Efforts should be made to expand home work through (a) better training for home workers, the provision of necessary tools and machines, and obtaining technical assistance when required; (b) establishing regional home work centers; (c) subsidies for certain extra costs,

such as transport of material, and travel of supervisors; and (d) organizing art handicraft, institutions for the handicapped, etc., so that it will be possible to increase educational opportunities for art handicrafters, provide them with appropriate equipment, and arrange for the purchase of material and the sale of their products through *one* organization.

10. There should also be a program for the supervisory control and follow-up of rehabilitation activities, which would include: (a) the systematic follow-up of the clients during work training, vocational education, and in their first job; and (b) periodical follow-up examinations of different groups of handicapped persons to estimate the effects of rehabilitation programs.

Of course, the question can be raised as to whether the Employment Service should be responsible also for the rehabilitation program, since many of the tasks are related to programs for social or medical care. However, there will probably be great advantages in making the Labor Market Organization responsible for the rehabilitation program, in view of the fact that its most important role is very often to find a suitable job and that it has better access than anybody else to available employment opportunities. Moreover, rehabilitation involves other labor-market measures that are already administered by the Labor Market Organization, e.g., programs for geographical and vocational mobility. The best coordination is probably reached if the labor-market policy also includes the rehabilitation program. It is more important than anything else that all the different means are brought to the service of the individual.

**Employment-creating measures.** Basic employment should be created by using general economic-political tools and their variations—fiscal, monetary, and credit policy. However, if economic policy is too liberal, it causes, as a rule, a general overstrain in the economy, which makes for continuous inflation. On the other hand, if the general policy is too restrictive, it is likely to cause continuous deflation, which will prevent progress. That is why economic policy must have tools at its disposal which create selective employment opportunities. It may also be necessary to reduce demand selectively, if aggregate demand becomes too large.

This is happening, for example, in Sweden, where labor-market policy includes measures to create employment opportunities as well as measures to prevent employment opportunities from demanding excessive amounts of manpower.

To create employment opportunities (beyond what is being done through general economic-political measures) is of great importance for leveling out seasonal fluctuations as well as for accelerating structural changes. The policies being used for this are of three different kinds:

1. Public works of many different kinds, both governmental and municipal.
2. Government orders to industry.
3. The use of investment funds to influence private investments.

The labor-market organization administers these measures. In Sweden the most important decisions are made centrally, but many decisions are delegated to the regional agencies, the County Labor Boards, or, in some cases, to the heads of the Employment Service Offices (e.g., short-time work for the handicapped). In this way we gain speed in action and a selective utilization of the tools available. Because the measures are administered by the Labor Market Organization, the necessary coordination with other labor-market policies is obtained. Timing is of great importance. Orders for public works should be issued at the proper time, as well as promptly withdrawn when they are no longer needed. The size of the projects and orders, their geographical location, and their time limits are often of decisive importance for their effect. No agency seems better fitted for planning these things than the labor-market administration, which constantly supervises the labor market.

**Demand-reducing measures.** Labor-market policy today does not have sufficient selective means by which the demand for labor can be moderated. In Sweden, however, a system of building permits, granted by the regional labor-market authorities, is applied. If there is no manpower available, a building or construction project can be delayed, since it cannot be started without a licence. In order to reduce seasonal fluctuations, no permission to initiate public or municipal works is granted during the summer months. These are just a few examples of selective demand-reducing measures. In Britain, a new system of special taxes on employment of manpower, which is currently attracting much attention, has recently been introduced. This type of measure can, of course, have a restrictive effect on the demand for manpower in some situations.

For a long time there has been a great need in parts of Europe for reducing the demand for manpower. However, the only approach used, on the whole, has been the adoption of a more restrictive general economic policy. This will probably be the case even in the future.

An important point in this connection is that the subsidies paid out during unfavorable market conditions and seasonal declines should be withdrawn in proper time—as soon as the first signs of a change in market conidtions are visible. However, the generally stimulating measures have, unfortunately, often been in use for too long a time. We can be more certain that the stimulating measures will be withdrawn rapidly if greater use is made of selective labor-market policy measures as a stimulus to employment in recessions. In other words, this consideration suggests the desirability of a more common use of the selective labor-market programs even in the framework of general economic policy.

The solution of the difficult problem of inflation—from which most European countries have suffered since the war—is above all to be found in a generally austere economic policy, which reduces total demand. This should be combined with measures which reduce demand for consumption as well as investment. It should then in its turn be combined with an active and selective labor-market policy, which in different ways aims at creating work and employment opportunities, where there is a need for them but only there. Despite the general reluctance to pursue an anti-inflationary policy for fear of unemployment, it must be recognized that today we have better means than ever before to keep unemployment down. Therefore they should be used.

**Personal and collective information about the labor market.** Information about the labor market, its need for manpower now and in the future, and changing geographical and vocational trends is of the greatest value, in order to arrive at the distribution of manpower resources that satisfies the need, and vice versa. An active *vocational guidance* and *vocational advice* program plays an important part in attempts to get the individual adapted to the labor market. Vocational guidance is of greatest importance to those young people who are still in school. But it is no less important for elderly people, who have to adapt themselves permanently to the changed needs of the labor market. It is therefore natural to consider vocational guidance above all as an instrument of labor-market policy.

The necessary labor-market information, which has to be combined with continued research work, must be generally and quickly available. The agency generating this information has to obtain the cooperation of the press, radio, and TV, as well as advertise and issue publications of its own or make contributions to those of others. It has to renew its own efforts continuously in order to influence the aspirations of the applicants and to stimulate them to increased mobility and adaptation, which will become more and more important in modern society.

## An Efficient Employment Service

Everything mentioned above may be called labor-market policy in the broadest sense. It has to be administered by the labor-market authorities, and here the Employment Service is the driving force.

What are the prerequisites for an efficient Employment Service? They are as follows:

The Employment Service has to be distributed all over the country. Even if we must accept the trend towards a concentration in larger places and centers, we should not forget that the Employment Service must reach all places where employers and employees want to make use of its services. Moreover, the Employment Service must have suitable and appropriate offices. In most countries the offices need renovation.

The Employment Service must have independent civil servants, who receive salaries that are competitive with those for other qualified people. Dealing with people is highly skilled work.

The Employment Service personnel must have many labor-market-policy tools at their disposal. This does not, however, mean that every Employment Service officer himself has to carry out or start to use every program. But he has to know what programs are available and when to use them. This depends on the situation of his clients—employers and applicants—when they meet the employment officer. The personnel must have good training and be continuously retrained. They must learn how to cooperate and learn the importance of coordination between the different labor-market-policy instruments. To be the manager of the Employment Service personnel is therefore an important task.

The strength of labor-market-policy measures depends in most cases on their being used at the proper time. The chances for this are greater if the tools are being used by the Employment Service officers, because they meet the people for whom the measures are intended. Labor-market-policy initiative and labor-market-policy measures are geared to the needs of the employers and applicants.

The carrying out of this labor-market policy must undoubtedly cost quite a lot. In Sweden, where the measures of labor-market policy have been used more extensively than in most other countries, we spend about 1 billion Sw. kr. a year on it (about $200 million for a population of 7 million). This is 3 to 4 per cent of the state budget and close to 1 per cent of the national income. The approximate costs for the different kinds of activities are as follows (in per cent):

| | |
|---|---|
| Administration (personnel and offices, etc.) | 10 |
| Geographical mobility | 5 |
| Vocational mobility | 20 |
| Location measures | 15 |
| Rehabilitation measures | 20 |
| Measures to influence the demand for manpower | 25 |
| Other, including information, foreign labor, etc. | 5 |

The figures may seem high compared with earlier years, when labor-market policy was regarded above all as a social-political task. But the amounts should be considered in relation to the profits the labor-market policy can yield to the nation. The aim of labor-market policy is, to a great extent, to influence manpower at the margin. Let's assume that the labor-market policy can avoid an unemployment rate of 2 to 3 per cent by creating a better adjustment between demand and supply, or that it can prevent inflation of 2 to 3 per cent by being used as a selective economic-political instrument during a period of generally restrictive economic policy, which creates a balance in the economy. Well, then, the costs are more than justified. Consequently we have to regard labor-market policy as one of the best means for creating a balance in economic policy.

## Conclusion

Labor-market policy has been subject to new thinking, and many new ideas have been generated in recent years in many different countries. But still there is much to do. The instruments of labor-market policy can be improved. And new ideas are coming. Thus, it will be possible to influence individual behavior on the labor market to an increasing extent by different means, for example, by taxation, pensions, holidays, and school enrollment. Part-time work and the manner in which working hours are distributed during the week and year are other items of interest to labor-market policy. The research findings of industry physiology can be, I am sure, of great help to labor-market policy in the future. Most countries have not started using these policies yet, but there is increasing recognition of the need to increase labor mobility.

The capital and credit markets have long since had their exchange where demand and supply for capital have been equilibrated. Let us make the Employment Service the exchange for manpower, which adjusts demand and supply in the labor market, taking the desires, needs, and interests of the individual into consideration. By doing this we best serve the nation as well as the human being.

# Discussion

## BY SAR A. LEVITAN

The message I get from Bertil Olsson is "look East, manpower planner." Of course, Mr. Olsson is not volunteering this advice. As a guest, he leaves it to us to deduce lessons and to benefit from the manpower policies and experience of Sweden and other Western European countries.

Mr. Olsson's paper is not intended as a blueprint for manpower policies, but it can properly serve as a checklist for policies and programs needed in the United States. For this purpose, it is a highly useful document. The thrust of his argument is that effective manpower policies are a *sine qua non* for a smoothly working economy. Such policies, he claims, can be designed as potent tools to fight inflation and to increase total production. Until recently, this possibility would have been only of academic interest for the United States. But, in the current situation, manpower policies and programs assume additional dimensions and have an immediate and pressing interest for us.

### The Good Life and Work Are Not the Same

Still, there is room for questioning an implicit basic assumption underlying Mr. Olsson's paper. He seems to assign the highest priority to raising national product and to increasing the total labor force. To achieve this end, he urges maximum utilization of manpower and the allocation of considerable additional resources to raising the national income without overheating an otherwise full-employment economy.

Assuming that the allocation of an additional 1 per cent of national income to manpower programs would increase total national production by a higher proportion, the desirability and wisdom of enticing some marginal groups into the work force might still be questioned. In view of our high standard of living, it may be more compassionate and wiser public policy to provide more adequate retirement benefits for the elderly and not to induce them to reenter or to remain in the labor force. When the economy operates at full employment, restraining monetary and fiscal policies may be preferable to programs aimed at inducing older people to work. In a highly industrial and productive economy, gainful employment and the good life are not necessarily identical, certainly not for old people.

It goes without saying that work opportunities should be provided for all those who desire gainful employment, but this policy cannot be equated with the encouragement of old people to work when they prefer leisure. Moreover, it has not been proved that effective techniques are available for training deficiently educated old people, or that the economic benefits from such training would exceed the social costs. In our own case, as long as vocational training, counseling, and related resources remain in scarce supply, it may be better to utilize the limited available resources to combat youth unemployment and to improve the quality of public services for the underemployed and disadvantaged who are already in the labor force than to impose obligations on oldsters who want leisure with an adequate income for a wholesome retirement.

## What Priority to Expansion of Manpower Programs?

As a first approximation, Mr. Olsson offers us a guidepost from Swedish experience. Specifically, Sweden spends about 1 per cent of national income for manpower programs and is moving towards doubling the resources allocated to manpower programs. Some have suggested that we might wish to follow the Swedish experience.

However, international comparisons present difficulties. It is not clear just what ought to be included under so general a rubric as "manpower programs." A rough estimate, based on Mr. Olsson's definition, indicates that we are spending about $3 billion a year on manpower programs, including aid to geographic areas of high unemployment. This sum accounts for only one-half of 1 per cent of our current national income. Thus it would appear that our allocation of resources for manpower programs lags far behind the suggested guidepost.

This standard leaves much to be desired. In the United States, a much larger percentage of youths attend school until they reach their eighteenth birthday, and relatively more go on to college than in Western European countries, where youths leave school to enter the labor force at a much earlier age. We spend billions of dollars for the "surplus" education of these youths, for education largely unused for productive purposes. Should these expenditures be included as part of manpower development programs? If the extra outlays for education are to be included as part of manpower programs, there is real doubt that we lag, as is customarily suggested, in allocating resources for manpower development.

Our higher unemployment rates, therefore, may not be due to the deficiency of conventional manpower programs and may result from many unrelated factors. Conversely, it is not clear how much the Swedish full-employment achievement is due to appropriate manpower policies. Furthermore, the Swedish economy has not avoided serious inflationary prices increases, averaging more than 4 per cent annually during the past decade. Inflationary pressures have accelerated even more sharply during recent years.

In the United States, at least, a strong case may be made for not hastily doubling the resources allocated to our present manpower programs. The cost of federally supported manpower programs to aid the unemployed, underemployed, and the disadvantaged (whether because of personal characteristics, discrimination, or because they are stranded in depressed areas) now adds up to a sizable annual total of about $2 billion—more than a tenfold increase during the past five years. Other advanced industrial countries do allocate a larger proportion of their national income to comparable programs. Assuming that it is desirable "to catch up" with our Western European neighbors, do we find the case for deliberate speed persuasive? Having started this decade with woefully inadequate and deficient manpower programs, particularly insofar as the disadvantaged are concerned, we have made rapid progress during the past half-decade, especially within the last two years. This record suggests the need for adequate digestion before we embark on further rapid advances.

A prime constraint on the further rapid expansion of manpower programs is, of course, the shortage of professional and technical personnel capable of administering and implementing these programs. Additional expanded demand for the limited technical resources would only dilute the quality of personnel and create further inflationary demand for their services.

## Major Programs

Concern over the quality of existing programs suggests that we need to assess their effectiveness before they are expanded, supplemented, or replaced by new ones. This is not the appropriate occasion for attempting a detailed evaluation of these programs. Still, some pertinent questions about them may be raised here.

**Youth programs.** Youth unemployment remains a pressing problem. Aside from conventional educational programs, the federal government has appropriated, during the fiscal year 1966, more than $600 million for three separate youth employment and training programs. These are the Job Corps (JC), Neighborhood Youth Corps (NYC), and the youth programs under the Manpower Development and Training Act. In addition, the U.S. Employment Service has recently inaugurated a special network of counseling and placement offices for youth, the Youth Opportunity Centers.

Expenditures per participant and expected results under the programs are markedly different. It costs about five times as much to support a youth in the JC as to provide him with employment in the NYC (about 30 hours employment per week at $1.25 an hour). At the same time, the payment to a youth trained under an MDTA course is $20 a week, or about half that received by out-of-school NYC enrollees. But NYC employment does not normally lead to the acquisition of any occupational skill, while MDTA training is presumed to equip the youth with a salable skill. Nevertheless, the higher pay under the NYC provides a special incentive to enroll in this program and thus to shun training for a particular skill.

An examination of the distribution of NYC enrollees would indicate that about three out of every four are attending school. The expenditure might well be justified if acceptable evidence suggested that the small outlay (an in-school youth works about 12 hours, also at $1.25 an hour) provides sufficient incentive for the youth to remain in school. No such evidence exists at present. And, if the House Committee on Education and Labor had its way, the $300 million appropriated for the NYC during the current fiscal year would be raised to $496 million during the next year. There may be ample justification for providing income maintenance to youths from impoverished homes attending school, but this is not the intent of the NYC.

The JC raises even more difficult questions. The underlying assumption of this program is that a youth from an impoverished home must sometimes be removed from his (or her) environment to undergo an effective training program. But no evidence exists that youths selected for JC training differ markedly from NYC out-of-school selectees. Experience during the past year and a half also raises doubts whether transplanting a disadvantaged youth, frequently from a city slum area, to an isolated JC center (perhaps located in a hostile environment where he is not welcome) is the best way to motivate acquisition of a basic education and a skill. Thus far about a third of the youths selected for the JC have left the program before completion of the training course, and little is known about the subsequent achievement of those who stayed until graduation.

**Training and work for disadvantaged adults.** The Manpower Development and Training Act of 1962 (MDTA), with its emphasis upon training the long-term unemployed, might have had some effect upon the rehabilitation of relief recipients and other impoverished persons, but relatively few of the disadvantaged qualified for MDTA training. During the first three and a half years, through the end of 1965, more than half of the workers selected for MDTA training had completed a high school education or better, and only one out of every fourteen MDTA trainees had completed less than eight years of education. Among relief recipients, one-third of the parents had less than eight years of education. About 11 per cent of all trainees selected for MDTA institutional courses and less than 2 per cent of the on-site trainees came from relief rolls.

Officials in charge of MDTA have apparently found it difficult to develop adequate training techniques for aiding the least educated. The tightening of the labor market experienced since 1965 will possibly reorient MDTA operations towards greater emphasis upon the training of the poorly educated and disadvantaged. During recent months, spokesmen for MDTA have indicated strong support for such programs, but we de not yet have data on the extent to which appropriate projects have been developed.

A work-relief program for adults is provided under the Work Experience Program (WEP) (Title V) of the Economic Opportunity Act. Estimates of the total employable or potentially employable relief recipients and other eligible needy persons vary widely, but the number certainly exceeds 1 million, and the administrators of the program in the Department of Health, Education, and Welfare (HEW) have placed the number closer to 2 million persons. According to the latest available data, only 56,000 were participating in the WEP. The total funds allocated to the program during fiscal 1966 amounted to $150 million.

The payment made to participants in the WEP is not realistic. It is intended to provide for the basic needs of the trainee, as determined by state relief standards. But since relief standards are normally woefully inadequate, the program offers little financial inducement for needy persons to participate in it. Furthermore, in some states, persons already on relief receive no additional payment for participating in the WEP, except for such supplementary expenses incidental to work as transportation and lunch. In this connection, it is most useful to recall Mr. Olsson's admonition that, if training is to be successful, the payment made to the trainees should substantially remove economic worries. Under the Economic Opportunity Act, an attempt is made to prepare needy persons for economic independence at less than bargain-basement rates.

According to some observers, another impediment to the effectiveness of the WEP is that the administrators are welfare oriented rather than work oriented. These critics suggest that the administrators have not taken due advantage of the present labor shortages in numerous labor markets to help place participants in the program in regular private or public jobs.

Estimates vary as to the number of employable persons who do not need work experience but still cannot secure jobs in an economy operating at a 4 per cent level of unemployment. It is safe to assume that the number exceeds half a million and may be closer to a million. Many of these people are stranded in areas of high unemployment, and others are unemployed for personal reasons or because of discrimination. Perhaps the most efficient way to provide employment for all these chronically unemployed, as was recently suggested by the President's Commission of Technology, Automation, and Economic Progress, is for the federal government to assume the responsibility as "an employer of last resort, providing work for the 'hard-core unemployed' in useful community enterprises." The underwriting of such a responsibility would be costly indeed. The annual cost of filling a job would be about $4500, assuming the workers are paid only statutory minimum-wage rates but are also provided basic education and adequate work supervision. The total cost of employing all employable but chronically idle disadvantaged workers would, therefore, run intially into several billion dollars annually. Obviously, such a program is not likely in the current economic setting and in the light of our Vietnam commitments. However, a start in this direction can be made under the WEP, and a good case can be made for the expansion of a public-employment program even under present conditions.

**Physically handicapped persons.** Vocational rehabilitation is the oldest of the programs considered here, dating back to 1920. Over the years the program has been expanded. The most significant changes occurred last year, when Congress amended the Vocational Rehabilitation Act. The goal of the 1965 amendment was virtually to double the annual number of participants in the program and also to improve the quality of the services by the provisions of additional funds for research and training. Past experience has shown that the average cost involved in rehabilitating a disabled person for gainful activity amounted to $1200.

The Administration has proposed that the funds for the rehabilitation program be nearly doubled during the fiscal year 1967. Bureau of the Budget estimates for the coming year indicate that a quarter of a billion dollars will be expended.

The distinguishing feature of the Vocational Rehabilitation Program (VRP) is its comprehensiveness. The Vocational Rehabilitation Administration (VRA) is authorized to help finance the rehabilitation process in all its stages, from referral to job placement. Typically, the disabled person may receive counseling, medical attention, a prosthetic device, training for either homemaking or a job, some maintenance expenses during the training period, and help in finding a job. Indigent persons receive these benefits free. Furthermore, the VRA also sponsors training of rehabilitation specialists and research to find better ways of rehabilitating the disabled. Thus, the VRA is involved in both the research and implementation aspects of vocational rehabilitation.

Dr. Ronald Conley has concluded on the basis of a cost-benefit analysis that annual returns to rehabilitated persons consistently exceed comparable outlays for vocational rehabilitation. But he suggested that the high returns may be due to a "creaming" process, and that vocational rehabilitation agencies tend to select applicants who are likely to achieve rapid rehabilitation.

Closely related to vocational rehabilitation are sheltered workshops operated normally by nonprofit private organizations. These workshops serve the function of easing the reentry of a rehabilitated person into the competitive world of work. They employed about 100,000 persons in 1965. In some cases, disabled people can never be rehabilitated fully enough to compete effectively in the free market place, and for these people the workshops may provide a place of permanent employment. Although the workshops usually produce goods for sale, the emphasis is placed not on quantity of output but upon teaching good work habits and upon giving actual work experience in a relatively protected environment. The 1965 amendments to the VRA authorized the making of grants to sheltered workshops (90 per cent of total costs) when occupational training is the core of a proposed workshop project.

**Disadvantaged areas.** The economic expansion during the past few years—and particularly during the last year—has reduced the number of depressed areas. Nevertheless, a number of chronic labor-surplus markets persist. At the latest count, unemployment in 17 major labor markets exceeded 6 per cent.

A period of overall high employment, when labor shortages exist in numerous areas, presents the most propitious time for the rehabilitation of depressed communities. In particular, it may induce employers to locate new enterprises, or to expand established businesses, in areas of surplus manpower. The federal program to aid depressed areas is now more than five years old; but, for more than four years, it operated in an economic climate in which labor surpluses were widespread. This fact has precluded concentration upon the rehabilitation of chronically depressed areas.

The general high level of unemployment which prevailed throughout the country during the first few years of the federal depressed-area program created a clamor by many communities to qualify for the benefits of the program. As a result, about a thousand counties, or one-third of the total in the United States, became eligible for aid under the Area Redevelopment Act. Because its meager appropriations were spread thinly, the impact of the Area Redevelopment Act (ARA) is difficult to measure. The Public Works and Economic Development Act (PWEDA), the successor program to the ARA, inherited the bulk of the areas eligible for assistance under the earlier program, and, under some provisions of the Act, new areas have been added. Whether the administrators of the new program will succeed in limiting the number of areas eligible for assistance in the current high-employment economy has not yet been determined.

Similarly, it remains to be seen whether the Appalachian Regional Development Act (ARDA) provides the proper tools for the rehabilitation of what is probably the most depressed region in the United States. Experience may show that the large area covered by the legislation does not necessarily represent a viable economic region. An area of 368 counties in 12 states, stretching from New York to Alabama, with a population of more than 17 million people, is eligible for special aid under the ARDA. The underlying assumption of the program is that the economic distress of the region is due to its relative isolation. Therefore, the emphasis of the program is upon the construction of roads, and only a small proportion of the total authorized funds is allocated to the development of human resources. Political and subregional conflicts have impeded the progress of the program, enacted in March 1965, and it is certainly premature to try to assess the probable impact on the region.

The economic justification for a program in aid of depressed areas is persuasive. Depressed economic conditions force people to migrate from their native communities in search of a livelihood, which in turn creates pressures on the growing communities for housing, schooling, and recreational and religious facilities for the immigrants. At the same time, the social facilities in depressed areas, poor as they are, go to waste; the deterioration of the economic fabric of communities is aggravated.

A realistic depressed-area program must also recognize that not all communities can be "saved." The solution for most of the unemployment in depressed areas with depleted resource bases may well lie in equipping the unemployed with skills marketable elsewhere and in helping these persons to migrate to more prosperous areas.

## Program Administration

Possibly the most telling deterrent to further rapid expansion of programs in aid of the disadvantaged and disabled is the present fractionalization of these programs. Mr. Olsson argues convincingly regarding the need to coordinate manpower policies and programs. He also recommends that manpower programs be closely integrated with fiscal and monetary policies. And in theory at least, we all say "Amen" to this approach. But if fiscal and monetary policies should be integrated with manpower policies, it might also mean that the latter would be placed at the tender mercies of the House Committee on Ways and Means and the Senate Committee on Finance. Few proponents of an effective (or what is now called an active) manpower policy would favor such a consignment.

Let me hasten to say that the need to coordinate manpower policy can hardly be denied. Charges that such coordination might lead to monopolistic manpower policies and programs and the dictum that "competition is good" are neither helpful nor germane. Nor is the assertion that decentralized decision-making is "necessary" in a pluralistic society a justification for fractionalization of manpower programs and the resulting confusion in their administration.

Friends of the recently expanded manpower program have evidenced an increasing concern about fragmentation and proliferation. It might be appropriate to cite the views on this subject of the two United States Senators from New York—both consistent supporters of manpower programs in aid of the disadvantaged. Fortunately for our purposes, invoking the aid of the two Senators from New York would not subject us to charges of political bias—and their views are helpful since I agree with both of them.

Senator Jacob Javits has indicated his impatience with the fractionalized manpower programs and has introduced legislation to prevent agencies from competing to service the same clientele. He also suggested the desirability of placing all training and job-creation programs under the auspices of one agency. Senator Robert F. Kennedy found that 28 federal agencies, bureaus, divisions, and commissions were charged with the responsibility for administering programs for the disabled, and he identified 18 separate federally funded programs responsible for vocational rehabilitation. The junior Senator from New York conceded that perhaps all the programs were needed, but he insisted that the programs should be coordinated and that the administrators of each program should have at least a nodding acquaintance with what their "competitors" are doing.

The fragmentation and overlapping of manpower programs would be of little concern if duplication and confusion were limited to Washington officialdom. The really disturbing problems arise at the local level and among the prospective clients of the programs. The "feds" are not in a position to bring viable and effective manpower programs to the communities. The initiative has to be taken at the local level, and few communities are adequately staffed in the manpower field to follow the myriad administrative regulations and rules issued by each of the federal manpower bureaus and agencies. Since the programs tend to overlap, a stern challenge is presented to community manpower leaders to design programs which fit the needs of the unemployed and the disadvantaged.

It is simple enough for a community to apply for a grant from the NYC to provide for disadvantaged youth attending school or for MDTA funds to train secretaries or nurses' aides. Few communities, however, are as yet aware that to train out-of-school youths they can get portions of the needed funds from several sources: the NYC pays the wages of trainees and some administrative overhead; additional money is available under community action programs (in the Office of Economic Opportunity); a special kitty, for demonstration and experimental projects, is administered by the Office of Manpower Policy, Evaluation, and Research in the Department of Labor; and the Vocational Education Act, administered by the Office of Education in HEW, also provides some benefits.

The obstacles to receiving federal assistance are, however, not insurmountable, and a few communities have achieved great success in the art of grantsmanship. They follow the federal regulations carefully, packaging manpower needs or aspirations to fit the magic "o.k. words" enunciated by the appropriate bureau; and, to mix a metaphor, they proceed to get various "pieces of the action" from the several federal spigots. The resulting mix is not necessarily the most effective program because, when the pieces are put together in the mold of the federal jigsaw puzzle, the picture may be incomplete, fragmented, and surprising. At best, the difference in sources of funds poses serious, if not insurmountable, obstacles to the design of integrated manpower programs. Expiration dates, extent of federal contributions, and criteria for allocation of funds vary among the several agencies, with resulting conflicts and difficulties in coordinating different parts of the same composite project.

The fragmentation of federally supported training programs assumes crucial significance when the impact upon the clientele is considered. Largely haphazard circumstances determine now whether a youth is assigned to a JC, NYC, or a Manpower Development and Training course. A rational program requires establishment of coordinated criteria to help decide to which program a youth is assigned, how he is to advance from one training program to another, and the compensation he is to receive under each. Similar confusion prevails in the training of adults. There is an urgent need to integrate work experience with MDTA programs, permitting a participant in the WEP to move into an institutional or on-the-job training (OJT) program conducted under the MDTA. Regrettably, there is little integration between the work-experience and the MDTA programs, and there is also little movement from the former to the latter. A similar need exists to integrate vocational rehabilitation with work experience.

The defects of the present system become particularly pronounced as labor shortages develop in an increasing number of communities and occupations. In a looser labor market, when jobs are scarcer, a training program may become a holding operation. But in the present labor market, as the demand for labor intensifies, the training programs become an integral part of the set of forces determining the supply of labor.

The urgent need in the United States is not for further proliferation and expansion of manpower programs but for consolidation and more effective administration of existing programs. The quest for further expansion will be justified when better evidence becomes available as to the effectiveness of the manpower programs that we now have.

CHAPTER **10**

# The Role of the Employer
# in Manpower Policy

## BY CHARLES A. MYERS

The central task of manpower policy is to facilitate the employment process and, in these times, to assist in the achievement of full employment with reasonably stable prices. In either case, the end result is the productive employment of people, and the employer's "role" in this process may seem so obvious as to need no elaboration. But the *responsibilities* of private and public employers in an effective national manpower policy are not so obvious and deserve some further consideration.

Some preliminary observations establish the ground rules under which I shall proceed. In the United States, and in most industrialized countries operating under a mixed system of private and public employment during peacetime, we have "pluralism in the employment process" (to use a phrase from the recent Report of the Employment Service Task Force). We do not require that all job openings and placements be channeled through a public employment service system. Employers use many sources and devices in recruiting new employees, and workers in search of jobs use many methods of finding them. Most labor markets work imperfectly, and governmental manpower policies are designed to reduce these imperfections. Since compulsory methods to improve the operation of labor markets are generally rejected, except in periods of national emergency, the relationship of employers and unions to governmental manpower policies is usually voluntary. Possibly the Civil Rights Act of 1964 is an exception to this generalization.

Most other public programs in the manpower field depend upon cooperation from employers. Examples are the federal-state employment service system; training programs such as those sponsored by the Manpower Development and Training Act (MDTA), Job Corps (JC), Neighborhood Youth Corps (NYC), and the Bureau of Apprenticeship and Training; and efforts to encourage the employment of physically handicapped workers. Some employers, particularly the larger ones with national, regional, or community standing, cooperate actively in some of these programs, as a number did in signing agreements with the President's Plans for Progress program to employ Negroes, before the passage of the Civil Rights Act. But in a pluralistic, mixed, private-enterprise system, most employers will use those methods of recruitment, selection, placement, and utilization of manpower which seem to work best for them. What they see as helpful or necessary varies with the tightness or looseness of the labor market in which they operate. It also changes as a result of their experience with different methods and approaches. If employers wish to preserve a pluralistic labor-market system, with great freedom for the participants, more of them will have to consider carefully their responsibilities for making the system work better.

Starting from these background assumptions or ground rules, I want to discuss five aspects of the employer's role in manpower policy: (1) cooperation with the federal-state Employment Service system; (2) revision of present hiring standards; (3) on-the-job and apprenticeship training; (4) effective utilization of employed manpower; and (5) participation in manpower advisory committees. There will be some review of experience in each area, with questions for the future. But the discussion will necessarily be rather brief.

## Cooperation with the Federal-State Employment Service System

It is probably a fair generalization to say that many employers use the Employment Service only as a last resort, for those job openings which they have been unable to fill by their usual methods of recruitment. It is also a frequent complaint that the referrals made by the Service are of unemployed workers who really lack the qualifications for the jobs employers have been unable to fill. In some communities and among a number of private employers, the "image" of the Employment Service is not too good. This perpetuates the well-known vicious circle of hard-to-place workers being referred to hard-to-fill jobs, which remain unfilled because the Service does not or cannot make referrals which meet the employer's hiring standards.

Unfortunately, a recent policy declaration adopted for 1965–1966 by the members of the U.S. Chamber of Commerce would simply perpetuate this situation. Some excerpts from the report are the following:

> The primary objective of the public Employment Service should be to find work for those unemployed who request its help. The Employment Service should not seek out those who are already employed, . . . . [and it] should not engage in any activity for employers not directly related to the normal placement function. It should not engage in such activities as advertising for job applicants, management consulting services, job analyses, and writing job descriptions and specifications.

This sort of recommendation is designed to limit funds available to the Service to improve and expand the assistance it can give both job-seekers and employers. If the Employment Service is restricted to being a placement service for marginal workers, "this will tend to reinforce the unfortunate image . . . which many hope to escape." [1]

The unanimous report of the Employment Service Task Force, discussed earlier in this conference, takes a much broader view of the role of the 2000 local offices of the Service when it insists that they become community "manpower services centers." The three employer members of the Task Force joined the labor and public representatives in the view that the tasks of the Service included "the maintenance of an active placement service for *all* workers and employers desiring assistance" (italics supplied), collection and dissemination of labor-market information, provision of employment counseling and testing services, special services for disadvantaged groups, and others. Legislation embodying the recommendations of the Task Force was introduced by Secretary of Labor Wirtz at a joint Senate-House subcommittee hearing on March 7, 1966, and a modified bill (S. 2974) was filed by the Clark Subcommittee of the Senate Committee on Labor nad Public Welfare on February 24, 1966. Hopefully, the bill will eventually be passed without emasculating amendments.

Will employers use these services more extensively under an improved federal-state system than they have in the past? That will depend on how effectively the staff of the local and state offices work *with* employers on *their* problems, rather than simply trying to "sell" the Employment Service by periodic employer visits. This is the service rather than the sales approach and requires a high quality staff.[2] A lot more effort needs to be put into demonstrating to skeptical or disinterested employers that a true manpower-services center can pinpoint future labor-supply problems, which will affect particular employers and industries, and help them work out solutions, in cooperation with other agencies such as trade and vocational schools and government training programs, as well as through the interarea Employment Service clearance system. The effective presentation of accurate labor-market information is a service which can be offered to employers not now using the public Employment Service system, as well as to those who do. The opportunity to provide services which employers need is especially great during growing labor shortages.

Employers, in turn, cannot expect more services for their tax dollars (which help support the federal-state system) unless they also take some initiative. How many have ever invited Employment Service representatives, interviewers, and counselors from the local office to tour their plants or offices, in order to become better acquainted with the nature of jobs on which they have filed vacancies, present or anticipated? I have always been impressed with the fact that frequently new firms entering a community see the Employment Service as providing helpful recruiting, testing, and screening services for them as they build up a work force. These employers have taken the initiative to seek help, and the local office staff has responded with the enthusiasm that civil servants often show when their efforts are sought and appreciated, rather than avoided and criticized.[3] Surely here is another vicious circle, and employers have as much responsibility for breaking it as has the staff of the Service. Some personnel officers may fear that increased use of the public Employment Service will limit their own need for staff.[4] But in my judgment, if they measure their contribution by the size of their own employment office staff, they have done a disservice to their company and to their profession.

Employers may reduce their work forces, as well as increase them or change their composition. When contract cancellations occur in defense industries, for instance, these employers clearly have an obligation to participate in an advance-notice "early warning system" so that the public Employment Service can develop plans to assist those laid-off employees who find difficulty in locating other work, possibly through enrollment in special training programs. An example of what can be done is the experience of the Long Island Defense Employment Study (of the New York Division of Employment) in relocating, placing locally, or retraining by September 1965 almost 500 of a sample of 2000 workers who were unemployed in March 1965 after layoffs by Republic Aviation and other Long Island plants.[5] A somewhat different situation is illustrated by the work of the Armour Automation Committee, which sought to mobilize community services (including the local office of the Employment Service) in relocating, training, and placing employees displaced by plant closures.[6] The early warning concept, as an employer obligation, applies also to employment changes resulting from technological change within existing plants or enterprises; but aside from the Armour experience, there is relatively little reported experience on the cooperation of employers thus affected with the federal-state Employment Service system *in advance* of actual job changes. Since there is not likely to be a legal requirement to list present and prospective job openings or reductions, it is all the more incumbent on employers to make the voluntary, pluralistic labor-market system work better.

Both the Task Force Report and the Report of the National Commission on Technology, Automation, and Economic Progress recommended use of computer technology to facilitate the matching of job-seekers and job vacancies. The Task Force was more modest in its suggestion that computers be used first in the present LINCS system operating in 17 major cities in 11 states; the Commission recommended that "a computerized nation-wide service for matching men and jobs be established." [7] These proposals deserve further study, for undoubtedly computer technology will be increasingly used for matching men and jobs. But successful operation presupposes that the self-interest of employers in a better search among job applicants will bring more employers to use this service than now use the federal-state Employment Service. Possibly, more rapid information on job vacancies and job applicants will encourage more extensive use of the public Employment Service.

Present labor shortages, dramatically illustrated by reports that firms are offering hundreds of dollars as "bounties" to their employees who can bring in new employees who will take unfilled jobs,[8] highlight another employer opportunity or obligation in manpower policy. If employers informed themselves better than many of them now do about the prospective changes in the composition of the labor force, the impending changes in the condition of the local labor market in which they operate, and other relevant external factors, they might do a better job of anticipating their manpower needs, especially in the critical occupations. Only a few large firms make any systematic attempt to relate their future manpower requirements to the forecasts they regularly make of sales, production, and capital spending. Manpower projections need to be based on both internal "systems" concepts and on external constraints. If even rough forecasts were supplied by major employers in a community to the public Employment Service, there would be better data on which to base more realistic and useful public manpower programs. It must be admitted, however, that data on present job vacancies are not generally available,[9] and these are easier for employers to supply, if they would, than are forecasts of future job needs or changes. There are many unrealized opportunities for employers to supply the kind of data on which they also depend for an accurate picture of the condition of the labor market.

## Possible Revision of Hiring Standards

When a firm has more job applicants than it can hire, it is understandable that hiring standards will be set high enough to afford a cut-off point in screening applicants. When the labor market becomes tight, standards are relaxed, and people are hired who would not be acceptable at other times. At least, this is the theory of employer behavior which has been used to explain how so-called structural unemployment would "melt" once the hot breath of increasing aggregate demand hit it. The experience of the Second World War, in which unemployment dropped to 1.2 per cent in 1944, is cited as proof of this point.

Undoubtedly, employers have relaxed their hiring standards in the areas of present severe labor shortage. But, as the internal staff report shown to me by officials of one large New England company indicated, some applicants and younger workers trained under the Economic Opportunity Act (poverty program) are "for the most part still unacceptable by our standards." In this company, hiring-in jobs are not kept long by newly employed workers; they are trained and upgraded as rapidly as possible. Like many progressive companies with or without union seniority provisions, this firm promotes from within; the ports of entry in the occupational structure are few. Consequently, in considering a job applicant, they look for the kinds of education, training, experience, and other qualifications which indicate that the new employee will be flexible enough to learn new jobs, rather than remain in the dead-end of a low-skilled job. Thus, hiring standards which seem high *for the particular unskilled job* are not high for the subsequent jobs to which the employee may be promoted. Admittedly, there is a mixture here of high hiring standards and good in-plant training for promotion, but the simple criticism that "hiring standards are too high" overlooks the importance of the special requirements of changing jobs and promotion from within.

A nagging question remains. How often is this valid point

used to explain why a firm cannot hire disadvantaged job applicants, whose employment would require more effort and more
training within the firm than outside? Clearly, some preemployment training in particular basic skills, or for simple literacy,
is the responsibility of public agencies; but the dividing line
between this and the employer's own responsibility is a hazy one
which shifts from time to time.

The civil rights movement certainly forced many employers to
"revise" their hiring standards for Negroes. The number seeking
qualified Negroes is much greater than it was five years ago, and
some firms go further and provide additional training for Negroes so that there may even be a sort of "discrimination in
reverse" against better qualified white applicants.

The growing number of teenagers, young adults, and middle-
aged women in the labor force also confront employers with a
similar problem in maintaining existing hiring standards. Young
workers, almost by definition, have little experience, and in some
cases they may be high school dropouts. Employers have been
hiring them in the absence of experienced and qualified applicants; and clearly more in-plant training has been necessary to
overcome the initial lack of qualifications. As for older women,
many of whom want part-time jobs, employers have been forced
to adapt working schedules to fit these desires and to do more
training. While I do not have specific illustrations, it is a reasonable presumption that some jobs have been redesigned and even
diluted, as they were during the Second World War, to permit
the employment of less-qualified applicants than employers
would normally like to hire. If the Second World War pattern
repeats itself, as it apparently has in some areas, more employers
will beat the bushes for new employees in rural or labor-surplus
areas, providing transportation and other inducements.[10]

All of these things, which employers may be doing in their own
self-interest when labor-market and aggregate-demand pressures
mount, are also consistent with their wider responsibilities in
providing employment opportunities for the less qualified and
more disadvantaged members of the labor force. Cooperation
with the various "outreach" programs designed to draw disadvantaged persons into the labor force and into productive employment is an example. The interrelationships of private re-

sponsibilities and public responsibilities in education, training, counseling, and placement are reinforcing; one cannot be effective without the other.

## On-the-Job and Apprenticeship Training

The preceding discussion has emphasized the connection between revising hiring standards and more on-the-job training. It is widely believed that many employers in this country have not devoted enough effort to on-the-job and apprenticeship training.[11] One reason may be that these cost money, and any individual employer can never be sure that employees trained at his expense will not leave if a better opportunity is offered by another employer, who has no training program. This has always been a possibility, but one hardly sufficient to justify an employer's doing no training at all. To the extent that in-plant promotion ladders have been established through union agreements or by personnel policies, the need for training as a part of the upgrading-promotion process is clear.

The failure of many employers to consider the consequences of inadequate on-the-job training programs in the past, when qualified job applicants were more plentiful, may account now for some of the persistent skill shortages.[12] The cumulative effect of neglect of training by many individual employers is reflected in the present tight labor market for many skills. If employers could not do the whole job, they could have demanded and supported better public education and training programs when shortages were only on the horizon, so that better qualified applicants would have been available in larger numbers now. One consequence of this overall neglect is the prospect that employees of relatively low competence in terms of education and aptitudes will be frozen in seniority and promotion ladders and will later block access to higher jobs by more competent, younger job applicants.

Can public programs and policies encourage more on-the-job and apprenticeship training by private firms? The Bureau of Apprenticeship and Training (BAT) of the Department of Labor now encourages the establishment of special training programs by employers, for five or more employees, with a reimbursement to the employer of $25 per week for each trainee to offset additional training and administrative costs. This is to be distinguished from MDTA, JC, and NYC training programs, which generally provide training off the job and usually pre-employment. Apart from the modest BAT program, there has not been much experience in this country with public subsidies for on-the-job training, either in the form of tax offsets or credits or of outright subsidies to the employer.

One exception is the program which MDTA has partially subsidized with the Chrysler Corporation. According to company sources, more apprentices are being trained for skilled jobs than the company alone had done before, and more mechanics and body repairmen are being trained jointly with Chrysler dealers.[13] Of course, Chrysler bears some of the costs in its own interest, but the public subsidy probably offsets some of the losses if trained employees leave for other companies and dealers. This type of public-private program needs to be extended to other employers and industries.

Contracting with private employers to run training programs in JC centers is probably a good use of employer training skills for groups of young people who have never had jobs, but public funds spent to encourage their employment and training *on the job* would probably be even more effective. If European experience is a good guide, the average cost per trainee of subsidized on-the-job training is less than in government training programs.[14]

One untapped source of labor supply is among the nation's physically handicapped persons, estimated by the U.S. Public Health Service to include up to 22 million persons limited to some degree by chronic disease and other impairments.[15] The The record of subsequent job performance of properly trained handicapped workers is good; yet it has taken the combined efforts of government, some insurance companies, and private agencies to bring this group to the attention of many employers. The training responsibility is largely that of the employer, once he is persuaded to tap this labor pool. The same training need applies to other disadvantaged members of the labor force, particularly minority groups.

In some cases, the training responsibility is shared with unions, which are (or should be) just as concerned as are employers with improving the qualifications of presently employed people through retraining. The issue of union limitations on the numbers and qualifications of apprentices can only be mentioned here, but it should be noted that employers have not always trained as many apprentices as union rules permitted.[16]

## More Effective Utilization of Employed Manpower

In addition to retraining and upgrading present employees, there are a number of other steps which some employers have already taken. One example is the use of more technicians and subprofessionals to support each professional. The ratio of technicians to engineers in American industry has been disgracefully low in the past. In a 1957–1958 survey of 90 companies, the ratio was 0.8 to 1, far below the suggested ratio of 5 or more to 1.[17] This reflects serious underutilization of scarce high-talent manpower, resulting also in frustration by professionals who feel their talents are not being fully utilized. If more technicians cannot be easily recruited, they may have to be trained in technical institutes and junior or community colleges which require strong employer support. It may also be necessary to redesign existing professional work to utilize more subprofessionals or to train skilled workers as technicians.[18]

Better attention to incentives, including financial incentives related to wage and salary structures and methods of wage or salary payment, can contribute to more effective motivation of employed manpower and hence to its better utilization. Many of the tested procedures of good personnel administration are relevant.

The central responsibility of management in all of this points to the continued need to develop and improve the quality of management itself. An increasing number of firms are aware of the importance of "executive development" and send key managers to external programs in universities and elsewhere. But fewer seem to realize the relationship between improved management, the organization structure, and the philosophy of top management in dealing with subordinates. This is a complex interrelationship, which has been the subject of considerable research by behavioral scientists over the past decade.[19] This research deserves continued study, discussion, and application by more managers as they seek ways of motivating people in their organizations to higher performance.

## Participation in Manpower Advisory Committees

At the national and state levels, government administrators of programs such as social security, unemployment compensation, and the public Employment Service frequently ask employer, labor, and public representatives to serve on advisory committees. The Employment Service Task Force is a recent example; the Federal Advisory Council on Employment Security is another. If the proposed "Manpower Services Act of 1966" (S.2974) is eventually passed, federal and state advisory councils would be established to advise the Secretary of Labor and state employment security officials "on problems relating to the manpower services and the unemployment insurance program." (Sec. 14).

Employer representation and participation in these advisory committees can bring the experience and wisdom of employers to the discussions and to the attention of administrators. But it also provides employers with a better understanding of the relationship between the support they can give to improved programs and administration, on the one hand, and the help they can receive from these programs, on the other.

If employers feel strongly about the importance of their policy advice and of their recommendations on better administration of existing, or new, programs, they should insist that their ablest representatives serve on these committees and attend all regular meetings. There have been occasions on which employers participation was less than might have been desired, although the same comment could be made about labor representatives.

While comparisons between the United States and smaller European countries are not always valid, it is worth noting that Swedish employers through their representatives apparently take a very active role in offering policy advice and in working out specific programs through the National Labor Market Board. In West Germany, the Federal Institute for Labor Placement and Unemployment Insurance is governed by two tripartite bodies, one of which deals with general policies and the proposed budget and the other with management questions. Similar committees have been established at the state and city levels. A recent review of this experience concluded with the following observations:[20]

> Certain features, especially of the Swedish set-up, would seem to have application in the United States. . . . The Federal-State Employment Service needs from employers and labor much more continuous understanding, consultation, and participation in policy formulation than is provided by the present fitful and feeble advisory arrangements. . . . And a high degree of participation . . . . would provide additional links between those (Federal and State) levels within the Service, would challenge bureaucratic complacency with fresh views, and would help improve the coordination between public and private manpower planning.

This succinctly expresses my own views.

## Conclusions

The principal conclusions of this paper can now be summarized.

1. Employers can take the initiative in getting better help on their recruitment, screening, and placement problems from the federal-state Employment Service system. While the staff of the Service could do much more than they have done to show employers how they can be helpful, more employer initiative is also needed if they are to get the maximum benefit from a public service which their tax dollars help to support. Possibly the growing shortages of labor will provide the opportunity for closer coordination of private and public manpower policies. Better job vacancy information is needed as is more rapid exchange of information through computer technology.

2. Present hiring standards will certainly be revised, although this will require more preemployment and on-the-job training as members of disadvantaged groups are hired along with others of lower educational backgrounds and those (particularly younger workers) lacking any prior job experience.

3. Some labor shortages would not have occurred so early if employers generally had done more on-the-job training and taken on more apprentices for skilled trades. Public subsidies may possibly be necessary to encourage training that is in the self-interest of all employers and of society, although costly for any individual employer if he loses trained workers to others who have made no investment in training. Employers' concern

for improvement of public and vocational education has been deficient in some areas.

4. Much can be done to improve the utilization of presently employed manpower. This includes upgrading, retraining, job redesigning, employment of more subprofessionals in relation to professionals, more attention to financial incentives, and improving the quality of management. The interrelationship of management development, organizational structure, and management philosophy needs to be pondered on by more managers, drawing on behavioral-science research.

5. Active participation of employers in federal and state manpower advisory committees will improve the policy-making and administrative capacities of the various manpower agencies and will also provide for better understanding and coordination between private and public manpower policies. In part, this is a communication problem, between employers and government and between federal and state levels. If employers desire better policies and administration in the public manpower field, carping criticism from the outside is not likely to achieve them. In a dynamic, pluralistic society, employers and government need each other if manpower policies are to be effective.

## NOTES

1. Glenn Miller, Frederick A. Zeller, and Robert Miller, "Some Factors Affecting the Role of the Public Employment Service," *Labor Law Journal,* XVI (April, 1965), 210–211. The authors conclude: "At present, in the world of reality, it is our opinion that complete escape form this image is neither practical nor entirely desirable." This view contrasts with the Report of the Employment Service Task Force, December, 1965.

2. William Redmond (Chief of Employment Service, California Department of Employment), "Effective Employer Relations," *Employment Service Review,* II (December, 1965), 25–26.

3. An example of employer initiative by an established but expanding company is the experience of the Raytheon Manufacturing Company, one of the largest firms in Massachusetts. In 1951 a large backlog of military orders required expansion of company operations in the state. Mr. Leslie E. Woods, Director of Industrial Relations and Personnel, developed a 14-point program with the State Employment Service, including listing of *all* job vacancies with the Service; advising applicants in radio, TV, and newspaper advertising to consult the nearest State Employment

Service office, temporarily assigning Raytheon personnel to these offices; plant visits by S.E.S. staff and some temporary assignments to the Raytheon employment department; arranging for out-of-state recruitment; study of jobs and job families by Raytheon personnel and state office people to assist recruitment; redesign of some jobs; and inauguration of exit interviews. For a full account, see Case 46, pp. 386–437 (including exhibits) in Ben Lindberg, *Cases in Personnel Administration* (New York: Prentice Hall, Inc., 1954).

4. See discussion of this point in Frank H. Cassell (Director, U.S. Employment Service), "Jobs for the Hard-to-Employ in Private Enterprises," in *Princeton Manpower Symposium on Critical Issues in Employment Policy* (Princeton: Princeton University Press, 1966).

5. Walter Langway, "Readjusting Laid-off Defense Workers," *Employment Service Review*, II (December, 1965), 6–8.

6. George P. Shultz and Arnold R. Weber, *Strategies for the Displaced Worker* (New York: Harper and Row, 1966).

7. *Report of the Employment Service Task Force*, p. 50.

8. "'Bounty' Hunters Seeking Workers," *New York Times*, April 17, 1966, p. 74.

9. An experimental program of job vacancy surveys in 16 labor-market areas was initiated in 1964 by the Bureau of Employment Security and the Bureau of Labor Statistics. A large proportion of the employers cooperated willingly. The survey was repeated in 1965, and two rounds of surveys in the 16 areas will be conducted in 1966. Norman Medvin and James Higgins, "Job Vacancy Studies," *Employment Service Review*, III (March, 1966), 25–29. For an analytical discussion of job-vacancy information, see John T. Dunlop, "Job Vacancy Measures and Economic Analysis," paper presented at Research Conference on *The Measurement and Interpretation of Job Vacancies* (New York: National Bureau of Economic Research, 1966).

10. Charles E. Silberman, "Business Can Live with the 'Labor Shortage,'" *Fortune* (May, 1966), 112–115, 238–248.

11. In-plant promotion and technological changes do involve considerable on-the-job training of an informal character. The importance of this for continuing adjustment to technological changes has been stressed in an unpublished Harvard economics doctoral dissertation by Michael Piore. "The Labor Market, Technological Change, and the Job Structure" (June, 1966). Preliminary findings by Piore and by Peter B. Doeringer in another related dissertation were reported by Doeringer and Piore, "Labor Market Adjustment and Internal Training," Industrial Relations Research Association, *Proceedings of Annual Meeting*, December 1965, to be published.

12. The President of the National Machine Tool Builders Association stated at the Spring 1966 meeting in Boston that "skilled help has vanished and our industry is now in the initial stages of an on-the-job training program. . . . The problem is to find the recruits to be trained." *Boston Herald*, April 22, 1966. For a critical evaluation of existing apprenticeship programs, see George Strauss, "Apprenticeship: An Evaluation of the

Need," in Arthur M. Ross, editor, *Employment Policy and the Labor Market* (Berkeley: University of California Press, 1965), pp. 299–332.

13. Statement of Wilbur E. Landis, Manager of Technical Education Department of the Chrysler Corporation, before Clark Subcommittee of Senate Committee on Education and Labor, *Daily Labor Report,* February 23, 1966.

14. Margaret S. Gordon, *Retraining and Labor Market Adjustment in Western Europe* (Washington, D.C.: Manpower Administration, U.S. Department of Labor, 1965), p. 83.

15. Howard A. Rusk, M.D., "Untapped Labor Pool: Training Makes Nation's Handicapped a Vast Source of Manpower Needs," *New York Times,* April 24, 1966, p. 79.

16. Sumner Slichter, James J. Healy, and E. Robert Livernash, *The Impact of Collective Bargaining on Management* (Washington: The Brookings Institution, 1961), pp. 77–82. See also Felician F. Foltman, "Apprenticeship and Skill Training—a Trial Balance," *Monthly Labor Review,* LXXXVII (January, 1964), 29.

17. Frederick Harbison and Charles A. Myers, *Education, Manpower, and Economic Growth* (New York: McGraw-Hill, 1964), p. 164.

18. Douglas Aircraft Company and the International Association of Machinists have begun a joint project to train skilled workers on the job and in evening classes as aerospace electronic technicians. This will involve 8000 hours of paid training and 700 hours of related evening training in four years. *Business Week,* January 8, 1966, p. 80.

19. For a review of some recent research, see Charles A Myers, "Behavioral Sciences for Personnel Managers," *Harvard Business Review,* XLIV (July-Augest, 1966), 154–156, 158, 160, 162.

20. Richard A. Lester, *Manpower Planning in a Free Society* (Princeton: Princeton University Press, 1966), pp. 93–94.

# Discussion

## BY WILLIAM G. CAPLES

Professor Myers' paper calls upon employers to cooperate in national manpower policies in five ways:

1. By greater utilization of the Employment Service system.
2. By revision of hiring standards and redesign of jobs.
3. By engaging in more on-the-job and apprenticeship training.
4. By more effective utilization of existing work forces.
5. By participation in manpower advisory committees.

I have comments on each of these propositions, but I should like to do so in reverse order.

I thoroughly agree that employers should participate in advisory committees such as the Employment Service Task Force and the Federal Advisory Council on Employment Security. I think that employer participation in these committees at both the state and federal level cannot but help be to the advantage of all concerned. Our participation gives us as employers an opportunity to make our views known with respect to questions of manpower policy and to learn more about the views and attitudes of our colleagues in government and labor. It gives us an opportunity to participate actively in the policy-making process rather than just having policy made for us by others. It must also be realized that, when we fail to take advantage of our opportunities to form policy, our case is weakened when we complain of the ultimate result.

With apologies to Ed Robie I sometimes think I am a living example of employer participation, but we at Inland have found that it is worth our while to be as well aware as possible of what is going on in academic, government, and labor circles.

When I say this, I am aware it has been suggested that the establishment of advisory committees has taken the place of political patronage jobs. I remember a clever article in *Harper's* some time ago which referred to membership on such committees as nonjob jobs, and suggested that they were primarily a method of making businessmen feel important by bringing them to Washington and arranging for them to have their pictures taken with the Vice President or the Secretary of Labor. No federal agency, it suggested, is complete without its advisory committee, and no businessman has really "arrived" until he has been named to at least one.

There may be an element of this type of motivation in the establishment of some of these groups, but I do not think that it is the primary motive or even a major one. As Myers pointed out, employer participation in tripartite groups is very common in Western Europe and is considered essential to realistic economic and manpower planning. I shall certainly do what I can to encourage my colleagues in the business community to participate in these groups. I think we have something to offer and to learn from them.

Myers' penultimate proposition was that employers should more effectively utilize their manpower, in particular by using more technicians and subprofessional employees to support scarce high-talent professionals. Here again, I have no quarrel with what he has to say. I should like to point out, however, that in many cities of the United States the public education system is not geared to training very many of the kind of people he describes. Employers working with the public schools in their own communities should certainly be encouraged to cooperate in the establishment of programs for technical and subprofessional workers.

We at Inland have had for the last twenty years a cooperative program with Purdue University for the training of technicians in mechanical engineering, electrical engineering, and steelmaking occupations. Under this program full-time Inland employees at our Indiana Harbor Works go to school during their free time but at company expense. It is a two-year, self election program which has been quite popular with our employees, and it has supplied us with the needed skills Myers describes.

The rapid growth of the two-year college and community college provides all employers with an opportunity to encourage this sort of post high school training in their own areas. It is important that employers participate in planning and training programs of this type, serving on boards where asked. It is essential that these programs be modern and up-to-date and train people to use equipment and procedures which are actually in use. To do this will require continuing cooperation between employers and educators. And, I might add, unions.

Professor Myers refers to the continued need to develop and improve the quality of management. I agree that this is of the utmost importance, but it is not easy; and Myers has taken the precaution in his paper of not telling us how to do it. I am sure that the top executives of any company which wishes to grow and prosper spend considerable time and effort working toward this objective; written and oral statements of these people rarely fail to state this as a primary objective.

## Using the Employment Service

Now, about cooperation with the Employment Service system. I don't believe that anyone has given more to the U.S. Employment Service than has Inland Steel. After all, we gave it Frank Cassell, its present Director. But of course we are Indian givers. When Frank has sufficiently stirred things up, we will have him back again (we hope), and, hopefully again, the question of what to do about the Employment Service system will have been resolved.

Professor Myers wisely points out that employers utilize what first works best for them, and that too often the Employment Service has been considered a desperation measure as far as recruiting is concerned. It is also true, he says, that the Employment Service is in a vicious circle. Employers will not use it until its procedures are improved; these cannot be improved without the cooperation of employers.

I agree with him that the Service should serve *all* workers— not just the unemployed or the handicapped. It should serve all workers and employers who desire its help.

I suspect most employers will not welcome what Myers calls the "service" rather than the "sales" approach. We should always welcome informed assistance, but I am not sure we always do. And, as he points out, the Service can be of great help—indeed,

almost indispensable—when an employer is staffing a new operation in unfamiliar territory. But as I said, what is suggested will
meet with more business opposition than approval.

In our company experience we have found a wide variation in
the competence of individual managers of Employment Service
offices. In some cases we receive relatively little help; in others
we get energetic and creative assistance. This seems to depend
entirely on the perdispositions of the individual who is heading
the local office. We strongly support efforts to improve the
quality of management in the Service. We would like to see
counselors, interviewers, and supervisory staff upgraded in quality and in pay. There is no logical reason for Employment Service specialists to earn less than their counterparts in private
personnel offices—their jobs in many ways are substantially more
difficult. Their work loads are higher; their clientele is more
varied and at least as difficult to handle; the kinds of jobs and
industries with which they should be familiar are also more
varied. If we bear these facts in mind, and then remember that
their salaries are likely to be considerably less than the salaries
of the personnel managers of the companies with which they deal,
it is easy to understand why the personnel managers are likely to
be more skilled and sophisticated than their counterparts in the
Employment Service. The Service should be recruiting the best
among personnel specialists. I realize that steps are being taken
in this direction, and I support them and sincerely hope they
are successful.

### Hiring and Training

Myers calls upon employers to revise their present hiring standards. Obviously, he wants us to revise them downward. I admit
that sometimes we set up requirements that we cannot statistically justify. Most of us would be hard put to prove that a
high school diploma makes a measurable difference in performance on an unskilled job. On the other hand, do we want to
reward dropouts at the expense of graduates? It is quite obvious
that we select what we believe to be the best people available,
given the selection methods we use (which, let us hope, are
objective and, within psychological limits, accurate); and we
want these people to do as much, not as little, of the job re-

quired as possible. This realistically meets with the least friction the problems created by seniority systems, a fact of industrial life Professor Myers does not mention.

With respect to training, I think it only fair to point out that most employers do engage in training to the extent that they feel it is needed in order to provide qualified workers for the jobs that need to be filled. Additional training benefits the employee by making him more mobile and more marketable. But in a tight labor market, this is a liability to the employer. We should remember this when we encourage employers to set up general apprenticeship programs for the skilled trades when in fact the employer does not need total skills. Too often they feel that all they are doing is setting themselves up for piracy, which experience has taught them is another fact of industrial life, particularly for large employers who do extensive training.

Subsidized on-the-job training should help in overcoming this obstacle. There is no question that in many occupations the best, if not the only, training available is that which an employer can provide. His equipment, methods, and facilities are those which the trainee will actually encounter in the world of work. His work rules and methods of supervision are those with which the trainee must learn to live when he is ready to hold down a job. It takes a great deal of money, invested in equipment and in the education of vocational teachers, to provide adequate vocational education in a school situation, but vocational training is necessary both in school and on the job. And while there is no question that on-the-job training has an important place, we should not expect it to be done at an individual employer's expense unless that employer believes he can justify its cost to the company's stockholders.

Unfortunately, as Myers points out, employers too often think of their needs for skills in the short run only, failing to recognize that training is a fairly long-term project for many skills. Again, seniority systems and layoffs which affect all long-term training are not mentioned. The fact that we do not need tool-and-die makers or carpenters or lithographers this week does not mean that we will not need them during the next few years. I hope that more of us can learn that we have to plan ahead and how to plan ahead not only in terms of research and development and capital investment and market development but also in terms of making sure that people are available in the trades, skills, and occupations which take more than a few quick weeks to train for.

One way to do this is to work with the Employment Service in developing better methods of predicting manpower needs and demands and in publicizing the work that is even now being done. Too many employers are not even aware of this work, the proceeds of which is made available in such publications as the *Monthly Labor Review* and the *Occupational Outlook Handbook*. Too many employers make no serious effort to predict their needs for skilled manpower any further ahead than the current season. This short-run outlook naturally results in skill shortages and piracy when demand rises. I should like to see a broad program, particularly aimed at smaller employers, to inform them of the need for long-range manpower planning and training programs and to tell them about information which is available to them.

I realize that making projections is a two-way street, and the government's projections cannot be any better than its information. Employers have an obligation to provide information on shutdowns, moves, and other major shifts in their labor force, so that these changes can be taken into account in making projections about regional or occupational shifts in demand for labor. I recognize that sometimes, for competitive or other reasons, employers may be reluctant to provide detailed information very far in advance. But I hope that methods can be devised so that they can be protected, which will encourage them to make the needed information available.

A major factor in manpower supply and utilization in the large urban areas—and apparently we are rapidly becoming a nation of large urban areas—is the public transportation system. This is a subject not covered in Professor Myers' paper. We must work out methods whereby large numbers of people can be moved swiftly and economically about urban areas to where their skills and services are needed when they are needed.

In conclusion, I should like to say that there is much to agree with and little to criticize in Myers' paper. This makes it very difficult for a commentator. It is more fun for the audience when a discussant has the opportunity to tear a paper apart than when he takes it point by point and says "I agree." This is the penalty which the audience has to pay when the author of the paper being discussed does so good a job.

# Discussion

## BY EDWARD A. ROBIE

In these brief comments I should like to do two things: first, give my reactions to the principal suggestions made in Professor Myers' excellent paper, and, second, briefly share with you some of the experience of a relatively large urban employer that may have implications for the question of manpower policy generally. The Equitable Life Assurance Society employs about 7000 people in the Home Office in New York and another 4500 in field offices in all 50 states. In addition, we have about 8000 commission sales agents. About 60 per cent of our salaried employees are female; about 40 per cent of our employees are age 25 or under, and almost half of these are teenagers. Our termination rate is about 25 per cent and we must therefore hire at an annual rate of almost 3000 people. This summer we will hire over 1000 teenage beginners in New York alone, most of them brand new high school graduates, and we will hire over 300 new college graduates or people with advanced degrees.

I agree with Professor Myers that in the manpower area, as in most other areas where there are substantial national problems, employers should realize more fully than many of us seem to do that the preservation of a relatively free system depends on how well the private sector recognizes and does its part of the job. Persistence of large ghettos in our major urban areas, with rates of unemployment far above national levels, simply cannot be either condoned or wished away. And the related problems of discrimination and high rates of Negro unemployment after years of deprivation are equally matters for concern and responsible action by those in the private sector of the economy.

A number of leading businessmen have begun to speak up about business' responsibility for helping to solve major economic and social problems; most recently, for example, we have had major addresses on this theme by Henry Ford, George Champion of

Chase, and Sol Linowitz of Xerox. I wonder if the time has not come for more major business corporations to assign to a top-ranking, highly competent executive the full-time responsibility for becoming informed about such major problems as unemployment, poverty and the administration of welfare, civil rights, public education, and housing, and for defining the proper role of the corporation in dealing with them. He would serve to focus the attention of the entire management in such a way as to stimulate creative thinking and action both inside and outside the corporation. What I am suggesting is quite different in scope and objectives from either lobbying or the so-called community relations and citizenship participation programs that some companies have recently developed. The role of a top-level, full-time executive would be not to relieve other members of management from becoming involved in developing and implementing solutions to major national problems but to stimulate them to greater involvement.

## Cooperation with the Employment Service

Professor Myers begins his treatment of specific areas for employer action with a discussion of cooperation with the federal-state Employment Service. I agree with his broad view of the Employment Service function, although I suspect that a majority of employers currently favor the narrow view of the Chamber of Commerce report. It seems evident to me that a sensible and efficient manpower program requires much closer cooperation between employers, educational institutions, and both government and private training and placement agencies than we have had in the past, and that the Employment Service occupies a key position in the development of such a coordinated manpower program.

But if the local Employment Service offices are to become the "comprehensive manpower service centers" that the Employment Service Task Force has suggested, then a number of questions arise as to what kinds of objectives these centers may appropriately seek as they work more closely with those who educate and train and with those who employ. Will they see their mission as controlling the labor market or as serving it within a pluralistic system? Will they actively seek to put private employment agencies and local services out of business, or will they seek rather to supplement them? Will they favor one employer or one category of employers over another or strive to serve all equally? Will they take over guidance functions that are an intrinsic part of the responsibility of high school and college administrators and teachers, or will they strengthen the effectiveness of these functions by providing needed and improved linkages with those doing guidance work in the schools? This last danger seems to me an especially important one since hard-pressed school boards are looking for all possible ways to save money, and are, in my judgment, far too ready to give up to the Employment Service or any other willing taker not just the referral function but much of the vocational-guidance function for those youngsters destined for jobs rather than college.

Better information on job vacancies strikes me as an especially vital challenge both to the Employment Service and to private and public employers who must cooperate to provide the basic data. Judging from the report in the March 1966 *Employment Service Review* by Medvin and Higgins, as well as by testimony at Congressional hearings in May, a great deal of progress on this has recently been made. Experimental surveys in 16 urban areas show that it is both feasible and practical to collect job-vacancy information by detailed occupation. The recent publication of the proceedings of the Conference on the Measurement and Interpretation of Job Vacancies by the National Bureau of Economic Research has made available in one volume a great deal of essential dialogue between top experts on the entire question. Certainly the collection and dissemination of job-vacancy information is far from a simple task. But in the light of the tremendous need for this type of information and the progress made experimentally over the past two years, I am distressed that the available funds for fiscal 1966 are the same as for the previous year. When good job-vacancy data become promptly and regularly available by market area, given the potentialities of computers for storing and analyzing such data, we should have, it seems to me, filled the most important informational gap that now exists in our planning for effective manpower utilization.

Furthermore, good job vacancy data might help to enlarge

what is already a growing area for private business: the service bureau. Many needed workers could be trained for a fee that worker-hungry employers would be happy to pay, or workers could be trained and organized into independent business units to serve customers in fields ranging from domestic service to electronic programming.

Professor Myers suggests greater initiative by employers in cooperating with the Employment Service. We have found that Employment Service personnel are sometimes not permitted to take the time to visit our company to become better acquainted with what we want and how we operate. Whether this is because of understaffing, or because our invitation was undiplomatically proffered, I do not know. More likely, it was because the invitation came from a single employer to regular counselors, and there must, of course, be a practical limit to such visits. Would it not be worthwhile for there to be established a regular program for Employment Service personnel to visit employers, sponsored jointly by the Service and by a prominent business group such as the Chamber of Commerce? This might be similar to the Business-Education days in many cities.

At the Equitable we have used the Employment Service rather extensively throughout the country. In New York City we have found private agencies more useful for obtaining experienced people, but in other parts of the country this has not necessarily been the case. Recently we had a severely limited amount of time to establish an office to administer Part B of Medicare in Nashville, Tennessee. This required about 75 people, most of them experienced, in a very tight labor market. And it was essential, of course, that this be an integrated group of employees. The Tennessee Employment Service proved most helpful to us; the quantity of referrals was not high, but the quality was good.

## Hiring and Training

Turning to Professor Myers' discussion of the possible revision of hiring standards, I find that he deals most realistically with several of the employer's problems in considering disadvantaged job applicants, especially the problem of promotional sequences.

I do not know if our experience is typical, but I must admit that our best efforts to match people and jobs seem to leave plenty of room for improvement. Even experienced interviewers have too little direct knowledge of the jobs for which they are screening or selecting people, and they probably have too much of a tendency to depend on tests, some of which are of questionable validity. They are working, moreover, in an extremely dynamic situation, with the quality and quantity of the applicants changing, and with the nature of the work for which they are hiring people also changing. Add to this the seasonal availability of high school and college graduates and heavy pressures to judge qualifications without discrimination, and you have a pretty harried manpower operation in a large company.

Under these circumstances, we believe it makes sense to keep our hiring criteria pretty flexible and to do a considerable amount of experimentation. One of our experiments has involved hiring a number of dropout teenagers, in cooperation with a New York City agency named JOIN. Why did we decide to do this? First, because we were concerned with the youth unemployment problem in New York, and we wanted to learn more about the characteristics and job potential of dropouts; and, second, because we know that early turnover is high among young high school graduates, and we saw dropouts as a new and possibly better source of labor for some of our lower-level clerical work.

We have learned a few interesting things from this experiment. The clearest distinction between our dropouts and our high school graduates has been in their records for absence and lateness rather than in ability to do the work. The firing rate for dropouts is much higher, and the voluntary quit rate is lower. It is too soon to judge promotional potential, although a number have been promoted. Most of these youngsters are Negro or Puerto Rican, with the kinds of deprived and chaotic backgrounds with which you all are familiar. They had sporadic school attendance before dropping out, and an established conviction of being imprisoned by "the system," and of going nowhere. What they need from us is not only the opportunity to move upward but also the kind of counseling and supervision that enables them to see, to feel, and to want to seize this opportunity. Actually, we have found their expectations higher and their patience lower

than is the case with most high school graduates, since they are
much more suspicious to begin with. Just to be put into any filing
or messenger job tends to reinforce their distrust, yet they have
the qualifications for little else. So we are now looking into supplementary educational programs, such as those being developed
by the National Association of Manufacturers and the Board for
Fundamental Education in Indianapolis. This program, known
as STEP, has had some early success with new methods of teaching basic subjects. We hope to be able to combine work and
education in a way that will both help the youngster and show
him or her how to move "up."

Even among high school graduates there has been a noticeable
change in New York City in 1966. There are fewer youngsters
available and, by our standards, they are of lower quality. We
are, therefore, taking substantially larger numbers who are
below our previous intelligence-test norms. And because the nonwhite population is increasing, we are taking a much bigger proportion of nonwhites for these beginning clerical jobs; our nonwhite hiring rate will probably jump from about 10 per cent
last year to close to 30 per cent this year.

These changes, of course, pose interesting and challenging training questions. We already train most of our own stenographers
and typists, but we may have to put more emphasis on spelling
and grammar and, for clerks working with numbers, on arithmetic.

In discussing training, Professor Myers refers to the great
expense of the JC experiment and suggests that public funds
to encourage on-the-job training for disadvantaged youth might
be "even more effective." Frankly, I think there is room for
continued experimentation with these intensive and comprehensive programs, particularly for the most difficult cases, and especially for boys. I rather doubt if enough supplemental services
can be provided in on-the-job training programs for the truly
hard-core youngsters. I see no chance that our urban schools can
bring about the minimum essential educational reforms in the
ghetto areas in less than five or ten years, and meanwhile we
appear to have thousands of youngsters needing substantial help.
For, example, I would favor the type of intensive program re-

cently proposed for the Bedford-Stuyvesant section of Brooklyn by a group known as Training Resources for Youth. This program would train up to 1000 unemployed boys in one of six service occupations, such as food service or appliance repair and service. It would be about as expensive as the JC, but I would bet on an extremely high placement record.

One other possibility might be a kind of "Neighborhood Youth Corps" applied to the private sector, rather than limited to public agencies as it has thus far been. But as Professor Mooney pointed out at Princeton last month, the NYC has suffered from lack of really meaningful jobs, lack of opportunity for advancement, poor supervisors, and inadequate incentives. Hence, the extension of the idea to private employers would certainly require special efforts to overcome these deficiencies.

It seems to me that Professor Myers' reference to rather broad public subsidies for on-the-job training of the unemployed is also worthy of more careful consideration than has yet been given it. There seems to be some interest in this approach, which, incidentally, was suggested as an idea for experimentation by the Chairman of the Equitable's Board, James F. Oates, Jr., at the Harvard Business School in 1964. We so far know little about the success of the Bureau of Apprenticeship training program which reimburses the employer $25 a week for each trainee, and it would be extremely interesting if someone familiar with it could tell us what kind of problems this has met. I am intrigued by the possibilities of a tax offset or direct payroll subsidy scheme, even though I recall that William Gomberg at Princeton last month expressed great lack of enthusiasm for a subsidized on-the-job training program at Chrysler for mechanics and body repairmen. He felt the government was merely subsidizing what the auto makers ought to do anyhow in their own best interests. But when there are substantial job needs that remain unmet for considerable periods and substantial numbers of unemployed people unqualified to fill them, reasonable incentives to business to help bridge this gap seem clearly in the public interest.

One brief word to supplement Professor Myers' reference to the physically handicapped. More work needs to be done in the design of buildings and factories to accommodate the handicapped. Last Sunday's *New York Times* contained an excellent summary by Dr. Howard Rusk on the current status of efforts to reduce architectural barriers to the handicapped.

In the section dealing with more effective utilization of employed manpower, Professor Myers correctly stresses the need for improved management. We personnel people are not as helpful as we should be in manpower planning for our firms. The speed with which the personnel shape of our organizations is changing is really quite remarkable. For example, between 1956 and 1966, the proportion of Equitable employees in the first four of our twenty-one salary grades went down from 80 to 60 per cent; the proportion in the middle grades, from five through ten, doubled from 15 to 30 per cent; and the proportion above grade ten also doubled from 5 to 10 per cent. Since our grade ranges have been adjusted upward for inflation about once every two years, this represents, theoretically at least, a true upgrading of the organization. We have made various projections for the next ten years. And we expect these trends to continue, with probably some relative slowing of the rate of increase in the middle levels.

In addition to analyses by levels, we should be more aware of such characteristics of our work force as the ratio of technicians to professionals. Most professional people seem to me to spend too little time in the most challenging tasks that lead to innovation and too much time on routine tasks that could be delegated. I admit to being one personnel man who has not made much of a dent in this problem.

This is, however, not only a question of management; it is also a question of the quality of education that future managers get before they come to business. Is education turning out a sufficient supply of really innovative leaders, whose future pioneering will enlarge the number of jobs available? Is there, as John Gardner has said, an "anti-leadership vaccine" being administered in our colleges? Is there any strong communication link between business—the main job-producing component—and education—the main people-producing component? I believe that the communication link is far too weak and is greatly in need of attention at both the secondary and more advanced levels.

In conclusion, I find little to disagree with in Professor Myers' paper and a great deal that stimulates positive comment. The note of urgency he sounded for employer involvement is fully justified if we are not to lose much more of our freedom of action than most of us want to occur.

CHAPTER **11**

# The Role of Organized Labor

## BY RICHARD A. LESTER

Generally throughout our history, organized labor has been a force for public improvement and promotion of the commonweal. However, its net contribution to national progress has varied from period to period. In certain decades, the American labor movement seemed somewhat out of tune with the times and had problems in adjusting its conventional views to significant changes in the environment. It may well be that we are living through such a period now.

Until the 1930's organized labor in this country tended to be dominated by the craft tradition. It was, in Perlman's term, largely "job-conscious unionism." Interest centered on control of jobs under union rules and collective agreements; political action was distrusted. A shift of view occurred in the 1930's, when much of organized labor adopted the philosophy and program of the New Deal. Government intervention was favored to promote collective bargaining, social insurance, minimum wages and maximum hours for men, and other forms of government intervention in and regulation of economic affairs.

Thus, organized labor in the 1940's and 1950's seemed to have an economic philosophy that was partly rooted in traditional job and craft protectionism while espousing, especially at the national level, a New Deal sort of progressivism.

Now in the 1960's we face a somewhat different set of economic problems and new ways of approaching old issues. High levels of employment and rapid economic growth have given rise to questions of wage-price policy, balance of payments, an active manpower policy, nondiscrimination in employment, cost-benefit analysis, and so forth. Not only have there been additional kinds of intervention by the federal government in the labor market but they have been accompanied by a demand for more rationality in the manpower field.

No longer are we content to rely on just monetary-fiscal policies and to accept without question the results of free collective bargaining and the thinking of local school boards. The quest for more rationality in the development and use of the nation's labor resources has led to serious questioning of the traditional ways of handling problems of occupational selection and labor mobility.

The actual and potential role of organized labor in the nation's manpower program needs to be examined in the light of developments in the economy and changes in thinking about manpower and effective use of human resources. The discussion here is largely in terms of national interests and government policy. No attempt will be made to examine arrangements for income maintenance or interlocational transfer rights achieved under collective bargaining. Generally, increased employment security for individual workers contributes to the welfare of the nation, but exclusive arrangements can provide gains for senior employees at the expense of younger employees or may mean reduced opportunities for youth.

## Labor's Uncertain Image

How has organized labor met the demand for greater equity and rationality in the preparation and use of the nation's manpower resources? Has it provided the proper moral leadership and presented a well-conceived, consistent program for work training, equality of job opportunity, and effective use of all the nation's manpower resources?

The principles of equity and rationality in the use of a nation's manpower present real problems for a set of sectional representation agencies as diverse, decentralized, and divided as those collectively known as the American labor movement.

Historically, organized labor in the United States has held strong moral positions based on equity, has vigorously supported free public education for all at an increasingly advanced level, and has taken other steps to improve the quality of parts of the nation's work force. Yet many individual unions have, by such means as membership and apprentice restrictions, pursued protectionist policies that have served to discriminate against equally or better qualified persons whom they have excluded from "the club."

The American labor movement has generally pressed for full employment through expansionist policies and competition in product markets in order to promote efficiency and the maximum Gross National Product. Yet, partly to avoid discrimination against, or unemployment among, their members and also in some cases to achieve monopoly-like gains, labor unions have sought to wall off work and to substitute for competition a "web of rules" and an unbalanced wage structure, both of which may have adverse effects on the efficient use of the nation's labor resources.

The confused image of organized labor partly arises from the divergent policies of individual unions. Craft unions like the building, printing, and metal-working trades are likely to be exclusionist and protectionist. They are apt to have little interest in and use for the public employment service. On the other hand, large industrial unions, especially outside the South, have generally been nondiscriminatory in membership and workshop policies and have been interested in building up the quality and use of the public employment service.

This unclear image also arises from the level of generality of different echelons in the labor movement. The central federation (the AFL-CIO) has a broad constituency and a political viewpoint. The affiliated national and international unions focus largely on collective bargaining within their jurisdictions. The horizon of local unions is likely to be even narrower. Self-interest representation concentrated on a small part of the economy, especially if that part has a sheltered local market, can prove to be quite parochial and exclusionist. Thus, the AFL-CIO may take positions, say on equal employment opportunity or on government training programs, that may be opposed in practice by many locals of its affiliated national unions.

In fairness to organized labor it should be stated that government in this country also experiences similar discordance of policy and conflicts of interest among the federal, state, and local levels. Indeed, local opposition to federal policies may arise from pursuit of parochial aims by local business, labor, or other interest groups.

Furthermore, it may seem a bit unrealistic to expect organized labor to promote a unified manpower program before scholars and the federal government have developed a convincing conceptual basis for determining what kinds of training and labor mobility are in the public interest. In order to achieve modification of apprenticeship practices and restrictive rules developed under collective bargaining, presumably it is first necessary, by systematic analysis, to prove that the efficient use of manpower in the national interest requires such changes. Even in clearcut cases, there may continue to be resistance by some unions, as the locomotive fireman's experience demonstrates.

Perhaps another reason that organized labor in the United States should not be expected to pioneer in national manpower policy is that a growing proportion of the economy is outside the realm of collective bargaining agreements. Organized labor seems somewhat removed from most of the growing job opportunities, most of the educational training for work, and most of the problems encountered by disadvantaged elements in the job market. To many youths and disadvantaged adults, certain parts of the labor movement may seem to have been creating barriers to their employment and to their career advancement through practices that reserve employment, promotion, and ample benefits for an in-group.

## Labor's Predicament and Opportunity

Organized labor in America has focused mainly on collective bargaining. By tradition, collective bargaining is democratic determination of wages and working conditions, and the results of decentralized negotiations have been accepted with little question. Before the mid-1950's, few asked whether the negotiated terms agreed or conflicted with the national interest. Indeed, until recent years, the national interest in the industrial-relations field was largely defined in terms of collective bargaining.

Lately, however, more and more emphasis is being placed on national planning. Collective bargaining is facing a challenge of rationality based on systematic analysis and new definitions of national interest. Indicative or guidance planning in many countries, including underdeveloped nations, has led to analyses aimed at the best use of manpower resources to promote economic growth. Naturally such reexamination has led to proposals for on-the-job training, institutional training for unemployed adults, improvement of the public Employment Service, and reform of general and vocational education and the collective bargaining system itself.[1] Questions are being raised about the economic validity of various manpower programs, about the effectiveness of the wage-benefit structure for manpower purposes, and about the inflationary pressures under varying degrees of unemployment.

Such questioning challenges the whole system of industrial relations built up since 1930. How can rational planning for use of the nation's labor resources be reconciled with two-sided, decentralized negotiations based on bargaining power and protection of sectional interests? What should organized labor's long-run goals be in the manpower field? What should the role of the labor movement be in national manpower planning and the implementation of that planning?

The challenge of planning for rational use of the nation's manpower resources raises a whole new set of problems for organized labor, while at the same time presenting it with a new range of opportunities.

The labor movement can hold fast to well-established practices and views and resist pressures to make training, wage-benefit structures, and labor mobility more efficient and effective for national manpower purposes. That would mean holding to the somewhat inconsistent position that organized labor is for planning everywhere in the economy except in the labor sector.

Or the union movement in America could reexamine the conventional views and traditional practices that obstruct manpower planning and develop a comprehensive program for labor that makes sense in the present and prospective environment. That is what the Swedish trade union movement did beginning some dozen years ago. It decided that, in a full employment economy, an "active labor market policy" is necessary to facilitate rational labor mobility, to avoid serious labor shortages, and to keep down inflationary wage-price pressures. A policy of dealing with manpower issues in the framework of a national economic program involves long-range planning for the training, transfer, and use of manpower resources and a wage policy compatible with a comprehensive manpower program. Of course, one should recognize that, for many obvious reasons, it was easier for the Swedish labor movement to join with the government in a comprehensive manpower program than it would be for the American labor movement.

Full participation by organized labor in this country in a comprehensive, rational manpower policy would serve to open up to the union movement new areas of interest and of opportunity for leadership and service. It would bring organized labor more fully into issues of educational policy, vocational guidance, and the employment problems of youth and disadvantaged adults. It should assist in eliminating inefficiencies in training, thus reducing workers' losses of potential income during training periods. And it would help to change the image of organized labor among youth and women and in the expanding white-collar and service sectors of the economy.

## Labor's Training Practices

Parts of organized labor face increasing criticism in the training area. That is not only because of discrimination against nonwhites in selection for apprenticeship. A large part of the apprenticeship system itself is inefficient and antiquated.

In its January 1966 report the Council of Economic Advisers said (p. 86):

Ways must also be found to expand more quickly the supply of skilled construction labor. Restrictions on entry not only retard the growth of industry but also have adverse social effects, since they tend to keep Negro youths out of attractive types of employment. To meet the needs of rapid growth and equality, vocational programs for skilled craftsmen must be stepped up.

In his March 1963 *Report on Manpower Requirements, Resources, Utilization, and Training,* the Secretary of Labor stated (p. 7):

Apprenticeship programs of the current magnitude will not supply enough skilled workers even to replace those who die, retire, or transfer out of their occupations in the years ahead—without any allowance for the large additional needs for journeymen to staff new positions expected in many trades.

The union complaints about that part of the report apparently discouraged discussion of apprenticeship deficiencies in the subsequent three annual reports, and, apparently, barriers have been placed on training under the Manpower Development and Training Act (MDTA) everywhere in the country in the skills subject to apprenticeship (except for some projects for preapprenticeship training outside the regular apprenticeship programs).

The yearly figures for registered apprentices in training have not changed much during the past fifteen years. They have fluctuated between 155,000 and 188,000, whereas the Department of Labor estimates that this country needs 230,000 skilled craftsmen a year just to replace attrition losses. Over three-fifths of the registered apprentices are in the building trades, and most of the rest are in the metal and printing trades.[2]

Weaknesses in present apprenticeship arrangements are evident. The average age of apprentices in training in this country is 23 years,[3] compared with 17 to 18 years in European countries. For the training actually obtained, the apprenticeship period in many cases is far too long—three years for a painter, four years for a carpenter, and four to five years for plumbers and pipefitters.[4] Such long periods discourage employer training of apprentices and discourage continuation of apprenticeship to completion. Although apprentice wages generally advance about every six months, the median pay of apprentices during apprenticeship is estimated at about 50 per cent of the journeyman's rate for painters, electricians, and machinists, at about 60 per cent of the journeyman's rate for plumbers, and about 70 per cent for carpenters.[5] Given the family responsibilities associated with the relatively high age of apprentices and their relatively low pay and inferior status, the apprenticeship dropouts (cancellations and suspensions) in the 1950's and early 1960's have, in almost every year, exceeded the completions of apprenticeship.[6] A dropout rate of over 50 per cent is probably the highest of any major training progrm in the country. It occurs because the sacrifice required is too great. One study in 1953–1954 showed that 40 to 50 per cent of the apprentices voluntarily discontinuing apprenticeship dropped out because they needed more money or had an opportunity to receive a journeymen's wage.[7]

Respectable apprenticeship programs, using modern methods of instruction and tools, could be developed for painters, carpenters, bricklayers, and some other skilled crafts that could be completed in a year or a year and a half. With more efficient methods, the amount of training now performed over a three-year period in many localities could undoubtedly be accomplished, with the same average output of productive work, in a much shorter time, and, therefore, with much less sacrifice on the part of the worker.

Given the inefficiency in training, the long time periods, and the relatively low pay, inferior status, and other restrictions, it is not surprising that only about a third of the practicing craftsmen today have been through a regular apprenticeship. A large percentage of the other two-thirds have had little or no systematic training for their particular skilled occupation.

In many localities, skilled building craftsmen are in short supply. In the Trenton area, for example, house painters have for more than three years been so short that owners of buildings have to wait a year or more, and much of the painting is of poor quality; the result is that homeowners frequently paint their own houses. Despite the fact that painters have been in such short supply, no training of painters is occurring anywhere under the MDTA. The same lack of training projects, with the exception of *preapprentice* training, applies generally to all the building trades. Invisible restrictions on training in the apprenticeable trades seem to exist under both MDTA and vocational education in the high schools.

All this has resulted in unfortunate impressions in the community, especially on the part of homeowners and their wives, who suffer from shortages of building tradesmen and who find it hard to understand how a good auto mechanic can be trained in one year but a painter, carpenter, or nonindustrial plumber officially requires three to five years of training. It is well to bear in mind that much of the work of the building trades is observed and paid for by individual consumers, who, therefore, have views on the training and efficiency of building craftsmen.

The consumer also knows that negotiated wage increases in the building trades have been rising rapidly. In 1966 the negotiated increases were commonly 7 to 8 per cent annually—a rate of increase percentagewise considerably above the rates in industry generally—"due in part to construction manpower shortages that exist in most areas." It is explained that, as the building manpower "shortages become become wider and more acute, the unions' bargaining muscles get bigger" and the building-trades employers are in a weaker position to resist union demands.[8] The union rates affect the nonunion scales in building, a fact which is significant to the general consumer because at least half of all dwellings are built under nonunion conditions.

Given these circumstances, it seems evident that the training of people for building occupations in this country needs thorough reexamination. Rationalization of training for building and other skilled trades is long overdue. France and West Germany have national practical tests and credentials for those who pass them, all under national supervision. A system of national tests and certification of competence open to all encourages efficiency in training and mobility among employers and areas of the nation. Clearly there should be considerable training for skilled building occupations like painters, carpenters, bricklayers, and residential plumbers under the MDTA, which can provide training and training allowances for periods up to two years. Clearly also there needs to be integration and coordination of various training programs for particular occupations—vocational education in high schools, apprenticeship training on the job and in classes, and MDTA training.

In the working out of such coordinated and rational training arrangements, the AFL-CIO could provide real leadership. The workers in this country and their labor movement have a vital interest in the whole gamut of training arrangements. In this connection the AFL-CIO ought to have a well-reasoned position with respect to legislative proposals, such as the Prouty-Curtis bill, which provide for such incentives to additional training as: tax credits under the corporate income tax allowed for expenditures on on-the-job training, levy of a training tax on payrolls with tax credits, grants for approved training expenditures by employers (as in France and Great Britain), or the training of disadvantaged workers in privately and publicly subsidized sheltered workshops which produce goods and services for sale (as in Great Britain and Sweden).

The American labor movement should also have a position, presumably favorable, with respect to government support for skill training so that employed workers could take such training on their own time in order to upgrade themselves to fill real shortage occupations. To meet the requirements in shortage occupations, a small subsidy in the form of instructional costs, transportation, and meal expenses for the worker, and perhaps a slight monetary incentive, would generally show a positive cost-benefit return for society and provide a real long-run benefit for the participating worker. The training allowances for workers under MDTA also need to be reviewed from the training viewpoint and separated from the particular state's unemployment compensation standard. Perhaps a trainee should receive a small bonus as an incentive for a good record and completion of a training program under MDTA. One would expect the labor movement to have a variety of proposals for expansion, liberalization, and improvement of public and private training in this country. A comprehensive and adequate training program for youth and adults is of great importance to workers and their families. The many facets of education and training, both pre-employment and on-the-job, should be of major concern to the American labor movement. The pieces need to be put in proper perspective and made part of a consistent total package.

## The Wage-Benefit Structure and Mobility

A national manpower program cannot disregard widespread imbalance in the structure of wages and employee benefits that would have perverse allocational effects. Presumably the inter-industry, interoccupational, and interregional differentials in pay and benefits should assist in the proper allocation of labor resources. At least they should not serve to maintain significant labor shortages and surpluses in particular industries, occupations, and areas. For instance, they should not encourage capable men to become office boys for railroads, janitors in automobile plants, or truck drivers rather than technicians, school teachers, or male registered nurses.

Studies of wages in 10 countries over the past two decades or longer indicate that industry, occupational, and regional wage rankings have been quite stable over relatively long periods of time. The studies also show that changes in wage differentials have not played an important role in labor allocation, that "the movements of labor have been preponderantly wage-insensitive." [9] One might conclude either (a) that the existing wage structure is not sufficiently off-balance to have important adverse allocative effects, or (b) that parts of the structure are perverse from an allocation viewpoint, but the economy does not suffer too much injury because adjustments are made through the attraction of job and promotion opportunities and on-the-job training.

One would expect collective bargaining to cause the wage-benefit structure to be influenced more by bargaining power, coercive comparisons, and ability to pay and less by manpower shortages and surpluses than would be true in the absence of unions. Under collective bargaining, all covered occupations tend to move up in unison regardless of labor-supply factors in particular occupations, and wage-benefit levels are often fixed for two or three years in advance whatever the manpower conditions.

Considerable doubt exists as to whether trade unionism in this country has served to make the wage structure more unbalanced from an allocation viewpoint than it would be without unionism. In a study of the wage structure in the United States published in 1955, Lloyd Reynolds and Cynthia Taft concluded that trade unionism had had a net beneficial effect on the wage structure.[10] It may be, however, that the situation has changed somewhat during the past decade with the contraction in blue-collar employment in mining, manufacturing, and railroading and the great expansion in employment in service lines, including government, where wage and benefit levels generally are relatively low.

In addition, negotiated employee benefits may have adverse effects on labor mobility. They tend to accentuate interfirm and interindustry differentials in compensation; expenditures on such benefits average two and a half times as high a percentage of payroll in high-paying as in low-paying firms and almost double the percentage of payroll in unionized firms compared to non-union firms.[11] More adverse is the effect on mobility of the non-transferability of benefits between firms and the gap in coverage that generally occurs with change of employer. In addition, seniority in agreements is an allocative factor that may help to immobilize parts of the labor force through strong ties to particular industrial plants.

These are complicated matters that cannot be adequately treated by citing past studies, particular cases, or abstract analysis. At this stage, any conclusions concerning manpower effects must be quite tentative. In view of the growing interest in these areas, the labor movement ought to give serious hought and study to the consequences for labor mobility of existing wage-benefit and seniority provisions in agreements and possible modifications, including transportable benefits, that are desirable from a labor-mobility viewpoint. Some unions have programs in these areas, but the AFL-CIO has not developed a well-reasoned position as a basis for leadership in these matters.

## Organized Labor and National Planning

The trade union movement has much to contribute to a national program for the most effective development and use of the nation's human resources. Labor early recognized that the terms and conditions of industrial employment could not properly be left to management determination restricted only by the very imperfect operation of market forces. Market forces in the labor sector tended to neglect vital human considerations and frequently (from a long-run national viewpoint) stimulated misapplication of resources, as, for instance, in the case of child labor and health-injurious working conditions. Market forces alone also proved to be rather inefficient in avoiding and correcting demand-supply imbalances in the labor market and corresponding unemployment.

Planning to achieve more rational programs for the preparation and utilization of human resources and to avoid the inflationary pressures of shortages in particular occupations and areas is an essential part of a program of full employment. Organized labor in this country must face up to the implications of that fact as central labor federations already have in a number of European countries.

The leaders of the labor movement in this country have strongly supported the Area Redevelopment Act (ARA), the MDTA, and a vigorous and comprehensive public Employment Service, which it believes may require nationalization of the present service. Organized labor has also supported some measures to increase labor mobility such as portable pensions and government support for the geographical transfer of jobless workers to areas of expanding job opportunity. Individual local unions have developed on-the-job projects under the MDTA, although the total number of trainees up to the beginning of this year was quite small—under 8000.[12]

The main deficiency is that the AFL-CIO has no well-formulated position and overall program in the manpower field. Instead of thinking big and taking advantage of recent developments, the central federation has tended to reaffirm past positions, while affiliated unions have pursued policies and practices that appear inconsistent and even contrary to the interests of workers generally.

In the manpower area, one can argue that the American labor movement has been missing a real opportunity to improve its posture and reputation with youth, women, and workers generally. We live in a world characterized by increasingly rapid obsolescence of occupational skills, by increasing importance of general education and continued training, and, in public affairs, by increasing stress on social goals and on comparisons of economic and social gains with economic and social costs. Many people, in and and out of government, are thinking in terms of more rational ways of using our manpower resources. They are looking toward a better adjusted labor force and a better adjusted society. More and more, there is recognition of the need for a comprehensive view of manpower problems within a framework of social and economic goals.

Not only does the labor movement need to develop its own concepts of national manpower policy but it should also request and receive the opportunity to participate effectively in the formulation and execution of the nation's manpower program. Of course, the National Manpower Advisory Committee under the MDTA has labor members, and the same is true of the regional and state committees. But organized labor and management should have more than membership on advisory committees that meet quarterly. For example, the federal-state Employment Service should have its own tripartite national board of governors as in Western Germany and Sweden. Organized labor and management should play a significant role in discussions about the annual manpower report of the President. They certainly should participate more fully in the determination of policies and programs of public vocational education and other preparation of youth for employment. In these and other ways, organized labor could be more fully integrated into the nation's manpower program.

Effective participation by organized labor in an active manpower policy means full engagement at the local level. Manpower programs must be implemented locally. But a manpower program needs national direction and oversight if local efforts are to be coordinated so that they can make meaningful contributions to a comprehensive set of goals. That is why the AFL-CIO at the national level needs first to develop the rationale for organized labor's full and effective participation. Only then will the whole movement, and especially the nationals and their locals, have a clear understanding of objectives and the sense of mission that comes with well understood aims. Union leaders must be convinced if traditional views and restrictive practices are to be modified in pursuit of a bigger and more important purpose.

Manpower policy is so pervasive that one country cannot serve as a detailed model for others. Nevertheless, if one wishes to consider the potentialities in terms of a concrete example, Sweden provides a case of a trade union movement that has made a significant intellectual contribution to manpower policy in a full-employment economy and that has effectively participated in policy formulation and implementation. Of course, the political and economic conditions and union-management relationships in Sweden have been especially favorable for the development of such a contribution by the Swedish labor movement.

The American labor movement needs to ponder its role in the kind of economy and society that we have now and are likely to have over the next decade. Manpower policy provides an excellent point of departure for serious reflection by the leaders of organized labor concerning the best ways for the labor movement to contribute to satisfactory work careers and meaningful lives for all the American people. Systematic analysis and forward planning for the use of the nation's human resources promise significant gains in terms of economic and social progress. Organized labor in America should play a large role in a national program for the effective development and utilization of the whole labor force of the country.

## NOTES

1. As an example of reform suggestions growing out of such analysis, see Allan Flanders, *Industrial Relations: What Is Wrong with the System? An Essay on its Theory and Future* (London: Faber and Faber, 1965).

2. Recently estimates have been made of the total career openings for craftsmen, foremen, and kindred workers during the decade 1965 to 1975. For selected building trades in construction operations, the total estimated openings for the decade are 670,000 (410,000 due to attrition and 260,000 for net growth); of that total, 245,000 openings will be for carpenters; 165,000 for electricians; and 130,000 for painters. See Allan F. Salt, "Estimated Need for Skilled Workers," *Monthly Labor Review*, LXXXIX (April, 1966), 368.

3. See *The Role of Apprenticeship in Manpower Development: United States and Western Europe*, Volume 3 of *Selected Readings in Employment and Manpower*, Subcommittee on Employment and Manpower of

the Committee on Labor and Public Welfare, U.S. Senate, 88th Cong., 2d sess. (Washington, D.C.: 1964), Appendix 7, p. 1224. See also p. 1357.

4. *Ibid.*, p. 1340.

5. Calculations from data in Appendix 9, *ibid.*, p. 1226.

6. *Ibid.*, Appendix 2, p. 1216.

7. *Ibid.*, p. 1186.

8. *Business Week*, June 18, 1966, p. 150.

9. See *Wages and Labour Mobility*, A Report by a Group of Independent Experts (Paris: Organization for Economic Cooperation and Development, July, 1965), pp. 15–17.

10. The basis of comparison was with a nonunion labor market and not just in terms of manpower demand and supply. See Lloyd G. Reynolds and Cynthia H. Taft, *The Evolution of the Wage Structure* (New Haven: Yale University Press, 1956), p. 194.

11. *Employer Expenditures for Selected Supplementary Compensation Practices for Production and Related Workers; Manufacturing Industries, 1962*, U.S. Bureau of Labor Statistics, Bulletin No. 1428 (Washington, D.C.: April, 1965), Table 48, p. 93.

12. See *Trade Unions and the MDTA* (Washington, D.C.: Manpower Administration, U.S. Department of Labor, January, 1966), p. 4.

# Discussion

## BY NAT WEINBERG *

Professor Lester's paper is extraordinarily difficult to discuss, first, because he ranges over such a vast territory and, second, because the labor movement itself is so diverse that practically nothing said about it is either wholly correct or wholly incorrect. A case can be made for or against organized labor on almost any issue, depending which part of the movement is placed in the spotlight. Diversity creates similar difficulties in giving advice to the labor movement. Most of Professor Lester's advice seems to me to be sound. But a great deal of it turns out, on closer examination, to prescribe actions already being carried out by some parts of the labor movement.

Professor Lester recognizes the diverse nature of the labor movement and the widely varying behavior of its component elements in manpower matters. He has taken pains at many points to state qualifications and note exceptions. Nevertheless, the total impression of labor's manpower role left by his paper seems to me to be unduly negative.

This is understandable in the light of his purpose, which, I take it, is to point out how the labor movement can improve its performance in the manpower field. But I think it would be wrong to leave the record uncorrected. So I will try to correct it at those points where, in my opinion, Professor Lester has withheld credit where credit is due, has blamed labor for the sins of others, has called upon labor to do what its limited power and the institutional framework prevent it from doing, and has, in effect, asked labor to sacrifice the welfare of its own members

* This paper is in response to Professor Lester's paper as presented at the Conference and, therefore, does not take account of the revisions subsequently made by Professor Lester. Quotations are from the original version of his paper. The views expressed are the writer's and not necessarily those of the United Automobile Workers.

in order to protect society against the consequences of irresponsibility by other groups. In addition, I will comment on a number of other issues raised by his paper.

## Policy Contributions

Professor Lester says:

The main deficiency is that the AFL-CIO has no well-formulated position and program in the manpower field. Instead of thinking big and taking advantage of recent developments, it has been content to operate in a piecemeal fashion and to reaffirm past positions.

This, I think, can be demonstrated to be an overstatement. Whether or not the position is "well-formulated" is, of course, a matter of opinion. But the AFL-CIO has a basic policy approach and a wide-ranging and integrated program. The most complete reflection of that policy and program (as it stood three years ago) appears in testimony presented to a Senate Subcommittee in May 1963 by UAW President Walter P. Reuther, speaking in his capacity as Chairman of the Economic Policy Committee of the AFL-CIO.[1] Not all the recommendations presented were original—many were drawn from European, particularly Swedish, experience; and not all are likely to win universal acceptance. They do, however, cover most of the problems raised by Professor Lester's paper plus many more, and an effort was made to integrate the separate recommendations into a coherent policy and program.

Mr. Reuther's statement sought to delineate the goals of manpower policy and to place the aggregate-demand and structural approaches in proper relation to each other. It presented a definition of full employment in qualitative as well as quantitative terms and outlined a program to achieve full employment while minimizing inflationary dangers. It called for democratic national economic planning and the integration of manpower policy with such planning. It advanced a program to minimize cyclical fluctuations.

The recommendations presented were so numerous and detailed that it is impossible here to do more than mention certain of the broad categories covered. It was proposed to create a single national manpower agency which, in addition to its direct administrative responsibilities, would have authority, subject to the President's approval, to intervene for purposes of coordination in all government actions having significant manpower implications. Recommendations were made for strengthening the public Employment Service and for the creation of machinery to provide early warning of—and to meet at both national and industry levels—manpower problems arising out of technological change. Detailed proposals were made to improve both the general educational system (including vocational education) and the retraining of adult workers. While urging a policy of bringing work to the workers wherever feasible—backed up by a comprehensive set of recommendations to rehabilitate and to prevent the creation of distressed communities—the statement also detailed a program to facilitate the relocation of workers when necessary. The statement anticipated the recent report of the Automation Commission in proposing that the government act as "employer of last resort" for those otherwise unable to find jobs. Measures were proposed to meet the special employment problems of members of minority groups, of young workers, of older workers, of women, and of handicapped workers. The statement proposed that unemployment be attacked through a more equitable distribution of available work opportunities to be achieved by increasing penalty pay for overtime work and by counter-cyclical adjustment of the straight-time workweek. A series of recommendations were made to lighten the burdens of unemployed workers in general, and of older workers in particular.

There is room, of course, for differences of opinion as to the merits of individual elements of the program. Nevertheless, I think it can be said that, if all the recommendations presented by Mr. Reuther on behalf of the AFL-CIO in 1963 were now in effect, the United States would be able to boast of having as advanced, as comprehensive, and well-articulated a manpower policy and program as any country.

The report of the Automation Commission reflects the fact that the manpower thinking of the labor movement has not been static since 1963. The labor members of that Commission both contributed proposals and were receptive to proposals advanced by the other members. It is neither fair nor accurate to say that the AFL-CIO has been unresponsive to new manpower developments or ideas.

## Legislative Contributions

Labor's contributions to the enactment of manpower legislation deserve more than the sentence of acknowledgement that Professor Lester gives them. The labor movement played a major role in the broad coalition that won enactment of the Employment Act of 1946. The AFL-CIO and a number of its constituent unions can legitimately claim a large share of the credit for enactment of such legislation as the ARA, the Accelerated Public Works Act (and their successor, the Public Works and Economic Development Act (PWEDA)), the MDTA, the Economic Opportunity Act, the Primary and Secondary Education Act, the adjustment assistance provisions of the Trade Expansion Act and the Automotive Products Trade Act of 1965, and the Fair Employment Practices Title (Title VII) of the Civil Rights Act of 1964.

In some cases, the initial impetus for enactment of the legislation came from the AFL-CIO. Many years of intense effort were spent in lining up the Congressional support needed for passage of a number of the measures—efforts that in some cases were continued after others had given up the fight as hopeless. It is doubtful that much of this legislation would be on the statute books today if it were not for the work of the AFL-CIO and some of its affiliates.

Title VII of the Civil Rights Act is a particularly significant case in point. No fair employment provision was included in the bill submitted by the Administration. The AFL-CIO spearheaded the drive for Title VII even though it is directed against discriminatory practices by unions as well as by employers, and it is noteworthy that the AFL-CIO is now pressing for strengthening the enforcement provisions of that Title. The labor movement proposed, saved from deletion, or strengthened important features of many of the other measures I have mentioned.

## Collective Bargaining Contributions

Professor Lester dwells at considerable length on certain aspects of collective bargaining which he considers to have negative effects from a manpower-policy standpoint. He entirely neglects the many positive contributions that collective bargaining has made toward cushioning the impact of economic and technological changes on workers, facilitating mobility (occupationally and geographically), and opening up job opportunities for workers who would otherwise be unemployed.[2]

Unions have sought, and to some extent have won, provisions for advance notice of layoffs to permit orderly planning to minimize hardships. The attrition method for avoiding displacement of workers when work-force requirements are reduced by technological change is being increasingly applied under union contracts. Seniority units are being broadened, area hiring pools have been created for workers laid off by corporations that have more than one plant in the same labor market, transfer rights in multi-plant corporations are being strengthened, and transfers are being facilitated through negotiated relocation allowances. Occupational mobility is being increased through union action to stimulate and improve employer retraining activities.

Hardships associated with layoffs are being alleviated through supplemental unemployment benefits, continuation of certain types of benefit coverage for laid-off workers, severance pay, the vesting of pension rights, and special early retirement pension provisions for displaced older workers.

Although the creation of jobs for the unemployed is the responsibility of government, unions in some instances have sought to make up for the failure of government to meet this responsibility by developing collective bargaining programs specifically designed to provide work opportunities for those who would otherwise be unemployed. This objective, in fact, was the central focus of the UAW's negotiations in 1964. Under UAW contracts negotiated in that year, employment opportunities were made available for large numbers of unemployed workers as a result of greatly liberalized early retirement pensions designed to encourage older workers to withdraw from the labor market,[13] through lengthened vacations and added paid holidays totaling 56 hours per year (equivalent to reduction of the workweek by more than one hour), and through the provision of added relief time for workers on assembly lines and similar operations which require the companies to hire literally thousands of additional relief men.

Some progress has also been made in winning collective bargaining provisions aimed at helping displaced workers to find new employment. The Armour Agreement is an outstanding although not highly successful example. The UAW has on occasion succeeded in informally working out arrangements under which companies have absorbed workers displaced by defunct competitors and suppliers.

In some industries contract clauses or company commitments in other forms have provided unions with more effective tools to police racially-discriminatory practices by management personnel.

Beyond these practical accomplishments, unions have developed demands for future negotiations designed to contribute to the solution of manpower problems. For example, conscious of the fact that employment opportunities are diminishing for workers with limited education, the UAW will seek in 1967 to make room for such workers in production jobs by providing preference for qualified blue-collar workers to fill vacant white-collar jobs.

Although collective bargaining at best can supply only limited and partial solutions to manpower problems, important sections of the labor movement are working vigorously and imaginatively to develop and apply those solutions.

### Blame for the Sins of Others

In stressing what he considers negative impacts of collective bargaining upon manpower objectives, Professor Lester at times holds unions responsible for problems that are attributable, with at least equal validity, to employers or government.

The shortage of apprentices is one case in point. Some unions undoubtedly have contributed to the problem. But important employers must share the blame. An outstanding, but by no means unique, example is the aerospace industry, in which, the UAW, the International Association of Machinists (IAM), and the Labor Department have for many years been trying in vain to persuade the corporations to establish apprenticeship programs. The aerospace corporations apparently find it less expensive to pirate journeymen trained by other industries. Journeymen in Detroit auto plants, for example, were targets of intensive recruitment by the West Coast aerospace industry during the Korean War. It is a well known fact, moreover, that companies with apprenticeship programs frequently employ far fewer apprentices than are permitted under agreement provisions establishing ratios of apprentices to journeymen.

Similarly, government and employers, rather than unions, are responsible for any loss of mobility that may be attributable to negotiated employee-benefit plans. Such plans are relatively rare in other countries in which social legislation is more comprehensive and the benefits more adequate than in the United States. Under governmental plans, benefit rights do not depend upon attachment to a particular employer. Negotiated plans are prevalent in the United States because of the need to fill in the gaps and to supplement the disgracefully inadequate benefits provided by our public programs.[4] Resistance by employer lobbyists accounts in significant part for the deficiencies of our social legislation, but governmental legislative proposals have been far short of what is needed. In order to minimize costs, employers resist union efforts to negotiate portability of benefits under the collectively bargained programs.[5] Opposition from employers has also resulted in pigeonholing of proposals to require minimum vesting provisions under the tax laws governing private pension plans.

## Limitations of Power and Institutions

Professor Lester cites the example of the Swedish labor movement as the model for U.S. labor to follow in the manpower field. Many in the AFL-CIO would like nothing better than the opportunity to emulate Swedish labor's manpower role. But that opportunity is not likely to be available, at least for some time to come, because of differences in both power relationships and institutions between the United States and Sweden.

The crucial fact is that the Swedish labor movement is far more powerful both economically and politically than the AFL-CIO. It has organized roughly 90 per cent of the blue-collar workers, 70 per cent of the white-collar workers, and a significant proportion of professional and lower-managerial employees. On the political front it is closely allied to the party that has governed Sweden almost continuously for more than thirty years. Through the combined power of its economic and political arms, flationary wage pressures in the index of labor cost per unit of output in manufacturing (which in May 1966 was 99.9 per cent of the 1957–1959 average). The source of such inflation of industrial prices as we have had is suggested by the price per unit of labor cost index, which in recent months has been at the highest levels reached at any time since July 1951, and by the fact that the seasonally adjusted ratio of profits before taxes to total income originating in nonfinancial corporations in the first quarter of 1966 reached a level higher than in any calendar year since 1956, despite the larger depreciation charges now permitted under the tax laws.

A few spectacularly large wage settlements in the construction industry attract a great deal of attention but do not prove very much—not any more, in fact, than the upward trend of salaries in the academic world which also has labor shortages and rigorous apprenticeship requirements.[9] The growing size of recent settlements outside construction is in large part a reaction to the acceleration of increases in living costs coupled with, and in significant degree caused by, inflated profits.[10] There is increasing evidence suggesting that the role of wages as an initiating factor in inflation has been exaggerated, to say the least, not only in the United States but elsewhere as well.[11]

Regardless of the sources of inflation, American unions are aware of its dangers, and some have shown their willingness to tailor their demands to the requirements of price stability. No group in America has made greater sacrifices in the anti-inflationary cause than the more than 200,000 General Motors workers who struck for 113 days in 1945–1946 for "wage increases without price increases"—offering to reduce their demands by any extent that might be required in order to avoid creating the necessity for a price increase.[12] In addition, the UAW has advocated ever since 1957 price-notification-and-hearings legislation that, among other things, would compel unions to furnish public justification for their demands if price-leading corporations in major industries alleged that those demands would necessitate price increases.

It should be apparent, however, that the labor movement cannot be expected to take the whole responsibility for price stability and to sacrifice the welfare and interests of its members other employment a realistic possibility do not sit around idly while waiting for recall on the basis of their seniority. Even those laid off for very brief periods often seek and find temporary work. (Employers may refuse to hire workers who retain recall rights with other companies, but that is not the fault of either the workers or their unions. Employer rejections of such workers would tend to be far fewer under full-employment conditions when the hiring of workers who are only temporarily available would often be the sole alternative to leaving job vacancies unfilled. Moreover, under full employment the unemployment insurance authorities would be able more effectively to test availability for work and to apply appropriate penalties to the few who might prefer to remain idle.)[16]

3. There is reason to believe that the labor forces of the United States and Canada—the only two countries where seniority and negotiated employee benefits are widespread and significant—are among the most mobile in the world. Any loss in mobility resulting from seniority (and fringe benefits) is therefore probably minimal.

4. Seniority makes a positive contribution to economic efficiency by avoiding the need to recruit and train replacements for workers who would not return to or remain with a firm in the absence of seniority. Since to my knowledge, there has been no measurement either of savings in recruitment[17] and training costs or of the cost of the alleged loss of mobility resulting from seniority, there is no basis for arguing that the balance is unfavorable.

5. Neither is there any basis for assuming that the judgments, or arbitrary decisions, or prejudices, or bribery (a not infrequent practice in the absence of seniority) of foremen achieves more efficient allocation of workers than does seniority—either within the plant or with respect to layoff or retention of workers.

6. The pace of work is increasingly controlled by machines, and the use of production standards (work quotas) is widespread in American industry. Under these circumstances, efficiency (in terms of output per manhour) tends to be the same regardless of whether seniority or any other basis is used in selecting workers to be assinged to particular tasks.

TOWARD A MANPOWER POLICY

## Allocational Effects

Professor Lester takes note of doubts as to whether the effect of collective bargaining on the structure of wages and fringe benefits has been beneficial or perverse from the standpoint of allocation of the labor force. It might be pertinent to note:

1. Current labor shortages are centered mainly in high-wage fields (where shortages might be greater if wages were lower) and in other occupations, such as nursing and primary school and secondary teaching, where the weakness of unionism may account for the fact that pay is relatively low.

2. Welfare as well as the criterion of resource allocation is relevant to wage structure. The Swedish labor movement follows a "wage solidarity" policy aimed at improving the relative position of workers at the lower end of the wage structure. In a full-employment economy this may have desirable allocational effects by shifting workers to firms and industries which are able to pay more because of greater efficiency; but the policy was devised for welfare reasons.[18]

## Apprenticeship and Training

There is a danger of going overboard on the subject of apprenticeship. I would not attempt to defend the present length of apprenticeship periods for all trades because, for one thing, I do not know very much about the subject. But it must not be forgotten that we are living in a time of rapid technological change that will require great flexibility and adaptability of workers in many of the skilled trades. The substitution of quickly trained, narrow specialists for rounded craftsmen could prove exceedingly costly in the long run. At the very least, it would certainly limit the mobility of the individuals affected.

It should also be noted that many union agreements, particularly in manufacturing, provide means for meeting manpower requirements when journeymen are in short supply and are less rigid in prescribing routes for attainment of journeymen status than many professions.

Insofar as the financing of training is concerned, labor has thought about the problem. Many in the labor movement are attracted to the principle of the British Industrial Training Act, which taxes all employers for training and provides for grants or loans to those employers who establish approved training programs.

Similarly, the labor movement has advocated sheltered workshops for the handicapped, for example, in the statement by Mr. Reuther previously mentioned. In addition, the UAW (and probably other unions as well) has proposed in bargaining, but has been unable to obtain employer agreement, to establish vocational rehabilitation programs for disabled workers.

## Labor and the Disadvantaged

The racially discriminatory practices of some unions are admittedly indefensible. They are not only wrong but costly to the labor movement as a whole in terms of public support. But other and quite important sections of the labor movement have devoted major efforts to the problems of the racially, educationally, and economically disadvantaged.

I have time for only a few examples. Long before the Civil Rights Act was passed, the UAW tried again and again to win contract clauses prohibiting discrimination in hiring. For more than twenty years it has had a Fair Practices Department to police discrimination by its local unions. It has expelled or placed administratorships over local unions guilty of discrimination. It was one of the initiating forces in the creation of the Civil Rights Leadership Conference nearly twenty years ago. It initiated the Citizens Crusade Against Poverty. It has facilitated the entrance of Negroes into the skilled trades by negotiating the removal of the high school diploma requirement as a prerequisite to apprenticeships. In cooperation with MDTA, it has established preapprenticeship training programs to prepare educationally disadvantaged youths—disproportionately Negro—to pass the examinations given applicants for apprenticeships. It has persuaded corporations to lower their hiring standards in order to open up job opportunities for workers with limited educations.

Other unions have engaged in similar actions. The AFL-CIO, its Industrial Union Department, the UAW, and other unions are helping the Delano grape strike, which holds great promise as the possible entering wedge for the large-scale organization of farm workers. Plans are being made for a major drive to organize the working poor. And, it should not be forgotten, large numbers of Negroes owe their job security and their promotions to union-won seniority provisions.

### Activity at the Operating Level

It must be conceded that the labor movement has not done nearly as much as it should to participate in manpower matters at the local operating level. It is one of the traditional failings of American unions that they neglect to follow up legislation which they initiated or were instrumental in enacting. Existing manpower legislation, as Professor Lester implies, offers only limited opportunities for labor participation. But full advantage has not been taken even of such opportunities as exist. One of several reasons—which I advance by way of explanation rather than excuse—is that neither the AFL-CIO nor its international unions are hierarchical organizations which can require action by their local constituents in matters of this kind. They can merely advise and prod, and the AFL-CIO as well as some international unions have done both. The UAW, for example, has established a headquarters Manpower Development and Training Service, and each UAW regional director has designated one of his staff members to stimulate and follow up on training and other manpower activities by the local unions in his region.

### Conclusion

There are many in the labor movement who share Professor Lester's view of manpower policy as an instrument for "a better adjusted labor force and a better adjusted society." They see it also—in combination with comprehensive and adequate social legislation—as the means for making workers less apprehensive of and more receptive to the changes resulting from economic and technological progress. They seek wholehearted adoption here in the United States of the view expressed by Prime Minister Erlander of Sweden, in a recent speach to the Economic Club of Detroit, who said that in his country:

We look upon it as a duty of society to protect an individual in a situation for which he is not himself responsible. Our philosophy is that the rapid and necessary changes must not create fear.

There are large and important sections of the labor movement which have a vision of the future and are working, on both the collective bargaining and legislative fronts, to realize it—a future in which everyone who wants to work has the opportunity to make full use of his highest capacities in a job which is rewarding to him and useful to society.

## NOTES

1. *Hearings* before the Subcommittee on Employment and Manpower of the Committee on Labor and Public Welfare, U.S. Senate, Part 1, May 20–23, 1963, p. 182.

2. See, for example, Derek Bok and Max D. Kossoris, *Methods of Adjusting to Automation and Technological Change* (Washington, D.C.: U.S. Department of Labor, 1964); Arnold R. Weber, "The Contribution of Collective Bargaining," in Proceedings of OECD North American Joint Conference on *The Manpower Implications of Automation,* Washington, D.C.: December 8–10, 1964; and Nat Weinberg, "Automation and Collective Bargaining Policy in the United States," published in German translation in *Automation, Risiko, und Chance* (Frankfurt am Main: Europaische Verlagsanstalt, 1965).

3. Early retirement would be desirable simply because of the nature of most jobs in the auto industry. However, withdrawal from the labor market was made a condition for receipt of special supplemental pensions by early retirees in order to assure that more jobs would be available to younger workers. During the nine months starting September 1, 1965, when this program went into effect, early retirements of UAW members from the Big Three automotive corporations numbered 14,400. At the monthly average rate of early retirements in 1962 and 1963, the last full calendar years under the preceding contract, the nine-month figure would have been 860.

4. Benefit inadequacy can be seen by comparing relationships between benefits and wage levels in the United States and in Western European countries.

5. Many unions are already giving the "serious thought and study to . . . transportable benefits" that Professor Lester urges. The Industrial Union Department of the AFL-CIO has in effect a multi-employer pension program cutting across industry lines which provides transportability. The Report of the Automation Commission "commends" for study to government agencies a UAW proposal to preserve the benefit rights of displaced workers. (See footnote to page 64 of the Report.)

6. This outline of the Swedish situation is admittedly somewhat oversimplified, but limitations of space leave no alternative.

7. The current situation, however, does not justify the phrase "high levels of employment" which Professor Lester applies to it. Our unemployment rate is still about twice the average for the advanced countries of Western Europe plus Japan, and it is about ten times the West German rate.

8. This is not to deny the possibility that collective bargaining could be an initiating cause of inflation but rather to stress that there is no persuasive evidence that it has been such a force in the United States.

9. In the period 1948–1964 as a whole, total employee compensation per manhour has apparently increased by about the same percentage in manufacturing as in construction.

10. Real employee compensation in the private economy has been lagging behind output per manhour for 10 years—a process that obviously cannot continue indefinitely without putting an intolerable strain on fiscal policy.

11. See for example, the OECD study, *Wages and Labour Mobility,* from which Professor Lester quotes. Particularly worth noting is the following paragraph from the foreword to the study written by the Chairman of Working Party No. 4 of the Economic Policy Committee of OECD:

> During the preparation of its second report, the Working Party had several discussions on the role of profits in the process of cost inflation. It concluded that "While it is difficult to disentangle the role of different elements in total costs, it seems probable that the failure of cost reductions to be reflected fully or immediately in prices is an important feature of the process by which costs and prices are levered up under conditions of cost inflation." As a result of the work of the Experts, the Working Party feels that it should have been rather more positive about the role of profits. In this connection, the evidence presented in Chapter VI of the Report suggesting a quite strong relationship between profits and changes in profits, and wage movements, is both interesting and significant. While this evidence is open to alternative interpretations, it seems to provide further support for the view that a successful incomes policy must cover prices, profits and other nonwage incomes as well as income from employment.

12. The UAW has also offered on other occasions to moderate its demands in return for price decreases or to reduce them if they were demonstrated to exceed what would be paid without raising prices. Arbitration or other impartial review was proposed to assure fulfillment of the union's pledges.

13. The Council of Economic Advisers has belatedly awakened to this obvious fact. In a speech to the Annual Meeting of the Chamber of Commerce of the United States on May 2, 1966, Gardner Ackley, the Council's Chairman, asked, "Does anyone imagine that labor will continue to show moderation in its wage demands when prices and profit margins are continually rising?"

14. Similar phrases are used throughout the paper.

15. He does note that "conclusions concerning manpower effects [of seniority and fringe benefits] must be quite tentative."

16. Seniority may have some effect on geographic mobility. Geographic mobility is, in any case, limited, and losses attributable to seniority would be offset to some unknown degree by the promotion of geographic mobility noted in the preceding point.

17. Aside from recruitment costs as such, there may be the cost of lost production while the job involved remains vacant. Recall rights based on seniority are conditioned upon the worker being available at short notice.

18. The plight of the low-paid could be eased by other means, for example, by transfer payments. These, however, would have adverse allocational effects by subsidizing inefficient employers.

# Discussion

## BY ADOLPH HOLMES

After considering the historical role of organized labor in the formulation of public policy in the United States, Professor Lester goes on to conclude that the labor movement should play "a larger role" in the formulation and implementation of manpower policy in this country.

History suggests that organized labor, once established as a powerful bloc in the economy, of necessity had to turn its attention first to such urgent issues as those created by the Great Depression of the 1930's. This orientation reflected the outlook, training, and educational background of the men who led the stronger and more progressive unions. These men and women were trained in economics, administration, and other disciplines which caused them to have a critical, and sometimes even a starry, view of the future of the labor movement. Hence, I submit, the shift away from "job conscious unionism" was not so much due to infatuation with the New Deal as to the growing sophistication of union leaders and their feeling of need to meet the challenges of the particular era. Employers utilized the services of efficiency experts, economists, and others skilled in bringing about maximum efficiency in producing goods and services. Organized labor needed the same professional services in order to obtain its share of the results of such increased productivity in the form of wage increments and other fringe benefits.

Once labor had established this foothold, it would then logically follow that trade unionism, reflecting the needs of its members and the tremendous growth of industrial unionism, should turn its attention to the political arena and work for favorable legislation. As time went on, the interest of the federal government in wage-price policy, manpower policies, and related matters made it imperative that organized labor answer a fundamental question: should it fully accept, or in some cases oppose, these new and broader economic policies?

The diverse points of view, policies, and practices adopted by local unions regarding restricted membership, particularly in the craft trades, suggests the extent to which parts of the labor movement were determined to maintain control of the supply of manpower. This control of supply, with an increasing demand for these craftsmen, naturally affected wages and prices. While the merger of the AFL-CIO into a central federation allowed one man or a small group to speak for the total entity known as the American labor movement, we must recognize that the leadership in many local unions does not necessarily reflect the same degree of sophistication which operates at the highest level. This provides further reason for supporting Lester's belief that we must move toward national planning in the use of our human resources.

It is somewhat paradoxical that Professor Lester observes that it is ". . . unrealistic to expect organized labor to promote a unified manpower program before scholars and the federal government have developed a convincing conceptual basis. . . ." Having said this, he then proceeds to reproach the labor movement for not doing exactly that. Yet, he has made clear the uncertain image of labor. The diversity described suggests the shortcomings of federations, whether they be of states or of local unions. We tend to lump the recalcitrant with the enlightened when we speak of the total group.

Nor can we ignore the factor of self-interest. If the "guide lines" were put forward as national policy, then labor displayed excellent instincts in repudiating them. It is hardly realistic to expect that the labor movement will transcend the parochialism of self-interest. But the labor movement could be expected to support ARA, MDTA, liberalization of workers' compensation laws, higher minimum wages, and similar proposals.

The federal government has accepted the fact that the supply of skilled workers is being restricted in particular parts of the labor movement and has somewhat reluctantly moved to intervene in the selection and enrollment procedures used in the apprenticeship trades in order to protect minority and other disadvantaged groups. This suggests that organized labor will do little to cope with this difficult problem on a voluntary basis because the alternative of punitive action by government will be available for those who are recalcitrant. However, we must recognize that it is precisely the political and institutional ties between the craft unions and the Department of Labor that permit the sort of monopoly implied by Professor Lester's quotations from the reports of the Council of Economic Advisers and the Secretary of Labor. This situation prevails at both national and state levels and operates most directly, although certainly not exclusively, through the various offices of the Bureau of Apprenticeship and Training (BAT). Admonition should be directed more to government than to unions, not because the unions are not culpable but because realistically they should not be expected cheerfully to surrender power. Professor Lester cites evidence of the insufficient number of registered apprentices. It is quite obvious that short-sightedness or other factors have been at work to cause this group not to expand over the past fifteen years. Of course, I fully agree with his recommendation that training periods can, and must, be materially reduced. But since the decisive factor here is not educational efficiency but collective bargaining strength, I find the discussion somewhat irrelevant. Again, pleas will not do it. Reviews of BAT regulations and the threat of establishment of competitive government training programs might. Enforcement of standards, establishment of uniform job-pay scales, changes in the ratio of apprentices to journeymen, and federalization of selection procedures are precisely what I have in mind.

With respect to the general problem of discrimination, including questions regarding apprenticeship and admission into the unions, the present range of manpower shortages is affecting the whole economy and causes me to be no longer concerned with an appeal to conscience and justice. There is ample evidence to demonstrate that this approach is ineffective. Because of the very political nature of local unions themselves, this is not an issue to be left to any democratic rank-and-file vote. What is needed here is obvious: rapid intensification of anti-discrimination laws (not manpower policy administered through existing agencies having flabby commitments to nondiscrimination, laboriously determining what is politically feasible and unwilling to rock the boat).

Regarding that portion of the paper which deals with labor's obsolete training views, I can only comment that it supports the need either for voluntary efforts on the part of labor itself to revise the entire apprenticeship procedure or for bold action on the part of government to redesign the procedure and to develop new training methods, with the objective of expanding the number of skilled craftsmen. Moreover, experience has shown that in industrial situations training can be provided in craftlike occupations in a relatively short period of time. Hence what is asked for here is nothing new but rather a hard look at a critical problem without holding present practices to be sacrosanct. European experience reveals that youths begin their apprenticeship at an earlier age than in this country, and certainly whatever manpower policies result from future study and evaluation should take this into consideration.

Finally, purely from a selfish point of view, labor should support on-the-job training programs. First, such programs should lead to an increase in the number of union members, and second, they help to retain those already in the ranks and offer them greater overall security. Surely, labor has some responsibility to its current membership in this area. The cost of the G. I. Bill of the Second World War has been repaid many times, largely because of improved skills and earning power.

Going on to another problem raised in Professor Lester's paper, I agree that there is a relationship between wage-benefit structure and mobility, but I find it difficult to see where, in fact, existing wage differentials have impeded mobility. To cite one perhaps extreme example, during the war period there was mass migration of farm workers from rural areas to the great shipyards and aircraft industries in the East and West. Lack of knowledge of new opportunities alone may be a deterrent to mobility; yet there is not much evidence of this in the available data. This is not always the case in European countries. I agree that we need to explore further the effects of interfirm and interindustry differentials in compensation, including differentials between unionized and nonunion firms. However, from our experience, it would appear that when knowledge of other opportunities is available persons will relocate. (A qualification does have to be made for the effect of seniority rights and retirement benefits, which are of considerable importance.) This is further substantiated by European experience, as well as by the very definition of a journeyman.

Professor Lester suggests that the labor movement should develop its own concepts of national manpower policy as well as participate in the formulation and execution of the nation's manpower program. It is unrealistic to expect organized labor to operate unilaterally in such an undertaking. He points to labor representation on the National Manpower Advisory Committee, as well as on committees at the regional and state level, but he believes that labor should have the opportunity to work through more active committees that actually formulate coordinated plans and that meet on a more frequent basis than at present.

In addition, the federal government should utilize labor representation in other ways, for example, as was done by the Commission on Automation, Technology, and Economic Progress. In this instance, technical assistance was made available to the Commission by the various academic disciplines and by labor. The points of disagreement were compiled into a minority report. I agree that some type of Manpower Advisory Committee could address itself continuously to this kind of activity, thereby becoming an asset to the Secretary of Labor not only as he prepares the Manpower Report to the President but more importantly by assisting him in the development of programs emanating from his department which affect the utilization of our nation's human resources.

CHAPTER **12**

# An Overall Evaluation
# and Suggestions for the Future

## BY JOHN T. DUNLOP

The ambitious assignment given me for this paper is to develop
an overall evaluation of manpower policy and to offer suggestions
for the future. It is not to provide a summary or further comments on particular papers. That has already been accomplished
by the discussants. Rather, the task is to ascertain where we
stand after four annual conferences of the Berkeley Unemployment Project. This period coincides with four years of an active,
if not hectic, national manpower policy. What have we learned?
In what areas are we most ignorant? What are the alternatives,
priorities, and needed next steps? For all the enthusiasm, political
innovation, and expenditures of recent years, these are stubborn
and embarrassing questions in an impatient world.

The discussion is divided into four sections: (1) The Concept
of Manpower Policy, (2) Manpower Concepts and Measurement,

(3) Administration of Public Manpower Programs, and (4) Future Developments.

## The Concept of Manpower Policy

The term "manpower policy" has come so much into vogue in recent years, and is used in so many different senses, that it deserves serious scrutiny. At times manpower policy is identified with public or even federal governmental policies or expenditures, although the development and training of most manpower, after enrollment in school, takes place in the private sector. At other times manpower policy has become so imperialistic that it appears to subsume all educational policy and even general economic policy, for example, as a part of manpower policy, to be appraised solely in terms of its manpower consequences. A discussion of manpower policy should start with a discussion of its limits and its relations to other policies.

It may be helpful to distinguish a narrow or pure concept of manpower policy from a broader or gross concept since many discussions range over both in some confusion. Pure manpower policies consist of measures to influence directly the labor market, given other institutions and policies. Thus, pure manpower policies are concerned with information on job vacancies and labor supplies, compensation, the location and requirements of jobs, career patterns, private and public employment agencies, and the like.[1] Pure labor market policy is concerned with the operation of labor markets *in a given framework*.

A gross concept of manpower policy is concerned with the impact of changes in this framework on the operation of the labor market. For analytical purposes it may be useful to identify six facets of this institutional setting: (1) general economic policy and the level of economic activity, (2) the educational system, (3) welfare programs, (4) civil rights programs, (5) the health system, and (6) military personnel arrangements.[2] Thus, a change in educational policy or in the draft will affect the quality, characteristics, and numbers in the labor force and the operation of the labor market. Changes in any one of these six in the framework of the labor market may be expected to result in changes in the demand for and the supply of labor and hence in the performance of the labor market. It is essential to distinguish the consequences of these gross measures from pure manpower policy. There has been a tendency to treat as manpower policies the gross changes in all these institutions and policies as well as pure labor-market activity within a given set of institutions. In thinking about labor-market policy it is essential to make clear what is treated as variable and what is regarded as fixed for the problem at hand.

The analytical perspective may be assisted by a schematic presentation:

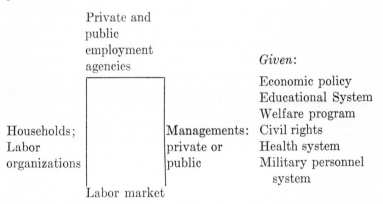

| Private and public employment agencies | | *Given:* |
| | | Economic policy |
| | | Educational System |
| | | Welfare program |
| Households; | Managements: | Civil rights |
| Labor | private or | Health system |
| organizations | public | Military personnel |
| | | system |
| Labor market | | |

Pure manpower policies are concerned with the technical operations of the labor market given the institutional setting and given the policies affecting each facet of this setting. A change in any one of these institutional policies, all other policies remaining unchanged, may be expected to have some impact on the labor market. Logically, it is important to know something of the size and direction of these partial effects in the labor market. Policy-making has often involved simultaneous changes in a number of these facets, and the separate effects have sometimes been conflicting. Moreover, changes in these institutional policies may be made for a great many declared purposes other than their direct manpower effects, and it is vital to assess the specific effects that they do have in the labor market.

The meaning and significance of this analytical perspective may be better appreciated if the discussion is made more specific. In the period 1964–1966 there was a dramatic demonstration of the impact of general economic policy on the labor market via the tax cut and increased military expenditures. It is this partial relationship—with given educational, welfare, civil rights, health, and military manpower institutions and policies—which is the special province of economists. Pure manpower policies and the partial relations between general economic policy and the labor market have been the preserve of economists, but these interests do not exhaust the gross concept of manpower policies. The analytical perspective advocated here suggests that economists and other specialists need to investigate carefully the interactions between changes in the educational system and policies, on the one hand, and the labor market, on the other. The same holds for the other dimensions of the institutional setting that I have listed. They are all legitimate fields for inquiry and measurement. Those of us who have studied labor markets, and the interaction between general economic developments and the labor market, tend to be self-styled manpower experts. But little do we know of the interactions between educational policies, welfare programs, civil rights measures, health programs, and military manpower policies, on the one hand, and the labor market, on the other. These partial relations are relatively unstudied and deserve considerable quantitative work.

Another illustration of this analytical perspective is provided by considering the partial relations between military personnel policies, i.e., the draft and military training, and the labor market. It is somewhat strange that in this conference on manpower policies there has been virtually no discussion of the urgent and controversial questions of recruitment and training of military manpower and the consequent effects of various policy alternatives on the labor market. What are the likely yields of different methods of recruitment? What are the consequences of different training procedures and expenditures in the military establishment? What training allowances and benefits should be available on leaving the armed forces? From the perspective of gross manpower policy, the armed forces might well be transformed into an even more extensive "educational institution" and provider of basic and specialized skills, particularly to disadvantaged groups. From the perspective of military policy and the efficiency of the military establishment, this might well be regarded an encumbrance to be avoided at all cost. A great many policies affect the labor market which are formulated with other primary objectives in view.

Occupational deferment is one of many ways in which the military personnel system affects the labor market. The Department of Commerce prepares a list of essential industries, and the Department of Labor prepares a list of essential occupations for the Selective Service System to be used ". . . when considering requests for occupational deferment of individual registrants and as a guide in selecting men with critical civilian occupations for the special enlistment program in the Ready Reserve under Executive Order 10650." [3] The list of 39 occupations includes veterinarians and osteopaths; it does not include high-pressure welders or shipfitters; it includes a machinist but not a sheetmetal worker or an electrician; it excludes a teacher of Spanish but includes one instructing in Swedish or Portuguese. There is no statement of the criteria by which this list has been drawn up, and there is apparently no regular procedure to revise the lists with changes in the labor market and military demands, although in March 1965 a programmer (engineering and scientific) was added, and a structural linguist was changed to a scientific linguist. My purpose is not primarily to criticize present policies but to make clear that the military personnel system in a variety of ways has impacts on the labor market and is a part of a gross concept of manpower policy, and further to recognize that many policy objectives other than labor-market considerations enter into this interaction.

The interrelations between welfare and civil rights policies and the labor market are even more complex, and it is essential in treating such questions that discussions of manpower policy have a clearly delineated analytical framework. It may be appropriate to advocate various civil rights or welfare programs for their own sake, apart from labor-market consequences. Thus, it is not necessarily the case that another billion dollars expended on training should go to the most disadvantaged if one were to apply the criterion of the largest net effect on the national product or the greatest reduction in unemployment. Yet a decision so to allocate the expenditure might be appropriately based on criteria emphasizing civil rights or welfare programs. Manpower specialists should be cautious about the tendency to imperialism in such matters. Civil rights and welfare programs have partial impacts on the labor market, and such relations are very much in need of study and measurement.[4] But civil rights and welfare programs cannot be entirely subsumed under manpower policies. The National Commission on Technology, Automation, and Economic Progress popularized the view of the labor market as a "shapeup" or queue,[5] with workers possessing higher education, skills and preferred employment characteristics at the head of the line. This is a useful view for many purposes, but welfare programs may be directed to those not in the labor-force queue at all. There may be a welfare queue as well as a labor-force queue, and it is not easy to classify certain people.

The discussion of manpower policy, in my view, will be more meaningful and rigorous if a distinction is made between narrow labor-market policies designed to influence the operation of that market within a given institutional and policy context and a gross concept which seeks to identify the various separate effects on the labor market of changes in general economic policy, educational policy, welfare programs, civil rights, the health system, and the military-personnel system. Manpower policy needs to understand the interrelations with these other programs and policies, but manpower policy as such cannot fruitfully encompass this larger universe.

### Manpower Concepts and Measurement

One of the most significant contributions that manpower specialists can make to manpower policies, defined narrowly or broadly, is the critical review and perfection of concepts and measurements. This responsibility should be felt keenly by those of us in the university community; this task has not been done well in recent years. There has been so heavy a preoccupation with policy prescription, and the opportunities to be heard sympathetically have been so great, that the basic work of improving concepts and measurement has been slighted. I hope that one of the results of this conference will be to highlight the inadequacy of our tools and the high priority that should be attached to their perfection if manpower policy-making is to flourish. The following discussion lists eight areas to which special attention should be devoted. They are ranked according to the priorities which I would assign, starting with our most serious deficiencies. In the event that you do not agree with this list or its priorities, you should be challenged to formulate your own list of the most urgent deficiencies in our theoretical and quantitative knowledge of the structure and functioning of the labor market.

1. The need to improve the occupational classification scheme for reporting employment—and to relate occupational categories to education, compensation, age, and other variables—is one of the most urgent of our deficiencies.[6] Dr. James G. Scoville has developed an occupational matrix grouping jobs by levels of job content and by job families.[7] Some effort is being made to improve the occupational data in the 1970 census.[8] But there are serious limits to securing occupational data from household surveys. It is not adequate to have wage data by occupation from one source using one classification scheme, employment data by occupation from another source using another scheme, and other data by occupation from still other surveys. The occupational description of employment and of patterns of change over time, including an analysis of the major determinants of occupational change on both the demand and supply side, is an urgent problem.

A brief comment is required on the publication of the long-awaited *Dictionary of Occupational Titles*.[9] It classifies each of the 21,741 separate occupations according to their relationship to Data, People, and Things and to the level of the function required of the job. A code of eight levels and the three relationships expresses ". . . the total complexity at which the job requires the worker to function." [10] It may well be that such a classification of jobs is useful for "placement, counseling, and related activities in public employment offices and for others concerned with the use of occupational information in vocational, personnel, and related services and activities," which is declared to be the primary purpose for which it was developed and prepared. But a comparison of the ranking of jobs by this code for a number of industries with the ranking of jobs by job-evaluation plans or wage schedules or promotion ladders casts very considerable doubt on the usefulness of the classification scheme of the new Dictionary for ranking occupations by job content, even in the same industry. A critical evaluation of the basic concepts and the logic of the new Dictionary is required.

2. There is widespread recognition that systematic data on job vacancies are an essential tool to improve labor-market policy. The experimental studies of recent years seem to suggest that a comprehensive program is feasible.[11] There are, however, a number of serious problems in interpretating job-vacancy data. Not the least of these relates to the difficulties of occupational classification of vacancies, since hiring-in jobs vary substantially among enterprises; and the largest proportion of job vacancies in most industries are filled by promotions and transfers within the internal labor market. In an economy of continuing high employment, characterized by both labor shortages and surpluses, job-vacancy data in some form are a significant labor-market signal. Our task is to improve the quality of the concepts and the measurement. One by-product of job-vacancy data is that they may constitute another incentive, among many, tending to develop manpower projection and planning activities in enterprises and industries.

3. One of the most significant, and yet most difficult, problems relating to the operation of the labor market concerns the "breadth of training" of an employee. What is the optimum range of training for incumbent workers in particular occupations? They can be too broadly or too narrowly trained. The concept of "breadth of training" and a means of measuring such breadth are needed. This problem is at the heart of both the design of the scope of a seniority district and the duration and characteristics of an apprentice program. In collective bargaining these problems involve the accommodation of complex competing and joint interests of managements, labor organizations, and employees (members). In general, the more broadly trained an employee the greater his security against layoffs, the greater his opportunities for promotion and employment, and the less vulnerable his skills to technological change. But the more broadly trained an employee the greater the time required for training and the greater the costs of training, as indicated by a loss of productivity to the enterprise during the training period. These are difficult considerations to balance, particularly when

the time horizon may be a whole career and when the thrust of technological change on skills is uncertain. Professor Richard Lester's belief that it should not require more than a year or a year and a half to train a carpenter, bricklayer, house painter, or other skilled worker, involves a view as to the appropriate scope of training.[12] It would be significant, for instance, to explore the consequences of different breadths of training of an economist, a nurse, a machinist, a plumber, and a sewing-machine operator. We need both the concepts and a great deal of empirical work in this difficult area.

4. One of the major deficiencies of our understanding of the labor market relates to the gross flows of workers between employment, unemployment, and outside the labor force, and the reasons for such moves. We have learned a good deal in recent years from the decennial and monthly censuses about the persons involved in flows between employment and unemployment, between employment and outside the labor force, and between unemployment and outside the labor force.[13] But we know too little about the reasons for these flows. For many years data on turnover, layoffs, and quit rates have been collected. It should be possible to integrate these infrequently used data into a closed system and to provide considerably more information and insights than we now have as to the reasons for these movements of workers into and out of the labor force.

5. The present labor-force concepts and data need to be supplemented with a very considerably increased emphasis upon the full career or life-time of the worker. In a world of rapid technological change affecting the durability and content of many job classifications and occupations, with greater geographical mobility, with increasing private and public concern over annual earnings and guarantees, with a rapid expansion of women in the labor force, and with demands for early retirement in some industries and partial retirement in others, the research community would do well to expend greater energy and resources on the study of working-life patterns of occupations and earnings not only in the professions but throughout the job structure. It is likely to take many years to develop significant concepts and useful data, and more inputs are needed in this area now. The present concern is not with career choices but rather

with a running inventory including data on occupation, education, income from various sources, unemployment, continuing training, mobility, and other related characteristics for various cohorts in the population. The computer makes the handling and use of such data feasible. The occupational characteristics and potentials of the labor force twenty years from now depend substantially on the course of work histories and experience over the next two decades.

6. The development of methods of projecting manpower requirements by occupational categories within individual enterprises and for industrial or geographical groupings is a priority field for private and public manpower activity. An associated need is to disseminate these methods widely. There is today a great deal more experimentation with projection techniques in large-scale enterprises than is generally recognized. At times, as in the case of technical and professional manpower in the aerospace and related science fields, these data are essential in bidding for contracts. At times, the projection is related to the planning of sales, output, and other dimensions of corporate development; at times, the interest is centered on managerial personnel; in still other cases, the projections are a part of capital budgeting.

There has been a considerable interest in manpower projections in a number of the professions,[14] including the many estimates of medical manpower and related proposals for medical schools and training facilities. Most of these projections of medical manpower needs have utilized atrocious methods, for example, a constant physician-to-population ratio.[15]

On an industrial basis, particularly for skilled occupations, it is important not only to improve the technique of projection but to secure a measure of consensus in order to influence apprenticeship and other policies. In the construction industry, we have recently secured a high degree of agreement on projections by craft published by the Bureau of Labor Statistics after a series of conferences involving discussions of craft definitions, the scope of the industry, and the assumptions on which the projections are predicated.[16] The distribution of these results to national and local joint committees may be expected to influence private policies. A continuing high employment economy will increase the interest in such techniques and studies and create the need for a considerable improvement in projection concepts and methods.

7. A significant contribution could be made by the study of the business enterprise as an educational institution. In any general view of the society, the business enterprise is a leading developer of skills, and it spends substantial amounts on human-resource development. Most business managers have not viewed their organizations as educational institutions, but the civil rights movement, labor shortages, and modern ideas of organization building are making this process of resource development more self-evident to large enterprises. Estimates of the full costs of training and comparative studies of the experiences of different enterprises and industries would be helpful. The problems of small business in this respect and the role of the trade association also deserve attention.

8. Cost-benefit techniques are currently "in," and there is little doubt that we shall see a great many studies in the government and in universities applying the technique to various training, welfare, or educational programs. Much of this is to the good, and these inquiries can have significant by-products in developing alternative approaches to achieving program objectives. But as a technical matter, very considerable improvements need to be made in the concepts and methods as applied to training programs. The measurement of benefits over long periods, the rates of interest, the handling of tax items, the differences between various concepts of social and private costs and benefits, and the question of foregone earnings all raise difficult conceptual and measurement problems. The theoretical and measurement issues involved in these studies need much more attention before there is any vast expansion in the number of such studies.

Public decisions on resource allocations in the manpower field will, for a long while, no doubt be almost entirely based on informed judgments and negotiations. But this should not preclude careful attention to priorities, ascertaining where public expenditures may be expected to yield greatest relative benefits and where private expenditures are likely to be least adequate. Lester Thurow's conclusion that it is ". . . rational for any indi-

vidual employer to avoid training women or young people, but
the same factors do not apply to society" provides a guide to the
relative direction of public expenditures. The same type of considerations suggest the importance of greater public concern with
training in small-scale enterprises and the need for greater attention to the possibility of an industry-wide tax or a tax credit
to stimulate training and skill development in a number of industries.

The list of eight areas to which primary attention has been
directed may not have included your favorite topic, and you
may wish to revamp the list in many respects. But at the present
stage of policy-making, attention to fundamental concepts and
basic problems of measurement should not be permitted longer
to languish. Manpower policy has reached a time for reflection,
administrative review, and consolidation.

### Administration of Public Manpower Programs

The federal government is spending perhaps between $3 and
$4 billion a year on manpower programs, rather narrowly de-
fined and outside the professions, through a variety of agencies
in the Labor Department, the Department of Health, Education,
and Welfare (HEW), and the Office of Economic Opportunity
(OEO). Among the major programs are those of institutional and on-the-job training, apprenticeship, the Employment Service, vocational education, vocational rehabilitation,
the Job Corps (JC), the Neighborhood Youth Corps (NYC),
the Work Experience Program (WEP), and area development
activity. I am sympathetic to the view that in recent years the
objective has been to develop legislative authorization and appropriations for manpower programs and that the appeal of
separate programs and agencies has probably advanced the activity. The appeal in behalf of separate groups such as youth,
the Negro, the handicapped, the unemployed, and distressed
areas has yielded greater legislative returns—probably because
of greater political appeal—than was likely from a comprehensive manpower program. The experience in raising federal
medical-research expenditures is analogous.

One can surely agree with Joseph Kershaw that ". . . an
excessively tidy administration ought not be the goal" and yet

hold that the time is at hand for some administrative consolidation. The overlapping among programs and the gaps left by all the programs raise the insistent question of whether the community cannot get a greater return for the expenditure. I think that the time is at hand for administrative change because the present arrangements in many local communities have become politically difficult. The different standards of eligibility for programs and the artificial classification of individuals among programs, the different scales of payment, the various ratios at which federal funds are matched, the different pay scales for administrators, and the jurisdictional and bureaucratic conflicts and power struggles are all sources of political difficulties.

Although this is not the occasion to detail proposals for administrative reform, three groups of ideas concerning administrative change indicate my conclusions, or biases, on the subject.

1. The scope of the Manpower Administration in the Department of Labor should, on balancing all considerations, be expanded to encompass some programs now administered in both HEW and the OEO. Any boundary line among agencies is difficult to draw and is likely to be controversial. But it should not be necessary to have so many different agencies involved in "outreach," counseling, basic education, occupational training, and placement. This perspective recognizes that there are many different groups of "consumers," "clients," or "customers" for these programs, and no one single program is appropriate for all. But the dividing lines, overlapping, and gaps among programs require more attention than can be achieved through interagency coordination. There will still be plenty of room for competition among agencies and programs. The expansion in the Manpower Administration is proposed in full recognition of the possible conflicts with the interests of some labor organizations. But the judgment is based on the view that this agency has the Employment Service with all its strengths and weaknesses, the most experienced manpower staff, and direct access to the best statistics on the labor market.

2. There is an urgent need to bring labor and management representatives, particularly at the state and local level, into a much more active role in the formulation and supervision of various manpower programs.[17] Government administrators and

educators alone cannot provide the orientation to the labor market that can be provided by leading representatives of management and labor in the community. The present diffuse advisory committee, too often used solely to report decisions already taken, is not adequate for viable manpower policy-making. Management and labor representation is essential in the decision-making process to provide informed opinion regarding the pattern of demand for various labor skills and qualities, to suggest new methods of training and new opportunities for employment, and to provide judgments regarding future conditions in the labor market. The representation of labor and management is also essential for what it contributes to industry and labor organizations in a community. In the process of developing labor and management leaders as community leaders, the continuing overview of the labor market and of conditions among the disadvantaged groups has an impact that must not be underestimated. It is for this reason that leading representatives of labor and management need to be involved in community manpower policy.

3. The last six months have emphasized that manpower policies should not be oriented solely to the disadvantaged, crucial as these problems are for our times. If the economy is to operate at a high level of employment, say, in the range of 3 to 4 per cent unemployment, then programs for treating shortages have no less an integral role than those oriented toward the unemployed and the disadvantaged. The interrelations between general economic policy and manpower policy cannot be ignored. While private incentives may be effective in meeting many of the shortages that arise, a variety of public policies also have a role. It is to be hoped that general economic policy will be effective in the future so that manpower policy can be administered so as always to be concerned both with shortages and with surpluses (including the underprivileged). Its exclusive preoccupation with one or the other may give distorted perspectives, since there is considerable internal mobility within the labor force. Moreover manpower policy cannot flourish in the exclusive domain of the social worker or educator. The criteria for the relative allocation of governmental manpower training

resources among shortages and surpluses is an administrative problem still to be explored.

## Future Developments

Any concern with future manpower developments would do well to begin by recognizing that the level of economic activity is a basic determinant of manpower policies. It is difficult to perceive the institutional changes in the labor market and the economy that a decade of high employment would bring, but that the transformations would be extensive and fundamental can scarcely be denied. The orientation of business policies toward training and manpower development would be extensive. The policies of union organizations toward training, admissions, and technological change should be expected to change in major respects. The aspirations of the community and what it expects of labor and management may also be counted on to change, to become more demanding with regard to wages and prices. A decade of continuing high employment would tend to create a new economy in important respects. It would also make more urgent the critical questions of manpower concepts and measurement discussed in an earlier section.

This section indicates a few of the institutional changes illustrative of the wider developments in manpower policy that we would expect to be associated with continuing high employment.

1. One of the major adjustments of tight labor markets would fall upon many seasonal industries. As other employments became relatively more attractive with continuing and expected steady employment, seasonal industries would be impelled to make a variety of changes. Attempts might be made to stabilize employment, to change the technological and market circumstances out of which seasonality is derived, to provide employment or income guarantees for all or a part of the labor force, to change the range of activities of the enterprise, to alter the method of allocation of the labor force, to create a new group of supplementary workers, and so on. A continuing period of high employment would compel careful review of policies in the garment, construction, resort, and other industries, particularly

where the labor force is not expanded uniquely to meet seasonal requirements.

2. One of the transformations in an economy of continuing high employment would be the development by the parties to collective bargaining of supplementary agreements, or articles in the basic agreement, dealing with training and investment in further education on the part of the employees. At times these programs would be financed by public funds, as at present with some MDTA contracts; on other occasions the parties would develop contributions to a joint fund to be administered as are many apprenticeship programs; and in still other cases the programs would be management initiated with union co-operation in their administration. It might take a while for the parties to collective bargaining to turn their attention to this subject, but I think that continuing labor shortages and the availability of funds, private or public, would attract the attention of the parties in the collective bargaining process.[18] A tax credit or an industry assessment plan would further stimulate these developments.

3. The national review of our policies for the recruitment and training of military manpower provides the occasion to reappraise the role of the military in the development of manpower skills and the opportunity to develop a general program for post-service training and education, not limited to college or professional education. A strong case can be made for providing under military auspices a greater degree of education and training during the period of enlistment and the creation of extensive rights to further training and education on leaving the services. These policies would move the military establishment somewhat in the direction of an educational establishment. The period of military service often creates new interests, develops some new skills, and changes family and community environments. The opportunity should be generously provided for the widest possible range of post-service training and education.

4. An economy of continuing high employment might be expected to develop new institutions for training and skill development in the local community. The general educational system is not enough, and the present vocational education programs are the weakest link in our manpower policies in most communities.

New facilities and institutions for training would be likely to develop in local communities. In some cases these might be an adjunct of the junior college or community college to provide training for technicians and the subprofessions. These training centers might be expanded to include the full range of skill development—outside the formal educational system and the business enterprise—to include job training and remedial education for the disadvantaged, as well as clerical, sales, and mechanical skills. In other communities these training centers might be discrete entities, not under the control of the educational system, created to fill a community need. These facilities would be on a large scale and could be expected to provide a wide range of training. Modern facilities in the community would provide a symbol of the commitment to training outside the educational system. These facilities would be available to the educational system, particularly for students near the end of their high school period and unlikely to go on to college. The responsible leaders of labor and management in the community would be expected to play a major role in shaping the policies of such a training center.

Thus in the continuing high-employment economy, training and manpower development would be performed not only by the formal educational system but also by the military establishment, by business enterprise, and by new community facilities.

## NOTES

1. See, for example, Report of the Employment Service Task Force, reprinted in this book, and E. Wight Bakke, *A Positive Labor Market Policy* (Columbus, Ohio: Charles E. Merrill Books, 1963).

2. This formulation abstracts from immigration and population policy.

3. *U.S. Department of Commerce List of Current Essential Activities; U.S. Department of Labor List of Current Critical Occupations,* December 1963.

4. Lester C. Thurow's paper in this book, "The Role of Manpower Policy in Achieving Aggregative Goals," is significant in this respect.

5. U.S. National Commission on Technology, Automation, and Economic Progress, *Technology and the American Economy,* Vol. I (Washington, D.C.: U.S. Government Printing Office, 1966), p. 23.

6. See John T. Dunlop, "Job Vacancy Measures and Economic Analysis"

in *The Measurement and Interpretation of Job Vacancies* (New York: National Bureau of Economic Research, 1966), pp. 38–45.

7. *The Job Content of the U.S. Economy, 1940–1970, An Attempt at Quantification* (unpublished Ph.D. dissertation, Harvard University).

8. Executive Office of the President, Bureau of the Budget, "Work of the Interagency Committee on Occupational Classification of the U.S. Bureau of the Budget," February 2, 1966.

9. U.S. Bureau of Employment Security, third edition, Vols. I and II, 1965.

10. *Loc. cit.*, Vol. I, p. xviii.

11. See *The Measurement and Interpretation of Job Vacancies*, pp. 331–487. Also the reports of the National Industrial Conference Board on the Rochester study in *The Conference Board Record* (May, 1965; September, 1965; November, 1965).

12. See his paper, "The Role of Organized Labor," in this book.

13. See, for example, William G. Bowen and T. A. Finegan, "Labor Force Participation and Unemployment," in Arthur M. Ross, editor, *Employment Policy and the Labor Market* (Berkeley: University of California Press, 1965), pp. 115–161.

14. See, for example, *Toward Better Utilization of Scientific and Engineering Talent, A Program for Action*, Report of the Committee on Utilization of Scientific and Engineering Manpower (Washington, D.C.: National Academy of Sciences, 1964), pp. 71–82.

15. For a critical review of these methods and studies as well as the development of improved techniques and projections for 1970, see Jeffrey H. Weiss, *The Changing Job Structure of Health Manpower* (unpublished Ph.D. dissertation, Harvard University, 1966). For an instance of a projection subject to criticism, see, *Physicians for a Growing America—Report of the Surgeon General's Consultant Group on Medical Education*, U.S. Department of Health, Education, and Welfare, 1959 (the Bane Report).

16. Allan F. Salt, "Estimated Need for Skilled Workers, 1965–75," *Monthly Labor Review*, LXXXIX (April, 1966), 365–371. (See table, p. 368.) Earlier projections were the subject of considerable controversy; see *Manpower Needs in the Construction Industry*, a summary statement prepared for the Building and Construction-Trades Department Executive Council, AFL-CIO, November 1963.

17. See Richard A. Lester, "The Role of Organized Labor" and Charles A. Myers, "The Role of the Employer in Manpower Policy," in this volume.

18. See Neil W. Chamberlain, "Corporate Long-Term Manpower Planning and the Union's Role," Labor-Management Institute, American Arbitration Association (unpublished).